T0206930

Practical R 4

Applying R to Data Manipulation, Processing and Integration

Jon Westfall

Apress®

Practical R 4: Applying R to Data Manipulation, Processing and Integration

Jon Westfall
Division of Counselor Education & Psychology
Division of Student Success Center
Delta State University
Cleveland, MS, USA

ISBN-13 (pbk): 978-1-4842-5945-0
https://doi.org/10.1007/978-1-4842-5946-7

ISBN-13 (electronic): 978-1-4842-5946-7

Copyright © 2020 by Jon Westfall

This work is subject to copyright. All rights are reserved by the Publisher, whether the whole or part of the material is concerned, specifically the rights of translation, reprinting, reuse of illustrations, recitation, broadcasting, reproduction on microfilms or in any other physical way, and transmission or information storage and retrieval, electronic adaptation, computer software, or by similar or dissimilar methodology now known or hereafter developed.

Trademarked names, logos, and images may appear in this book. Rather than use a trademark symbol with every occurrence of a trademarked name, logo, or image we use the names, logos, and images only in an editorial fashion and to the benefit of the trademark owner, with no intention of infringement of the trademark.

The use in this publication of trade names, trademarks, service marks, and similar terms, even if they are not identified as such, is not to be taken as an expression of opinion as to whether or not they are subject to proprietary rights.

While the advice and information in this book are believed to be true and accurate at the date of publication, neither the authors nor the editors nor the publisher can accept any legal responsibility for any errors or omissions that may be made. The publisher makes no warranty, express or implied, with respect to the material contained herein.

Managing Director, Apress Media LLC: Welmoed Spahr
Acquisitions Editor: Steve Anglin
Development Editor: Matthew Moodie
Coordinating Editor: Mark Powers

Cover designed by eStudioCalamar

Cover image designed by Freepik (www.freepik.com)

Distributed to the book trade worldwide by Apress Media, LLC, 1 New York Plaza, New York, NY 10004, U.S.A. Phone 1-800-SPRINGER, fax (201) 348-4505, e-mail orders-ny@springer-sbm.com, or visit www.springeronline.com. Apress Media, LLC is a California LLC and the sole member (owner) is Springer Science + Business Media Finance Inc (SSBM Finance Inc). SSBM Finance Inc is a **Delaware** corporation.

For information on translations, please e-mail editorial@apress.com; for reprint, paperback, or audio rights, please email bookpermissions@springernature.com.

Apress titles may be purchased in bulk for academic, corporate, or promotional use. eBook versions and licenses are also available for most titles. For more information, reference our Print and eBook Bulk Sales web page at http://www.apress.com/bulk-sales.

Any source code or other supplementary material referenced by the author in this book is available to readers on GitHub via the book's product page, located at www.apress.com/9781484259450. For more detailed information, please visit http://www.apress.com/source-code.

Printed on acid-free paper

Dedicated to the little people in my life: Kaden, Ryleigh, Ryan, Amelia, Loretta, Rhett, Grant, and Walt.

May a love of reading all sorts of books (even boring ones like this!) be with you for life.

Table of Contents

About the Author

Jon Westfall is an award-winning professor, author, and practicing cognitive scientist. He teaches a variety of courses in psychology, from introduction to psychology to graduate seminars. His current research focuses on the variables that influence economic and consumer finance decisions, as well as retention and persistence of college students. With applications to psychology, information technology, and marketing, his work finds an intersection between basic and applied science. His current appointments include Associate Professor of Psychology, Coordinator of the First Year Seminar program, and Coordinator of the Psychology program at Delta State University. Prior to joining the faculty at Delta State in 2014, he was a Visiting Assistant Professor at Centenary College of Louisiana and the Associate Director for Research and Technology at the Center for Decision Sciences, a center within Columbia Business School at Columbia University in New York City. He now maintains a role with Columbia as a research affiliate/variable hours officer of administration and technology consultant.

In addition to his research, Dr. Westfall also has career ties in information technology, where he has worked as a consultant since 1997, founding his own firm, Bug Jr. Systems. As a consultant, he has developed custom software solutions (including native Windows 32 applications, Windows .NET applications, Windows Phone 7 and Android mobile applications, as well as ASP, ASP.NET, and PHP web applications). He has also served as a senior network and systems architect and administrator and been recognized as a Microsoft Most Valuable Professional (MVP) 2008–2012. He currently is the owner and managing partner of Secure Research Services LLC. He has authored several fiction and nonfiction books and presented at academic as well as technology conferences and gatherings. A native of Ohio, in his spare time, he enjoys knitting, crocheting, creative writing with the Delta Writers Group, and a variety of other hobbies.

For more information, visit jonwestfall.com, listen to him weekly on the MobileViews podcast (mobileviews.com), or follow him on Twitter (@jonwestfall).

Acknowledgments

Writing a book is never an easy task and is seldom the task of just one individual, even in a sole author work. I am indebted to my wife, Karey, for her support throughout this process. It can't be easy to have a husband who pounds out thousands of words at a time on weekends, on road trips, and in hotel rooms. Yet she has never complained once.

I'm also thankful for my parents, Alan and Dianne, who instilled a love of reading and learning in me early in my life. Writing is only possible after spending a ton of time reading, whether it be fiction or nonfiction. I'm thankful to my friends who have listened to me talk about this project and provided feedback (Steve Jocke, Jason Dunn, Matt Rozema, and my longtime podcasting partner Todd Ogasawara). Other friends who have supported me without knowing it (by providing inspiration for projects, or stories in this book) include Christy Riddle, Tricia Killebrew, Kristen Land, Darla Poole, Kesha Pates, Jontil Coleman, Elise Mallette, Jackie Goldman, Andrés García-Penagos, Sally Zengaro, and many others in the extended Delta State family. I'd also like to acknowledge my students, for whom many of these projects originally were designed, for inspiring me to continue creating. I also am lucky to have the support of those at Apress, especially Mark Powers, Steve Anglin, and Matt Moodie.

On a personal level, I'd also like to thank the Delta Writers Group (Michael Koehler, Katy Koehler, Jason Hair, and Dick Denny) for providing a ground for sharpening my writing and critique skills regularly. I also gain so much support from friends and family, including Nate and Kristen Toney, Sarah Speelman, Maggie Ditto, Heather Hudgins, Ashley Newman, Dan, Sue, Scott, Emily, Greg, Janet, Mark, and Brenda Himmel, Margaret Lee, Christine and Carl Morris, Don Sorcinelli, Tony Rylow, Trella Williams, Eric Johnson, Elke Weber, Karen Fosheim, Carol Beard, Maria Gaglio, Hope Hanks, Tom Brady, and many others.

Introduction

In 2007, as I was finishing up my last full year of graduate school, I learned about R. At the time, most of my data analysis was done in SAS or SPSS, and I had grown weary of the headaches of trying to find a properly licensed computer to run my data. A longtime fan of open source software, I started noticing more and more of my colleagues talking about R, and I began exploring it. In 2009, when I took a position at the Center for Decision Sciences, working with Eric Johnson and Elke Weber, I found it to be a nearly R-only. Coupled with my background in scripting languages and other programming duties, I jumped right in. Today I consider myself an R evangelist, having given multiple talks on the platform, incorporating it into my courses, and now writing my first book on the subject.

R, in my opinion, is wildly misunderstood outside of its core user base. Even within its base, many are only familiar with what they use R for – statistics, visualizations, data formatting, and so on. Outside the base, many of my colleagues view it as intimidating, given its command-line appearance. Many have shared with me that they "really wish they could learn R" but that they "can't afford the time" to devote to it. My hope is that this book shows that you really can't afford to *not* learn R, because once you know it and recognize its power, your time frees up. How? The report that used to take 25 minutes now takes 25 seconds. The PowerPoint deck that you needed to update every week to send to your boss now is automatically created and sent, all without you having to lift a finger. The analysis that you used to have to spend an entire class period explaining how to run in SPSS is now run with 3–4 lines of R code (allowing you to spend that class period explaining what the analysis does, not which menus to drill into to run it). R saves you time, and in this book, my goal is to show you how you can use it in a myriad of ways in your life, hence the "Practical" label.

To do this, we'll start by explaining what R is and how to get up and running with it. Chapter 1 assumes no knowledge of R, so if you've just heard of it or picked up this book thinking "I don't even know where to begin," you're in the right place. Chapter 2 then discusses how to get data into R to work with – whether that be a series of columns in a spreadsheet or finding specific items on a web page or document. Chapters 3 and 4 get into data analysis by collecting data using open source tools (which might end up saving you money over commercial options). Chapter 5 gives you some everyday applications for how to use R to format and manipulate data. Chapters 6 and 7 ramp up your automation skills, while Chapters 8–10 bring R to the cloud, allowing you to run your analysis anywhere you need to, and have it report back to you.

The specific code in this book is just the beginning, however. My goal is to give you tools through examples, inspiring you to mix and match as appropriate to your needs. For example, Chapter 5 discusses sorting data based upon rules, and Chapter 10 includes code to download the latest news headlines. Imagine needing to know the number of times a certain word appears in news headlines over a 10-day period of time. While there is no explicit example, by grabbing code from Chapters 5 and 10, one could easily write code to collect and process the data, and using tools introduced in Chapter 8, schedule it to run every day. After 10 days, pull the data and sum it up, and you're all set.

More than anything, my goal here is to inspire innovation with an extremely powerful tool, R 4, to make your life easier and your work more enjoyable. I don't know about you, but I'd rather spend time thinking critically about something than spend hours counting rows in a spreadsheet or computing statistics on a hand calculator. I'd rather talk with others about my findings rather than spend an hour wrestling with PowerPoint to make 30 slides filled with data and analyses (see Chapter 7). Do more of what matters to you, and let R do the rest.

I hope you are inspired, and look forward to seeing what you create!

CHAPTER 1

Getting Up and Running with R

Welcome to the first chapter on the book that covers every pirate's favorite programming language and statistics package, R. With that very bad joke out of the way, let's talk about what this book is: your Practical R recipe book for three broad areas – research, productivity, and automation. In the first part of this book, I'll give you the essentials to getting up and running with R and apply those to two research projects you might find useful in your work: a market research study and a psychological process-tracing study. In the second part, I'll talk about how R can be used in your workday to enhance your productivity – less data science, more useful scripting environment. And finally, in the third part, I'll use R to automate some seriously complex tasks, turning R into your personal assistant through two projects in Chapters 9 and 10. Along the way, you'll find that R fits in many different areas of your life and that no job is likely too big for it!

So, the actual business of this book: helping improve your life in practical ways by using R. Before we can do much of that, we'll need to fill in a bit of background on this programming language that is over two and a half decades old, yet still unknown to many who could benefit from it. In this chapter, I'll cover

- What R is... and what it's not!

- The R landscape – its history and influence

- How R is installed and used

- How to write a basic R script, to create the traditional "Hello World" program that's required by law to be in all programming books[1]

---

[1]OK, so it probably isn't really required by law, but certainly feels like it!

© Jon Westfall 2020
J. Westfall, *Practical R 4*, https://doi.org/10.1007/978-1-4842-5946-7_1

Along the way on our journey, I'll share with you how I came to use R in the examples written here and how I continue to find new uses for R in my daily life. So let's get started.

What Is R

In my experience, many people come to R after having heard about it from someone else. And when you hear about it from someone else, you tend to get just one view of what R is and where it came from. So in this section, I'll try to give you the most holistic and encompassing view of what R is, as well as what people think it is. According to the R-Project homepage, R "is a language and environment for statistical computing and graphics." Further, they elaborate that R is

- An effective data handling and storage facility

- A suite of operators for calculations on arrays, in particular matrices

- A large, coherent, integrated collection of intermediate tools for data analysis

- Graphical facilities for data analysis and display either onscreen or on hardcopy

- A well-developed, simple, and effective programming language which includes conditionals, loops, user-defined recursive functions, and input and output facilities[2]

If you're like me, you find that this description really doesn't help you much in understanding what R is or what it does. It almost sounds too elegant or refined to be a tool that you'd use every day. As a programmer for over 20 years, I think of programming languages much more as a means to a definite end, while this R language seems to be more ethereal and mysterious. This is one of the reasons I think people have trouble understanding what R is, and why R can help them. They feel they're not the "target" audience since they lack a PhD in statistics or computer science, and that it may just be easier to continue doing what they've done in the past, manually. It is unfortunate when you see someone take out a hand calculator to do something that R can do for them, simply because they've "always done it that way" and "don't think they have the time to

---

[2] www.r-project.org/about.html

learn a new tool." As you'll see in this book, R is a free and flexible tool that most anyone can incorporate into their lives.

So who evangelizes for R in the real world? Typically people who have used it for one particular niche scenario or another. Here are a few examples:

- The professor who wants to give her students a low-cost (e.g., free) alternative to pricey statistics packages, so she writes a few example scripts and posts them in her statistics or research methodology course.

- The IT manager whose firm asks him to compile the annual budget spreadsheet, and he finds it's really inconvenient to wait 10 minutes for Excel to load up just to realize he has the wrong version of the file.

- The marketing professional who has a bunch of data from a research survey, but no idea how to analyze it. A friend slips him an R script to calculate basic frequencies and generate a report.

- The secretary who has to update a department's web page and writes a script in R to take data from a spreadsheet, format it nicely, and spit out HTML that she can copy and paste into the web page's CMS (content management system) software.

- The student who is just learning about concepts in mathematics that longs for a computer-based graphing calculator that can easily be accessed, modified, and shared.

If you don't see yourself in any of these scenarios, that's fine and somewhat the point – many people find themselves using R for a task, but don't realize that it can do so much more. Think of R like a Swiss Army knife, but instead of 15–30 tools, it has 15,000 tools named packages, tools that anyone can write and share. Those tools do everything from generating reports (a package named `knitr`) to adapting and smoothing fMRI data (`adaptsmoFMRI`) to sending email (`mail`). If you're seeking to do something, you can probably do it in R.

Oh yeah, and it's free. R is an open source software product licensed under the GNU General Public License, and while commercial versions of R exist, the base product will always be free. What you get with the commercial packages typically consists of greater optimization for large data operations, specially designed packages, and support contracts that allow you to call someone when something breaks. However, none of those enhancements are required to download and start using R today.[3] Ironically, it is this very powerful advantage R has that I feel has actually hurt its adoption in many scenarios. As a professor, I often encounter people in education and IT that tend to believe that there is no such thing as a free lunch. When I explain that R is free, I can get sideways glances that seem to say "Oh sure, it's just as good as the $6000 statistics package we buy." And they're right – it isn't just as good, I firmly believe it's better. How so?

- Commercial statistics packages require their owners to update them, which may mean that a feature remains unimplemented or a bug unfixed until the next major version. R is maintained by a team of individuals who can push up updates quicker – and if they can't, you can always go in and fix it yourself or add it, since it's open source.

- Commercial statistics packages have a limited user community since there is a cost of entry that may be above many individuals. And while R may be experiencing stiff competition from languages such as Python, it's still ranked higher in popularity than any other statistical package (#7), compared to Matlab (#11), Scala (#16), Julia (#27), or SAS (unranked).

- R has an established history spanning over 25 years and an avid following among statisticians and scientists. Despite that, it's amazing to me how many people ask me about R by starting the conversation "So, tell me about this new thing, R?"!

- R is accessible, even to beginners, through graphical user interfaces like RStudio and Jamovi (both open source products I'll discuss later in this book).

- The multi-thousand dollar statistics package costs multi-thousand dollars a year. My budget doesn't have that kind of space, and I suspect yours doesn't either.

So what is R? R is a versatile programming language that tends to be heavy on statistics and scientific computing, but can be used for nearly any other task you might want to throw at it. And if that task is hyperspecialized in science or math (such as the

---

[3]All you need for that is a few minutes, a computer, and desire to learn.

multilevel regression that we will run in Chapter 4), you might find it much easier to find packages to accomplish it in R than a more common language, such as Python. R is powerful, established, and accessible.

What R Is Not

If R sounds like it's your savior when it comes to data processing, analysis, visualization, reporting, automation, and calculation, then it's very possible that it is. But it's also possible that you're delusional, because R does have a few things it isn't so good at, at least not right now. Here are some warning signs that you might not be ready for R yet (in which case, buy this book and keep it for later), or that R might not be the best tool out there (in which case, still buy this book and give it to a friend).

First, R can be very user-unfriendly, for a few reasons. First, the folks behind R, as of this writing in 2020, are still a little bit stuck in the 1995 Internet. What do I mean?

- The R Project homepage sports a clean design, but isn't the easiest to navigate. As you'll see in a few pages, downloading R is not as easy as "go to the homepage, click the big Download button."

- R gurus tend to be highly educated and specialized, which can mean that they don't always appreciate what it's like to start out. I've seen posts in R support listservs that make me think "Oh honey, bless your heart" – for those who haven't spent time in Southern United States culture, this roughly translates to "He asked a beginner question, and you just asked him questions only an advanced user would even know how to answer." It's a supportive community, but it can take things for granted.

- R is fundamentally a scriptable, command-line interface. The official graphical user interfaces for R are not pretty nor do they have many of the design elements that we've come to expect in a Web 2.0 era. Firing up R will make you feel like you've gone back in time, and it's possible that the official maintainers are fine with this since more polished GUIs, like RStudio, exist.

Second, R can also be unintuitive for those raised after the command-line era in computing. For many today, scripting is not something they are familiar with doing. In my own classes, I've found that asking an 18-year-old to "download a file and open it in R" can be very challenging in the era of cloud computing. Tools like Jamovi, which is built upon R but incorporates responsive design, help mitigate this problem. Also, R does not always provide the most intuitive error messages when things go wrong. Someone unfamiliar with searching the Web to fix a typo or mistake may find R especially challenging.

Further, R does not run natively on iOS. It can run on a Chromebook and on an Android device if those devices allow a Linux mode in settings. While it may seem weird to consider someone using those devices to run R, we'll see in Chapters 6, 7, 9, and 10 projects that one might want to be able to run from an iOS or iPadOS device, and in some cases, I'll show workarounds for those scenarios. There are ways to access an RStudio Server on iOS as well as use Remote Desktop software such as VNC; however, it can be limiting for someone who lives their life on an iPhone or iPad. R runs fine on macOS, Windows, and Linux.

And finally, R can require a bit of future-proofing to ensure it will always run the way you need it to. We'll discuss this more in future chapters, but for now, the short version is packages are updated regularly by their maintainers. If a maintainer needs to re-work a package, to take out a function or add new functionality, it may break your script. This means that for any mission-critical application, you'll want to keep copies of the specific versions of your packages. As I said, I'll walk through this later in the book.

There you have it – my most compelling arguments for why R might not be the best for you. Obviously, I don't provide them to scare you away, but rather to make sure you're going into your R adventure with realistic expectations. After all, I can't help you in a practical and actionable way if you're angry with me for the remainder of the book!

The R Landscape

In this short section, I want to give you a bit of an overview on how R has evolved over time, with special attention on the moving parts that make it somewhat unique in the programming world. The best way I can think to do this is a timeline (See Figure 1-1).[4]

---

[4]Made with the R, of course, the timelineS package. Code available on GitHub under `1-1.timeline.r`

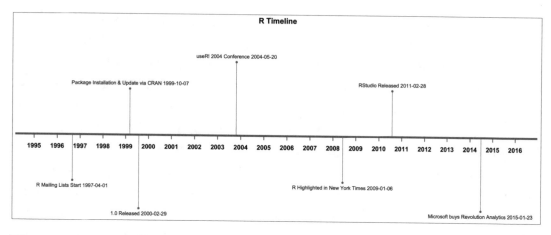

Figure 1-1. *R Timeline*

R can trace its inspirations back to the S programming language of the mid-1970s, with work on R starting in the mid-1990s. It's always hard to pin down exact dates, but the earliest recorded conversations on R tend to center around the mailing lists that began in 1997. A hobby at that time, R became "useful" around 2000, with CRAN (the Comprehensive R Archive Network) supporting not only copies of the source files and compiled binaries but also packages that had been submitted. With R's ability to download and install packages (via the `install.packages()` function) as well as update them, the user was able to easily add functionality to the basic package with just a few keystrokes. Looking at my timeline code, you'll notice the very first line installs the `timelineS` package, which it needs in order to create the timeline that you see.

By the mid-2000s, R had begun to attract a devoted user base, with the first official R conference, *useR!*, being held in 2004. The spirit of the future of R was present here, with keynotes on new features, "Users become Developers," and data science precursors to the "Big Data" movement of today. Graphing with R and using R as a teaching tool were also covered. With this activity, it was inevitable that those with an eye for profit would begin to notice and utilize R.

In 2007, the first major corporation to make R a centerpiece was founded: Revolution Analytics. Revolution's business was to support an open source product, R, add their own enhancements, and provide a version to their clients for large volume or niche specifications. Revolution R would become so popular that Microsoft would purchase them in 2015, with Microsoft building R into many of their cloud business applications and releasing a free version of R based on the work done by Revolution. In parallel, smaller software groups began writing enhancements for R, with perhaps the most notable being the specialized integrated development environment (IDE) RStudio, released in 2011. At that time I was using R daily and remember being really psyched by what RStudio had brought together – it felt like R was really growing up! Today RStudio, Inc. offers free versions of RStudio Desktop, RStudio Server, and Shiny Server, as well as maintains packages such as RMarkdown (for adding R into markdown documents easily) and knitr (for creating rich reports from within R that export to HTML, Markdown, or TeX). We'll be talking about those products throughout the book.

As you can see, R has come a long way in a fairly short amount of time. Today it's a serious contender in the data science space, with many companies finding ways to use R to increase their own productivity and profitability, while the core software remains free and open to the public. It's pretty amazing to consider that if you were to buy this book and then run through my examples on a computer running Linux, the only costs to you would be the physical products – the book and the hardware – everything else would be free of charge thanks to open source!

How R Is Installed and Used

Now that we've talked about R, it's about time that you're able to get it up and running on your computer. The process is fairly straightforward, albeit a tiny bit unintuitive.

One might think that all you'd need to do is head over to the official R Project homepage at www.r-project.org (See Figure 1-2) and click a Download button. Being the modern web era, you'd expect it to detect your operating system and tell you "Here's the installer for your computer, most recent stable version." R isn't going to do that. In fact, going to the homepage you will see a Download heading on the left, but it's just a heading that you can't click.

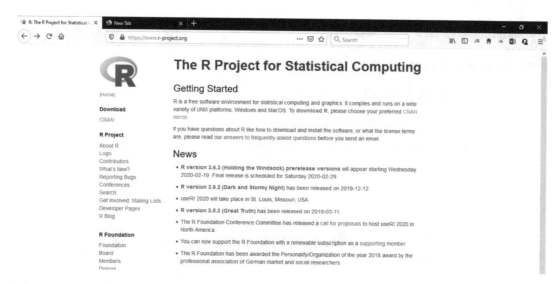

Figure 1-2. *The R Project Homepage*

Under that Download heading, you see a link for CRAN, the Comprehensive R Archive Network that I mentioned earlier (See Figure 1-3). Clicking that, you're asked to pick a mirror from the list of nearly 100 separate R mirror sites around the world. If the World Wide Web ever suffers a major break in connectivity, I'm sure you're happy to know that while you might not be able to stream your favorite show or use your favorite social media app, you will likely still be able to get to an R mirror and download the packages you need to adequately analyze and graph your ensuing depression!

Anyway, today I typically advise people to use the Cloud option at the top of CRAN, which will automatically find a near mirror to you. From CRAN's homepage, you do see installation links for the three major desktop platforms: Linux, macOS, and Windows.

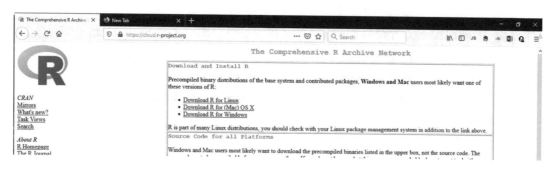

Figure 1-3. *CRAN Homepage*

Installation on Windows

For Windows users, you'll want to follow these steps:

1. Click "Download R for Windows".

2. Click "base" (See Figure 1-4), which indicates that you'd like to download the base installation of R with its included packages.

Figure 1-4. *Base Installation Option*

3. Finally, click the Download for Windows option (which will include the current R version number; See Figure 1-5).

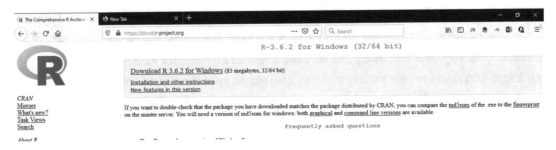

Figure 1-5. *Download Executable Installer*

4. Once the executable file has been downloaded to your computer, double-click it to install. You'll likely get a warning such as the following one (See Figure 1-6) that reminds you that this is a software installer, and it will make changes to your system. Accept it to move forward.

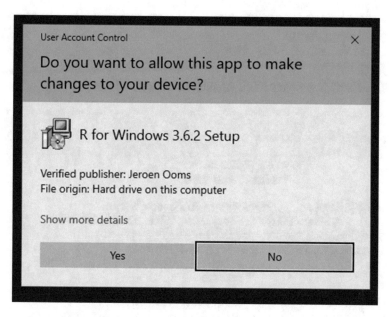

Figure 1-6. *Security Prompt*

5. Finally, you'll get an installation wizard (See Figure 1-7) that you
    get the joy of pressing "Next" to several times. Accepting the default
    options is fine, as we can easily change them later if need be.

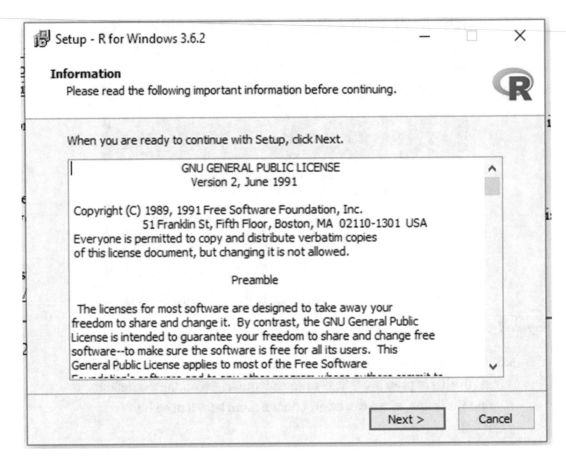

Figure 1-7. Installation wizard

Congratulations – you should now have R installed on your computer. Going to your Start menu, you should see an "R" program group. You'll notice two versions of R inside there, one labeled "R i386" and "R x64" with the version number after them. This is by design, with the i386 option allowing you to run 32-bit R and the x64 allowing 64-bit. For most things today, you'll likely want to use the x64 option. In rare cases, you may need the 32-bit option if you're using a package that hasn't been updated yet to support the 64-bit version. One thing to note is that the packages you download for each version are specific to it, so if you find yourself using both versions interchangeably, you'll be frustrated thinking "Didn't I already download that package?!?" when you try to run your code.

Go ahead and launch the 64-bit version, and you should see a screen similar to the one as follows (See Figure 1-8), ready for you to start work!

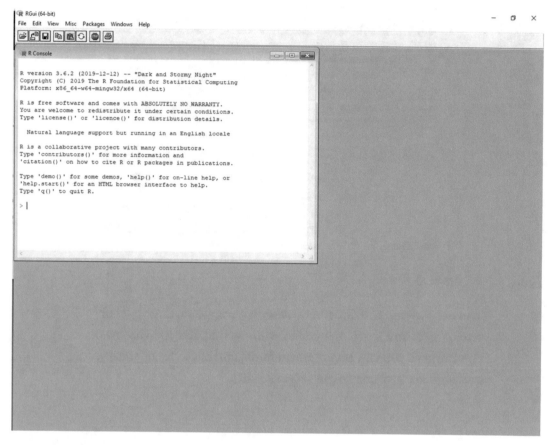

Figure 1-8. *R x64 Running on Windows*

Installation on macOS

Those on a Mac have a similar installation routine as Windows. From the CRAN homepage

1. Click "Download R for (Mac) OS X".

2. Click the first package under "Latest release", in the following figure; it's R-3.6.2.pkg (See Figure 1-9).

R for Mac OS X

CRAN
Mirrors
What's new?
Task Views
Search

About R
R Homepage
The R Journal

Software
R Sources
R Binaries
Packages
Other

Documentation
Manuals
FAQs
Contributed

This directory contains binaries for a base distribution and packages to run on Mac OS X (release 10.6 and above). Mac OS 8.6 to 9.2 (and Mac OS X 10.1) are no longer supported but you can find the last supported release of R for these systems (which is R 1.7.1) here. Releases for old Mac OS X systems (through Mac OS X 10.5) and PowerPC Macs can be found in the old directory.

Note: CRAN does not have Mac OS X systems and cannot check these binaries for viruses. Although we take precautions when assembling binaries, please use the normal precautions with downloaded executables.

Package binaries for R versions older than 3.2.0 are only available from the CRAN archive so users of such versions should adjust the CRAN mirror setting (https://cran-archive.r-project.org) accordingly.

R 3.6.2 "Dark and Stormy Night" released on 2019/12/12

Important: since R 3.4.0 release we are now providing binaries for OS X 10.11 (El Capitan) and higher using non-Apple toolkit to provide support for OpenMP and C++17 standard features. To compile packages you may have to download tools from the tools directory and read the corresponding note below.

Please check the MD5 checksum of the downloaded image to ensure that it has not been tampered with or corrupted during the mirroring process. For example type
md5 R-3.6.2.pkg
in the *Terminal* application to print the MD5 checksum for the R-3.6.2.pkg image. On Mac OS X 10.7 and later you can also validate the signature using
pkgutil --check-signature R-3.6.2.pkg

Latest release:

R-3.6.2.pkg
MD5-hash: 83741657f6abdc0c3c6e10f5d5d65ca0
SHA1-hash: e07a717ab4489326c96747f2f5601e28ea9d7306a
(ca. 77MB)

R 3.6.2 binary for OS X 10.11 (El Capitan) and higher, signed package. Contains R 3.6.2 framework, R.app GUI 1.70 in 64-bit for Intel Macs, Tcl/Tk 8.6.6 X11 libraries and Texinfo 5.2. The latter two components are optional and can be ommitted when choosing "custom install", they are only needed if you want to use the tcltk R package or build package documentation from sources.

Updated 2019/12/15: A notarization has been added to the installer package to simplify installation on macOS Catalina (the payload is identical). See above for the current checksum with size 81,045,295. The previous package was signed but not notarized and had a SHA1 checksum of 4a38acac6341a06770d1fedad127df086d9aaf82 and size 81,042,225. (Thanks to Bob Rudis for support and testing!)

Note: the use of X11 (including tcltk) requires XQuartz to be installed since it is no longer part of OS X. Always re-install XQuartz when upgrading your macOS to a new major version.

Important: this release uses Clang 7.0.0 and GNU Fortran 6.1, neither of which is supplied by Apple. If you wish to compile R packages from sources, you will need to download and install those tools - see the tools directory.

NEWS (for Mac GUI)

News features and changes in the R.app Mac GUI

Figure 1-9. *macOS Package*

3. The package file will download. After it's complete, double-click it to launch. You'll get an installer window that, like its Windows counterpart, you can accept the defaults and click "Next" until you get the success message (See Figure 1-10).

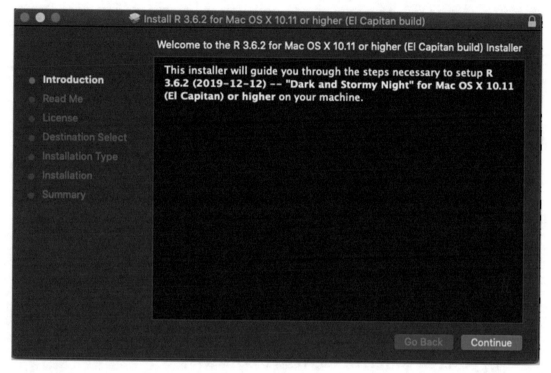

Figure 1-10. *macOS Installer*

Once the installer finishes, you'll find R in your Launchpad – just look for the giant R icon similar to the one shown here (See Figure 1-11).

Figure 1-11. *R Icon on macOS*

Launching it should provide you with a screen similar to the one as follows (See Figure 1-12), and from that point, you're ready to work!

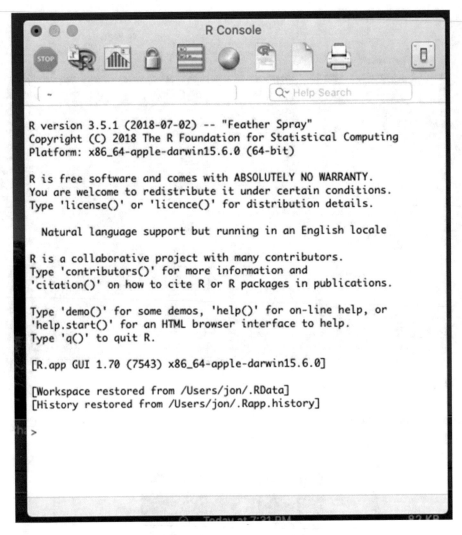

Figure 1-12. *R Running on macOS*

Installation on Linux

Installation on Linux is, oddly enough, either much easier than the other platforms or much more complex, depending on how geeky you'd like to be. R is available pre-compiled for four common Linux distributions: Debian, Red Hat/Fedora, SUSE, and Ubuntu. Here are the quickest ways to install the most common pieces of R for each of distribution:

- For Debian or Ubuntu, run apt-get install r-base-dev as root or as a normal user through sudo.

- Note that for Ubuntu, only the latest LTS release is available from the Ubuntu servers. You can install the latest stable builds by following the instructions at `https://cloud.r-project.org/bin/linux/ubuntu/README.html`.

- For Fedora, run `yum install R` as root or as a normal user through `sudo`.

- For Red Hat Enterprise Linux (RHEL), CentOS, Scientific Linux, or Oracle Linux, you can add the EPEL repository as described at `https://cloud.r-project.org/bin/linux/redhat/README` and then issue the same `yum` command earlier.

- For SUSE, you can use the one-click installation links available in Section 1.4 of `https://cloud.r-project.org/bin/linux/suse/README.html`, choosing the appropriate link for your version of openSUSE.

In many cases, these are a bit easier than on Windows or macOS, since the command does all the work of downloading the file and installing it. However, if you're a Linux aficionado, you may also want to install R from source, which is a bit more time-consuming and beyond the scope of this book.

Regardless of how you get it installed, to run R on your Linux machine, you simply run the command R – remembering that Linux is case-sensitive. r will not work, as you can see in the following image, it must be R. Assuming you issue the appropriately cased command, you'll get the R version and copyright, similar to the Windows and macOS version earlier, with a prompt waiting for your first R program to run (See Figure 1-13).

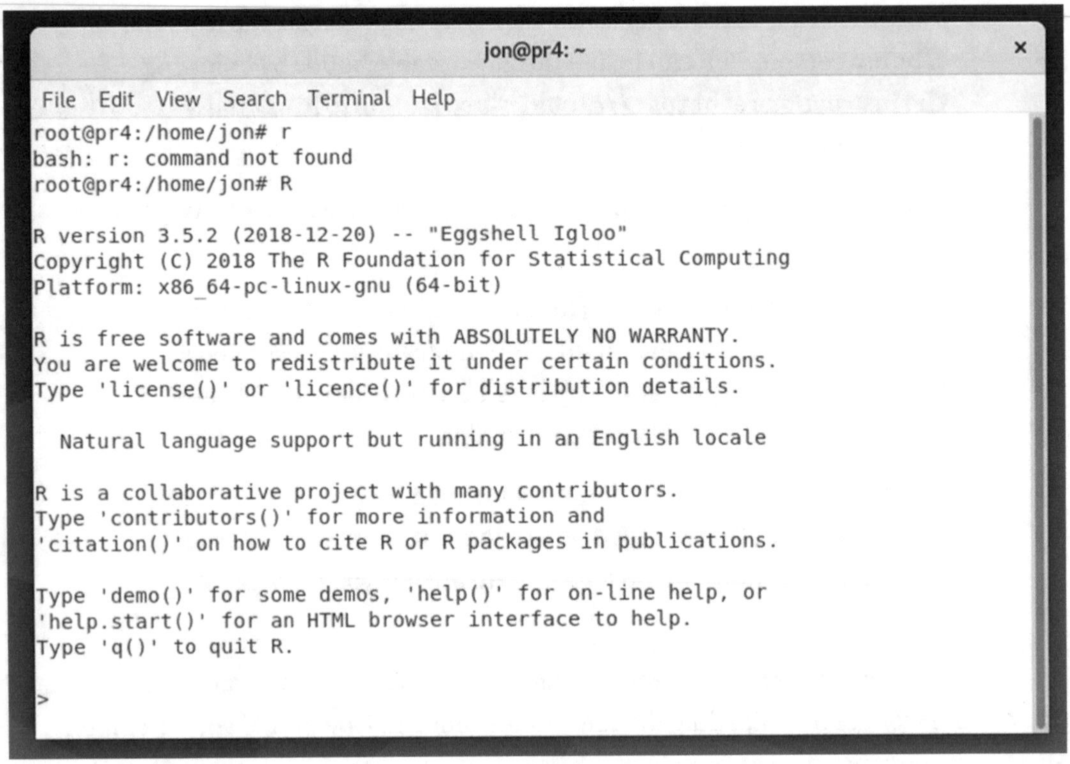

```
                                jon@pr4: ~                                  ✕

 File  Edit  View  Search  Terminal  Help
 root@pr4:/home/jon# r
 bash: r: command not found
 root@pr4:/home/jon# R

 R version 3.5.2 (2018-12-20) -- "Eggshell Igloo"
 Copyright (C) 2018 The R Foundation for Statistical Computing
 Platform: x86_64-pc-linux-gnu (64-bit)

 R is free software and comes with ABSOLUTELY NO WARRANTY.
 You are welcome to redistribute it under certain conditions.
 Type 'license()' or 'licence()' for distribution details.

   Natural language support but running in an English locale

 R is a collaborative project with many contributors.
 Type 'contributors()' for more information and
 'citation()' on how to cite R or R packages in publications.

 Type 'demo()' for some demos, 'help()' for on-line help, or
 'help.start()' for an HTML browser interface to help.
 Type 'q()' to quit R.

 >
```

Figure 1-13. *R Running in Linux*

How to Write a Basic R Script

Now that you have R installed on your computer, you're ready to play around with it a bit. R is a command-line interface at its core, which means you can open R and type the following command:

2+2.

R executes this, as seen in the following image, and happily tells you that there is one returned result, the number 4. Getting a little more fancy, you can try this:

x <- 2
x + 2

This also returns 4, as you just assigned the value of "2" to a variable named "x" and then added x + 2 or 2+2 once more. If the assignment operator "arrow" (really a less than sign and a hyphen) looks strange to you, you can also use an actual equals sign in most cases. The following code will also give 4.

```
y = 2
```

Or

```
x + y
```

We now have completely useless variables named x and y, but their point has been demonstrated as you reminisce nostalgically back to basic arithmetic (See Figure 1-14).

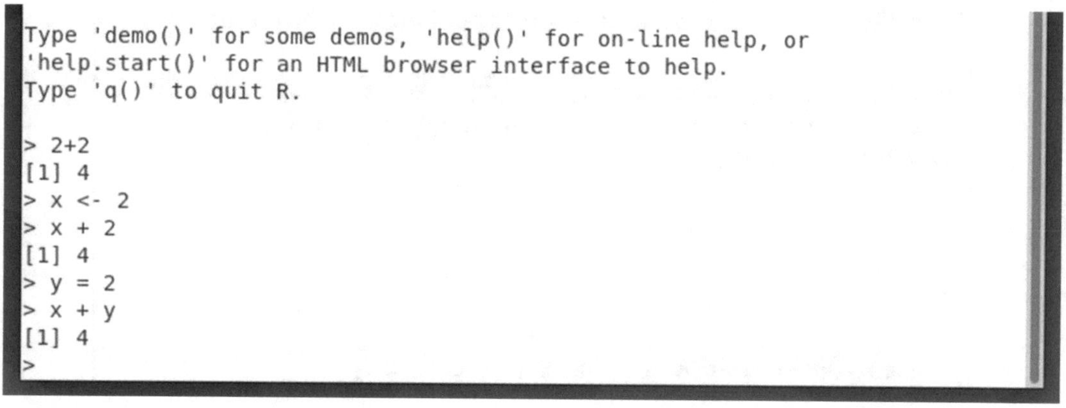

```
Type 'demo()' for some demos, 'help()' for on-line help, or
'help.start()' for an HTML browser interface to help.
Type 'q()' to quit R.

> 2+2
[1] 4
> x <- 2
> x + 2
[1] 4
> y = 2
> x + y
[1] 4
>
```

Figure 1-14. *Basic Operations in R*

You may wonder how we would do something a bit more automated? This is accomplished by piping a script into the R command-line interpreter. You can do this from the command line by writing a script, saving it generally with a .r file extension, and then providing it as an argument to the R command. Typing this in a terminal will execute the code and provide the output R -f 1-2.domath.r (See Figure 1-15).

```
jon@Jonathans-MacBook-Pro Chapter 1 Code % R -f 1-2.domath.r

R version 3.6.2 (2019-12-12) -- "Dark and Stormy Night"
Copyright (C) 2019 The R Foundation for Statistical Computing
Platform: x86_64-apple-darwin15.6.0 (64-bit)

R is free software and comes with ABSOLUTELY NO WARRANTY.
You are welcome to redistribute it under certain conditions.
Type 'license()' or 'licence()' for distribution details.

  Natural language support but running in an English locale

R is a collaborative project with many contributors.
Type 'contributors()' for more information and
'citation()' on how to cite R or R packages in publications.

Type 'demo()' for some demos, 'help()' for on-line help, or
'help.start()' for an HTML browser interface to help.
Type 'q()' to quit R.

> x <- 2
> 2 + 2
[1] 4
>
jon@Jonathans-MacBook-Pro Chapter 1 Code % []
```

Figure 1-15. *R Running a Script from Command Line*

You can also open a new R script in the Windows and macOS versions by going to the
File menu and choosing New Script (Windows) or New Document (macOS). You'll get a
new blank text window near your R interpreter window (See Figure 1-16 and 1-17).

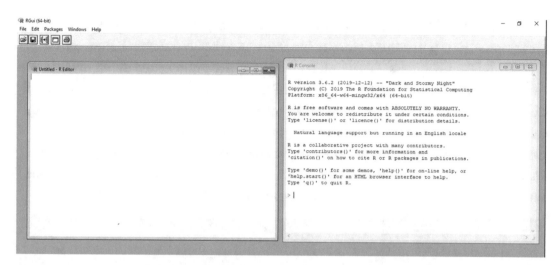

Figure 1-16. *New Script on Windows*

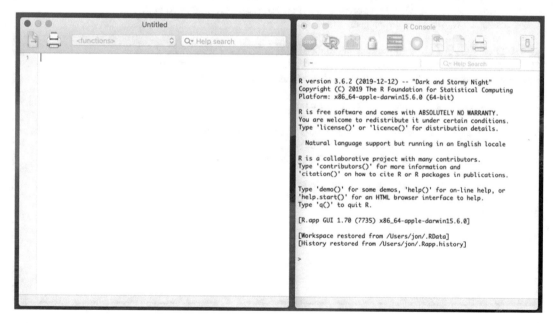

Figure 1-17. *New Document on macOS*

You can type the same commands into the script window as I had earlier. To execute them, you can put your cursor at the top and execute line by line by pressing Ctrl+R or choosing Run Line from the Edit menu (Windows). On macOS, you use Cmd+Enter or choose "Execute" from the Edit menu. To execute the entire script at once, you can either select all of it and press the shortcut key for your operating system or use the "Run All" command from the Edit menu (on Windows only).

I'll stop and take a moment to address something slightly annoying in the last paragraph – the fact that the menu structures are so radically different between R on macOS and R on Windows. Because R is an open source product and different teams are responsible for different elements, the macOS GUI and Windows GUI can seem radically different even though the same code works equally well on both. It's one of those things that makes it difficult to teach with R since your students may have different screens depending on their operating system. Further complicating matters is that R on Linux also has a GUI that can be invoked with the R -g Tk command, which doesn't have the same wording either – it doesn't even have an Edit menu! (See Figure 1-18).

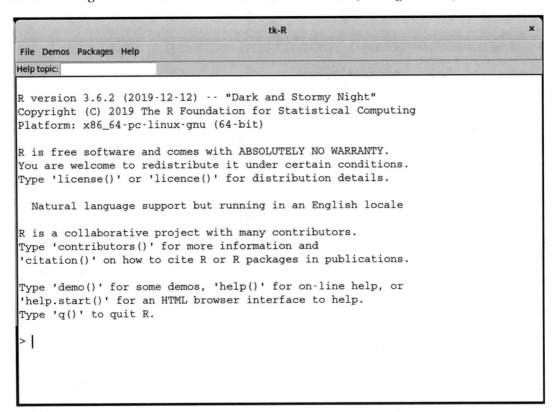

Figure 1-18. *R's Tk GUI on Debian Linux*

Hello World

We're nearly at the end of the chapter, so it's time for a Hello World program, a time-honored tradition since 1974 with another monoalphabetic programming language, C. Admittedly, it's not that much to look at:

```
print("Hello World").
```

If you find that a bit underwhelming, well… it is. As mentioned though, R can do some fancy graphics work, such as the timeline earlier in the chapter. So let's jazz it up a very little bit. Try this code, executed in Figure 1-19:

```
install.packages("BlockMessage")
library("BlockMessage")
blockMessage("Hello World")⁵
```

```
> blockMessage("Hello World");
      [,1]
[1,] "X    X              XX    XX              X    X              XX        X"
[2,] "X    X               X     X             X    X               X        X"
[3,] "X    X               X     X             X    X               X        X"
[4,] "XXXXX    XXX         X     X      XXX     X    X    XXX    X XX     X       XX X"
[5,] "X    X  X   X        X     X     X    X   X X X  X    X   XX   X    X     X   XX"
[6,] "X    X  XXXXX        X     X     X    X   X X X  X    X   X     X         X   X"
[7,] "X    X  X            X     X     X    X   XX XX  X    X   X          X     X   X"
[8,] "X    X   XXX        XXX   XXX    XXX     X    X    XXX   X          XXX     XXXX"
```

Figure 1-19. *Output of Block Message*

As you can see, that's a little fancier. The blockMessage() function actually has quite a few customizable commands. To get help on it or any other function in R, all you need to do is place a ? in front of the function and press Enter. The help should automatically launch and take you to information on that command. Try it by typing ?blockMessage in your R window after running the preceding code (See Figure 1-20).

---

⁵1-3.blockmessage.r in this book's code package.

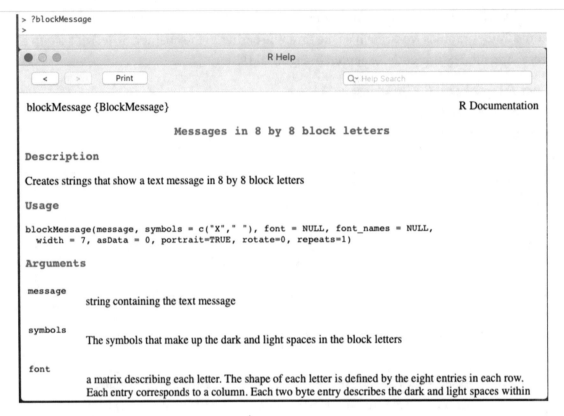

Figure 1-20. *The Help for the blockMessage Function*

Wrapping It All Up

We've covered a lot of ground in this chapter, from a background on what R is and what it is not, to a brief history of R, to getting R up and running on your computer. The rest of this book is dedicated to putting R to good use now that it's there. Here's a quick preview of what we'll be covering:

Chapter	Summary
2 – Feed the Beast: Getting Data into R	We'll talk about how to get your data into R, how it's stored, and how to hook R into dynamic data sources such as a database. We'll also talk about basic web scraping – getting a website's data into R!
3 – Project 1: Launching, Analyzing, and Reporting a Survey Using R and LimeSurvey	Ever have to give a survey out as part of your job? Want something a bit more in depth than the reports SurveyMonkey or another platform can provide to you? Want something... FREE? Then this is the chapter for you.

(continued)

Chapter	Summary
4 – Project 2: Advanced Statistical Analysis Using R and MouselabWEB	Sometimes you need to know what grabs someone's attention, and in this chapter, we'll use another free tool to see how people behave when searching for the best product on a website!
5 – R in Everyday Life	So maybe you're not a scientist or market researcher. Maybe you just want R to help you out day by day. In this chapter, we talk about using R to automate data formatting, reporting, and more.
6 – Project 3: The R Form Mailer	Mail Merge, the ability in Microsoft Office to send out customized emails or letters using a spreadsheet is a real timesaver. What if you could do that without the hassle of pointing and clicking? What if you could script it? Now you can!
7 – Project 4: The R Powered Presentation	We know that R can create graphics, it can create text, and it can crunch numbers. What if we put those all together with audience participation? Get ready for the Best. Presentation. Ever.
8 – R Anywhere	It's annoying that R can only run on your computer. What if R could run in the cloud? Then you could access it anywhere. That's what we'll explore in this chapter.
9 – Project 5: The Change Alert!	The world is full of change, but we don't always feel like we know about it far enough in advance. What if you had a script searching for changes in reports or web pages and notifying you nearly instantly when they occurred? In Chapter 9, we'll cover exactly that.
10 – Project 6: The R Personal Assistant	So R can do a lot for us, but the best personal assistants do everything behind the scenes. In this final project, we'll have R prepare a daily report for us and then find ways in which our other technological servants, such as an Amazon Echo, can deliver this vital information to us at our command.

It's time you lived your life a bit more in tune with that favored swashbuckling stats package, R. I'm glad you've decided to join me on our voyage!

## CHAPTER 2

Feed the Beast: Getting Data into R

Before R can be truly useful to you, you'll probably have to get more data inside of it than just basic arithmetic problems or greetings to the world. This can be tricky in some cases, and daunting in others. R has tremendous support for a wide variety of data types and sources, and we'll cover the most common types and use cases in this chapter. My goal here is to

- Explain the different types of data that R can work with and how that data is stored

- Explain the basics of connecting R to flat files, databases, and published data on the Internet through web scraping

- Give examples for entering, importing, or scraping data with R

- And finally, explain writing of data objects to native RData format as well as other formats for interchangeable use

We'll begin by talking about how data is stored in R and the types of data that R can automatically classify and use appropriately.

The Data Object

In researching for this chapter, I ran across a very nice and detailed overview of data types in R[1] that is thankfully licensed using Creative Commons, so I can point you toward it and mention a few of the more salient points here – I don't want to reinvent the wheel by getting too technical too quickly regarding how data is stored.

---

[1]`https://swcarpentry.github.io/r-novice-inflammation/13-supp-data-structures/`

To begin with, we have to remember that R is a programming language that works by using objects to represent pretty much everything. A numeric variable? Object. The output of a statistical test? Object. The collection of error messages you just got back after making a really big mistake? Object! And since everything is an object, R must give you ways to analyze those objects.

Here's a quick and easy way to inspect an object – try this code:

```
x <- 2
y <- 2L
x
y
str(x)
str(y)
```

You'll notice something interesting here – you stored the same value (the output on Lines 3 and 4 is the same – [1] 2 – despite the fact that you put the letter L in after the number on Line 2). What's going on here? Well, that L told R to store the same value, 2, as an integer instead of a floating point number. The str() commands confirm that, showing x to be num and showing y to be int. Aside from integers and numbers, what other data types does R support?

Data Type	Description	Example
Character	Strings of characters	Yes
Number	A decimal or real number	3.2
Integer	A whole number value	2 entered as 2L
Logical	True or False	FALSE
Complex	A number made up of real and imaginary parts	8+3i
Raw	A vector of raw data, in a protocol known to the user raw data types can store binary data, such as images or other files	

In addition to the preceding data types, R also supports structures of data, or a structure with multiple data objects and types. These are listed as follows:

Structure	Description	Example Code to Create	Example Code to Modify
Atomic vector	Atomic vectors contain a one-dimensional number of items.	`vector("logical", length=3)` will produce a vector with three items, all defaulting to FALSE.	The `c()` combine function can add items to vectors. R also supports missing data in vectors represented by the term NA, which functions like `is.na()` or anyNA() can check for. Additionally, one might find NaN if a mathematical operation produces a value that is not a number.
List	Sometimes referred to as a generic vector, lists are more flexible and can have mixed types of data.	`x <- list(grp1 = "name", grp2 = 1:5, grp3 = FALSE)` will create a list of three named items, each with their own lists inside.	Many different commands export their results as lists. This means that you can "peal" off different parts of a result. Using the code to the left, one could type `x$grp1` and get `"name"` in return.
Matrix	Matrices are an extension of vectors or lists, just in two dimensions.	`x <- matrix (nrow = 3, ncol=2)`	You can modify individual elements within an array by reassigning them. For example, `x[2,2] <- 3` will put 3 into the second row, second column of the matrix you created earlier.
Data frame	The powerhouse of data structures. Most large datasets you work with will be this type. Data frames can have named columns and nested structures and be easily modified and queried.	`x <- data. frame(idnum = 1:26, alpha = letters[1:26])`	You can reference specific columns in a data frame (e.g., x$idnum) or rows (x[1,], or exact cells (x[1,2]). You can also use the `head()` and `tail()` commands to view the first and last six items in the data frame.

(continued)

Structure	Description	Example Code to Create	Example Code to Modify
Factor	A collection of nominal values – labels without quantity, if you will.	`gender <-factor(c ("male","male","f emale","female"))`	Factors work a bit differently than lists because R keeps track of the levels of a factor. So removing a value (such as removing the last two "female" values and replacing with NA) will not modify the levels of the factor. Additionally, using the `relevel` command will change the reference level for the factor. In the example to the left, female is the reference level. `relevel(gender,"male")` would make male the reference level.

Now that we have a bit of an understanding of the types of data R can store, let's actually get some in there. And we'll start with a dataset already included!

Playing with a Built-in Dataset

R ships with a large number of built-in datasets through the `datasets` package that's included in the base installation. I discuss them here for several reasons: First, sometimes it is easiest to demo concepts in R when everyone has a "level playing field" so to speak – we're all working with the same dataset that is reloaded every time we restart R. This makes it easy to write examples that are easily replicated by all. Second, the built-in datasets, because they are reloaded, can be modified to your heart's content without worrying about affecting real data permanently. They're an excellent playground.

To see a list of these datasets, one simply needs to issue the `data()` command. Several interesting datasets are listed as follows:

Dataset Name	Description
AirPassengers	Monthly airline passenger numbers from 1949 to 1960
ChickWeight	Weight of chicks based upon age and diet type
HairEyeColor	Hair and eye color of a set of stats students
USArrests	Violent crime rates by state for 1973
presidents	Quarterly approval rating for the US President from 1945 to 1974

Several other datasets are included, but I think the five mentioned earlier give us some things to play around with. First, let's explore one of them – USArrests. To see the entire dataset, type USArrests. If you're like me, you'll run out of screen space with the list that fills your R console (See Figure 2-1).

```
                                    R Console
[-]                                            Q▾ Help Search

rtoriuu         13.4    333     80 31.9
Georgia         17.4    211     60 25.8
Hawaii           5.3     46     83 20.2
Idaho            2.6    120     54 14.2
Illinois        10.4    249     83 24.0
Indiana          7.2    113     65 21.0
Iowa             2.2     56     57 11.3
Kansas           6.0    115     66 18.0
Kentucky         9.7    109     52 16.3
Louisiana       15.4    249     66 22.2
Maine            2.1     83     51  7.8
Maryland        11.3    300     67 27.8
Massachusetts    4.4    149     85 16.3
Michigan        12.1    255     74 35.1
Minnesota        2.7     72     66 14.9
Mississippi     16.1    259     44 17.1
Missouri         9.0    178     70 28.2
Montana          6.0    109     53 16.4
Nebraska         4.3    102     62 16.5
Nevada          12.2    252     81 46.0
New Hampshire    2.1     57     56  9.5
New Jersey       7.4    159     89 18.8
New Mexico      11.4    285     70 32.1
New York        11.1    254     86 26.1
North Carolina  13.0    337     45 16.1
North Dakota     0.8     45     44  7.3
Ohio             7.3    120     75 21.4
Oklahoma         6.6    151     68 20.0
Oregon           4.9    159     67 29.3
Pennsylvania     6.3    106     72 14.9
Rhode Island     3.4    174     87  8.3
South Carolina  14.4    279     48 22.5
South Dakota     3.8     86     45 12.8
Tennessee       13.2    188     59 26.9
Texas           12.7    201     80 25.5
Utah             3.2    120     80 22.9
Vermont          2.2     48     32 11.2
Virginia         8.5    156     63 20.7
Washington       4.0    145     73 26.2
West Virginia    5.7     81     39  9.3
Wisconsin        2.6     53     66 10.8
Wyoming          6.8    161     60 15.6
>
```

Figure 2-1. *The Last 40 or so Lines of the USArrests Dataset*

This might be a bit overwhelming to see, so perhaps we should try to only look at the top or the bottom. Being alphabetically challenged myself, I'll choose the last six items with the `tail(USArrests)` command. Looking at it, I'm kind of glad I didn't live in Virginia in 1973. But is that 8.5 really bad compared to the murder rate nationally in that year? I can use the `max(USArrests$Murder)` command to get the maximum number and `mean(USArrests$Murder)` to get the arithmetic average (See Figure 2-2).

```
> tail(USArrests)
              Murder Assault UrbanPop Rape
Vermont          2.2      48       32 11.2
Virginia         8.5     156       63 20.7
Washington       4.0     145       73 26.2
West Virginia    5.7      81       39  9.3
Wisconsin        2.6      53       66 10.8
Wyoming          6.8     161       60 15.6
> max(USArrests$Murder)
[1] 17.4
> mean(USArrests$Murder)
[1] 7.788
```

Figure 2-2. *The Last Six Lines, Plus the Maximum and Mean*

8.5 seems higher than average (7.778), but is far lower than the maximum. This might get me wondering what the distribution of murder rates was. Perhaps I should look at a histogram with hist(USArrests$Murder). See Figure 2-3.

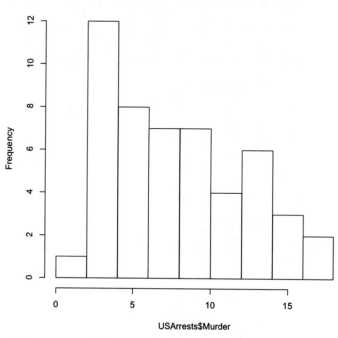

Figure 2-3. *The Histogram of the Murder Rate*

Hmm... 8.5 does seem to be a bit on the higher end of that graph now that I see it. And wow... Vermont must really have been safe with only 2.2!

While we're here, it's also useful to point out that the functions above all take several arguments to customize them. If we wanted to customize the X or Y axis labels in that histogram, we could do so easily – try this command on your own: hist(USArrests$Murder,xlab="Murder Rate").

Now that we've played around with that data, let's look at the two time series datasets we have from earlier – presidents and AirPassengers (See Figure 2-4). Doing a quick str(presidents) command will tell us that this is a data type Time-Series – that wasn't one that I had mentioned earlier, now is it?

And here we find the real power of R – complex real-world data structures. In this case, time series is a data structure that can accommodate data on a given time interval, whether they be months or years.

```
> AirPassengers
     Jan Feb Mar Apr May Jun Jul Aug Sep Oct Nov Dec
1949 112 118 132 129 121 135 148 148 136 119 104 118
1950 115 126 141 135 125 149 170 170 158 133 114 140
1951 145 150 178 163 172 178 199 199 184 162 146 166
1952 171 180 193 181 183 218 230 242 209 191 172 194
1953 196 196 236 235 229 243 264 272 237 211 180 201
1954 204 188 235 227 234 264 302 293 259 229 203 229
1955 242 233 267 269 270 315 364 347 312 274 237 278
1956 284 277 317 313 318 374 413 405 355 306 271 306
1957 315 301 356 348 355 422 465 467 404 347 305 336
1958 340 318 362 348 363 435 491 505 404 359 310 337
1959 360 342 406 396 420 472 548 559 463 407 362 405
1960 417 391 419 461 472 535 622 606 508 461 390 432
> presidents
     Qtr1 Qtr2 Qtr3 Qtr4
1945   NA   87   82   75
1946   63   50   43   32
1947   35   60   54   55
1948   36   39   NA   NA
1949   69   57   57   51
1950   45   37   46   39
1951   36   24   32   23
1952   25   32   NA   32
1953   59   74   75   60
1954   71   61   71   57
1955   71   68   79   73
1956   76   71   67   75
1957   79   62   63   57
1958   60   49   48   52
1959   57   62   61   66
1960   71   62   61   57
1961   72   83   71   78
1962   79   71   62   74
1963   76   64   62   57
1964   80   73   69   69
1965   71   64   69   62
1966   63   46   56   44
1967   44   52   38   46
1968   36   49   35   44
1969   59   65   65   56
1970   66   53   61   52
1971   51   48   54   49
1972   49   61   NA   NA
1973   68   44   40   27
1974   28   25   24   24
```

Figure 2-4. *Output of Both Commands*

Let's finish our walk-through of datasets with some pressing questions about ChickWeight dataset. Namely, which diet produces the fattest chicks? First, let's look at what the ChickWeight dataset is, structurally (See Figure 2-5).

```
> str(ChickWeight)
Classes 'nfnGroupedData', 'nfGroupedData', 'groupedData' and 'data.frame':
     578 obs. of  4 variables:
 $ weight: num   42 51 59 64 76 93 106 125 149 171 ...
 $ Time  : num   0 2 4 6 8 10 12 14 16 18 ...
 $ Chick : Ord.factor w/ 50 levels "18"<"16"<"15"<..: 15 15 15 15 15 15 15 15 15 15 ...
 $ Diet  : Factor w/ 4 levels "1","2","3","4": 1 1 1 1 1 1 1 1 1 1 ...
 - attr(*, "formula")=Class 'formula'  language weight ~ Time | Chick
 .. ..- attr(*, ".Environment")=<environment: R_EmptyEnv>
 - attr(*, "outer")=Class 'formula'  language ~Diet
 .. ..- attr(*, ".Environment")=<environment: R_EmptyEnv>
 - attr(*, "labels")=List of 2
 ..$ x: chr "Time"
 ..$ y: chr "Body weight"
 - attr(*, "units")=List of 2
 ..$ x: chr "(days)"
 ..$ y: chr "(gm)"
```

Figure 2-5. *ChickWeight Structure*

We see that we have 4 variables and 578 observations. Chick is an ordinal factor, likely the ID number assigned to the chick. Diet is the diet version that the chick received. Time is the number of days old, and weight is, well, the weight of the chick. I wonder if we have an equal number of observations for each diet? I'll take a look with the `table(ChickWeight$Diet)` command (See Figure 2-6).

```
> table(ChickWeight$Diet)

  1   2   3   4
220 120 120 118
```

Figure 2-6. *ChickWeight Diet Table*

Looks like we have a few more chicks on Diet 1 vs. Diets 2–4, but we have over 30 in each group, so we could assume normality... probably. Just to be on the safe side, let's look at the distributions with a simple plot: `interaction.plot(ChickWeight$Time, ChickWeight$Diet,ChickWeight$weight)` (See Figure 2-7).

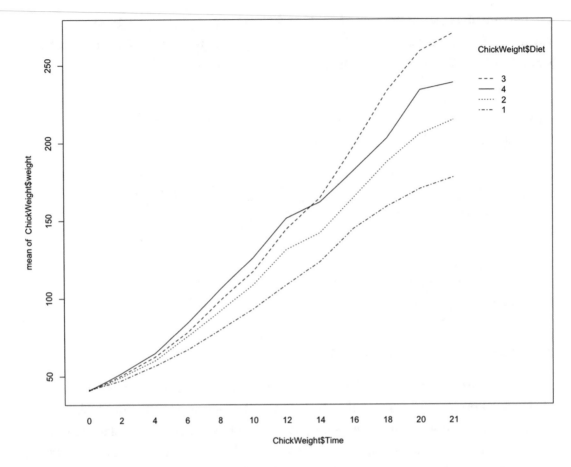

Figure 2-7. *ChickWeight by Time by Diet*

The plot shows me that it certainly looks like Diet 3 produces the heaviest chicks at 21 days. I wonder if that's true, and by true, I mean based upon inferential statistics. Let's take a look at a linear model by issuing the commands here:

```
fit <- lm(weight ~ Time * Diet, data=ChickWeight)
summary(fit).
```

This returns our linear model output shown here (Figure 2-8).

```
> fit <- lm(weight ~ Time * Diet, data=ChickWeight)
> summary(fit)

Call:
lm(formula = weight ~ Time * Diet, data = ChickWeight)

Residuals:
     Min      1Q   Median      3Q     Max
 -135.425 -13.757  -1.311  11.069 130.391

Coefficients:
             Estimate Std. Error t value Pr(>|t|)
(Intercept)  30.9310     4.2468   7.283 1.09e-12 ***
Time          6.8418     0.3408  20.076  < 2e-16 ***
Diet2        -2.2974     7.2672  -0.316  0.75202
Diet3       -12.6807     7.2672  -1.745  0.08154 .
Diet4        -0.1389     7.2865  -0.019  0.98480
Time:Diet2    1.7673     0.5717   3.092  0.00209 **
Time:Diet3    4.5811     0.5717   8.014 6.33e-15 ***
Time:Diet4    2.8726     0.5781   4.969 8.92e-07 ***
---
Signif. codes:  0 '***' 0.001 '**' 0.01 '*' 0.05 '.' 0.1 ' ' 1

Residual standard error: 34.07 on 570 degrees of freedom
Multiple R-squared:  0.773,   Adjusted R-squared:  0.7702
F-statistic: 277.3 on 7 and 570 DF,  p-value: < 2.2e-16
```

Figure 2-8. *Linear Model Output*

For those of you who haven't taken stats in a while, I'll walk you through the output:

- Time is a significant predictor with a positive estimate – this means that all things being equal, the chicks go up 6.84 grams on average per day.

- Diets 2 and 4 are not significantly different from the baseline Diet 1, but Diet 3 is marginally worse. This seems at odds with what we saw in the plot where Diet 3 seemed much better.

- That's why we have those interaction terms – they show us what's really happening. As time goes up, all diets do better, but the one with the largest difference is Diet 3!

Linear models compare things relative to a baseline level – in this case Diet 1. What if we were to make the baseline level Diet 3? Would we see that all diets were significantly worse? Remember that relevel command I talked about earlier? Let's modify our code a bit and see what happens (See Figure 2-9):

```
ChickWeight$Diet <- relevel(ChickWeight$Diet, 3)
fit <- lm(weight ~ Time * Diet, data=ChickWeight)
summary(fit)
```

```
> ChickWeight$Diet <- relevel(ChickWeight$Diet, 3)
> fit <- lm(weight ~ Time * Diet, data=ChickWeight)
> summary(fit)

Call:
lm(formula = weight ~ Time * Diet, data = ChickWeight)

Residuals:
    Min      1Q   Median      3Q      Max
-135.425  -13.757   -1.311   11.069  130.391

Coefficients:
            Estimate Std. Error t value Pr(>|t|)
(Intercept)  18.2503     5.8972   3.095  0.00207 **
Time         11.4229     0.4590  24.887  < 2e-16 ***
Diet1        12.6807     7.2672   1.745  0.08154 .
Diet2        10.3833     8.3399   1.245  0.21364
Diet4        12.5418     8.3567   1.501  0.13396
Time:Diet1   -4.5811     0.5717  -8.014 6.33e-15 ***
Time:Diet2   -2.8137     0.6491  -4.335 1.72e-05 ***
Time:Diet4   -1.7085     0.6548  -2.609  0.00931 **
---
Signif. codes:  0 '***' 0.001 '**' 0.01 '*' 0.05 '.' 0.1 ' ' 1

Residual standard error: 34.07 on 570 degrees of freedom
Multiple R-squared:  0.773,   Adjusted R-squared:  0.7702
F-statistic: 277.3 on 7 and 570 DF,  p-value: < 2.2e-16
```

Figure 2-9. *Releveling of ChickWeight*

Ah, just as I suspected, with the comparison against Diet 3, all four diets are significantly worse than Diet 3. We have our winning diet to produce fat chicks![2]

One important thing to note about the last section on linear models – it's included here as an example of how you can easily run a complex statistical test within R in just a few lines. We'll use linear regression throughout the book a few more times, and if you're not familiar with it, I highly suggest background reading to understand the assumptions that are made when interpreting a model. An excellent primer, if you're not familiar with regression diagnostics and assumptions, can be found at `www.sthda.com/english/articles/39-regression-model-diagnostics/161-linear-regression-assumptions-and-diagnostics-in-r-essentials/`. Throughout this book I skip some of these steps in order to move us to the findings a little quicker; however, if you are planning to publish your results in a scientific journal, be sure to check your diagnostics and assumptions before reporting a completed model.

As you can see, working with data in R is pretty straightforward, but so far our data has either been typed in or it's been pre-loaded into R. How do we get larger datasets? That's what we'll cover in the next section!

---

[2]In all of the years I've written things, I never thought I'd get to write that last sentence and it be completely accurate and non-pejorative.

Getting Data into R

In this section, we'll cover the most common ways that we can get data into R:

- Typing it in or piping them in via a script

- Reading it in from a flat file

- Getting it in via a database server

- Scraping it off of the Internet

I'll take each one of these areas and give you some of my favorite methods; however, it's important to recognize that at the end of the day, all we're doing is piping data from one place to another, and that can take various forms. These are some that I believe are most intuitive, but you'll likely see others as you explore R further.

Typing in Data or Piping It In

As you've seen, we can get data into R by simply typing it in via the console or a script. This is fine for a small set of values and for teaching demonstrations, although it will get out of hand fairly quickly. Those of you who are familiar with the SAS language might recall that SAS allowed for data to be placed directly in analysis script files through the `datalines` or `cards` commands. R allows a similar method that looks like this, the output of which can be seen in Figure 2-10:

```
OurData = ("
Student Pretest Posttest
A 25 27
B 23 23
C 21 22
D 23 29
E 23 24
F 21 19
")
Data = read.table(textConnection(OurData),header=T)
t.test(Data$Pretest,Data$Posttest,paired=T)[3]
```

---

[3]1-1.textConnection.r

```
> OurData = ("
+ Student    Pretest Posttest
+ A 25 27
+ B 23 23
+ C 21 22
+ D 23 29
+ E 23 24
+ F 21 19
+ ")
> Data = read.table(textConnection(OurData),header=T)
> t.test(Data$Pretest,Data$Posttest,paired=T)

    Paired t-test

data:  Data$Pretest and Data$Posttest
t = -1.2286, df = 5, p-value = 0.2739
alternative hypothesis: true difference in means is not equal to 0
95 percent confidence interval:
 -4.123069  1.456403
sample estimates:
mean of the differences
            -1.333333
```

Figure 2-10. *Output of the Preceding Code*

I refer to this method as the textConnection method, since it uses that built-in function to take the data out of the first several lines and create a data frame. I really like this method for teaching as it allows me to show off data directly in R, without having to open Excel or another application to show it there before running the statistics on it. And before we move on, for the stats nerds and geeks out there, the paired t-test done indicates that the students did not do so well – no improvement between pretest and posttest. Want to lend them a hand? Change Student F's posttest grade from 19 to 25. Now the p-value drops to 0.052. Not great, and an example of p-hacking, but since this is fake data, we can do what we want!

What about larger datasets though? Something I can't have all in one file? Let's work with that next!

Reading Data in from Text and Excel Files

In order for us to read data in from a file, we're going to need some data. What better place than Data.gov, the homepage for open data from the United States government? I chose to download a dataset from a United States Department of Education program named My Brother's Keeper, a project that aims to improve the expected educational and life indexes for men of color. I downloaded a CSV (comma-separated value) file with the ludicrously long name of userssharedsdfratebrthsyaw1819raceethncty20002012.csv.

Once I got this extremely long named file on my computer, I had to store it somewhere that I can access with R. This typically isn't a problem unless you're running on an operating system that sandboxes files to prevent one application from modifying another. In my case, I put it in my Downloads folder, which on my computer is at /Users/jon/Downloads. The exact command I used to read this into R and store it in an object named data was

```
data <-
read.csv("/Users/jon/Downloads/userssharedsdfratebrthsyaw1819raceethncty
20002012.csv");
```

And being that I'm on macOS Catalina, I received the following warning message (See Figure 2-11).

Figure 2-11. *macOS Catalina File Access Warning*

This is a security measure that my computer is taking to make sure that malicious apps don't go mucking around with my personal files. It adds a bit more work though compared to how things used to be. Wouldn't it be great if I could just download this straight from the Web? Turns out I totally can – because this works as well:

```
data <- read.csv("https://inventory.data.gov/dataset/cedbc0ee-d679-4ebf-
8b00-502dc0de5738/resource/ef734bd0-0aff-4687-9b8a-fc69b937be63/download/
userssharedsdfratebrthsyaw1819raceethncty20002012.csv");
```

Note   If you're downloading a particularly large file, you may want to use this version of the code that downloads the file first – also useful if you want to keep a copy of the file for later:

```
download.file("https://inventory.data.gov/dataset/cedbc0ee-d679-4ebf-8b00-
502dc0de5738/resource/ef734bd0-0aff- 4687-9b8a-fc69b937be63/download/
userssharedsdfratebrthsyaw1819raceethncty20002012.csv", "data.csv",
method="auto", quiet=FALSE)
data <- read.csv("data.csv");
```

We've now seen one of the most powerful and versatile ways that R can save you time – it has full Internet access and can download files directly into its own memory. Think about what this means:

- If your data is stored on a web server and updated regularly, your R script can download a fresh copy each time, no need for you to download it first.

- If you want to share your script with someone else, you only need to send them the actual script, not the data file.

- If you use a service such as Google Sheets, you can publish a specific file to CSV by going to File and then "Publish to the web" and then using the URL provided in your script (remember that using "Publish to the web" does allow anyone who has the URL to access the data; See Figure 2-12).

Figure 2-12. *Published CSV File in Google Sheets*

So far our data has been in plain text – all the CSV file format does is place commas between each data value. We can actually tweak the read.csv() command's big brother, read.table(), with a ton of options to fit how our data is formatted, for example:

- header lets R know if the first line of the text should be treated as the header. This defaults to true for read.csv() and false for read.table().

- sep lets R know what the separator character is – a comma in read. csv() and a blank space in read.table().

- quote lets R know if it should place quotations around the imported data.

- dec lets R know the character used for decimal points.

- row.names and col.names are vectors that tell R what to call the rows and columns, respectively.

By mixing and matching arguments as needed, we can read many different plain text formats into R. Data not in plain text? That's a little trickier. The main culprit in this space: Microsoft Excel.

Reading in Microsoft Excel Data

The short answer here is: don't. If at all possible, I generally advise people to convert their data to CSV by using the Save As copy in Excel. This ensures you get exactly the data you want, without having to worry about sheets or strange formatting.

But if you really want to read data in from Excel, you do have options: the readxl package (a part of the tidyverse packages) or the openxlsx package. The following code will show you how to do this with the openxlsx package:

```
install.packages("openxlsx")
library(openxlsx)
data <- read.xlsx("/Users/jon/Downloads/Births-to-young-adult-women_
verified.no-chart.two-tabs-with-rates.xlsx")
```

Replacing the path with the appropriate path on your computer, you'll get the data into R, and the added benefit is that the openxlsx package can also be used to write data back to Excel, as we'll look at later. I still believe that plain text is easier and more flexible, but I recognize that sometimes in the business world, you need to speak Excel!

And sometimes you also need to speak "Database"!

Reading Data in from a Database Server

Database servers house everything from the combined financial records of the largest companies in the world to the blog posts of an angsty teenager. And while tools certainly do exist to download data from them to CSV file, it's often easier to skip that step and directly connect to the database from R. While this is primarily to retrieve data, it could also be to store data as well.

One of the largest and most well-known database servers around is MySQL and its fork, MariaDB. The workhorse of many websites, it's the MySQL database that houses data we often might want to download and analyze in R. Thankfully a package exists to do just that, named appropriately RMySQL. With this package, we can directly connect up to a MySQL database and drag the data down into R (other database users may wish to look at the RODBC package). Let's walk through how to access MySQL data using that package.

First, we need to be able to connect to the server. Most database servers on the Internet are protected by a firewall of some sort (or at least they should be). This means that even if we have the database credentials to our favorite WordPress blog, we can't just connect straight up to the server and download the content. We'd need to establish a secure connection to the server first. This can be done via a corporate VPN, for example, or through tunneling the connection over something that is, generally, available via the Internet: Secure Shell. The SSH protocol allows, if properly configured, for you to tunnel your traffic through the Secure Shell protocol and access services on the other side. You can do this via a simple command line; however, I prefer to use a graphical tool that lets me toggle the connection on or off. On macOS, I tend to use Core Tunnel, a screenshot of which is as follows (See Figure 2-13). On Windows, MobaXterm provides similar functionality.

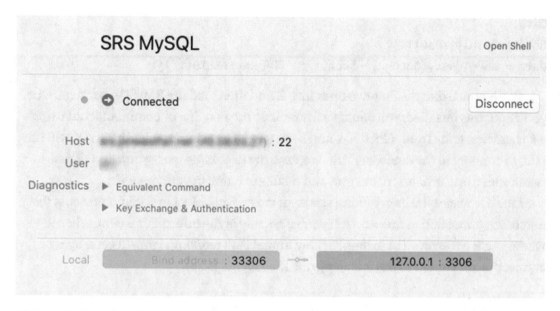

Figure 2-13. *Core Tunnel Routing a Database Server to My Local Machine*

The tunnel created earlier routes the database server, which normally runs on port 3306 of the destination machine, to port 33306 on my local machine. I prefer to add an extra digit or change the local port number just in case I want to have multiple tunnels open at the same time – imagine, you could use R to copy data from one database on Machine A to another database on Machine B, using a script that you could modify as needed!

Now that we have the connection set up, let's look at the following code:

```
install.packages("RMySQL");
library("RMySQL");
username <- "pr4";
password <- "pr4";
database <- "pr4-database";
dbconn <- dbConnect(MySQL(), user=username, password=password,
dbname=database, host="127.0.0.1", port=33306);
dbListTables(dbconn);
results <- dbSendQuery(dbconn, 'select * from secretstuff');
data = fetch(results, n=-1);
```

```
data
dbClearResult(results);
data = dbGetQuery(dbconn, "SELECT * FROM secretstuff");⁴
```

You'll notice that the first two lines install and then load the RMySQL package. Once you've got this installed, you could easily remove the first line or comment it out using a # character at the front. Lines 3, 4, and 5 are used to create variables the script will use later to connect to the database. You'd replace my username, password, and database name with the username, password, and database name in your scenario.

Line 6 is where the heavy lifting starts – it creates an object in R that represents the database connection to the server. If you've got any of the information wrong, here's where you'll get errors. For example, if my tunnel isn't working right, I'll get a "can't connect" error similar to the following one (See Figure 2-14).

```
> dbconn <- dbConnect(MySQL(), user=username, password=password, dbname=database, host="127.0.0.1",
port=33306);
Error in .local(drv, ...) :
  Failed to connect to database: Error: Can't connect to MySQL server on '127.0.0.1' (36)
```

Figure 2-14. *A Can't Connect Error from RMySQL*

Assuming you don't have any errors, your database connection has been created and stored in an object. I chose to name my object dbconn although you could name it whatever you want. Next, I decide to test to see if the database connection is working by listing the tables in the database using the dbListTables() command, and it returns one table, the ominously named secretstuff (See Figure 2-15). Sounds like an interesting table.

Let's actually view what's in that table. I've given you two examples of code that do the exact same thing, in order to talk about why you might want to use one over the other. Lines 8, 9, 10, and 11 do the following actions:

Line	Code	Action
8	results <- dbSendQuery(dbconn, 'select * from secretstuff');	This line sends and executes the SQL query to the database. In this case, it translates to show all variables and lines from the secretstuff table.

(continued)

---

⁴1–2.mysql.r

Line	Code	Action
9	`data = fetch(results, n=-1);`	The previous line created an object named `results` which is the raw data coming back from the MySQL database. This line, using the `fetch()` command, parses those results and loads them into a data frame named `data`. The n option tells it to load all of the results into one data frame.
10	`data`	This shows the data, so we can see if we returned the right items we were expecting.
11	`dbClearResult(results);`	This line frees the memory associated with the results and closes the query, allowing us to use `dbSendQuery()` again if we like.

Now the more astute of you that are working ahead may have noticed that Line 12, the innocent looking data = dbGetQuery(dbconn, "SELECT * FROM secretstuff"); actually did everything Lines 8, 9, and 11 did. So why go through the extra work?

```
> install.packages("RMySQL");
--- Please select a CRAN mirror for use in this session ---
trying URL 'https://cloud.r-project.org/bin/macosx/el-capitan/contrib/3.6/RMySQL_0.10.19.tgz'
Content type 'application/x-gzip' length 1760084 bytes (1.7 MB)
==================================================
downloaded 1.7 MB


The downloaded binary packages are in
        /var/folders/nt/z82_3xdd3m9fdg7623m3j69m0000gn/T//Rtmp3eOoVw/downloaded_packages
> library("RMySQL");
Loading required package: DBI
> username <- "pr4";
> password <- "pr4";
> database <- "pr4-database";
> dbconn <- dbConnect(MySQL(), user=username, password=password, dbname=database, host="127.0.0.1",
port=33306);
> dbListTables(dbconn);
[1] "secretstuff"
> results <- dbSendQuery(dbconn, 'select * from secretstuff');
> data = fetch(results, n=-1);
> data
  id vault                       treasure occupied
1  1   687              Potter Family Vault        Y
2  2   713 Something wrapped in brown parchment      N
> dbClearResult(results);
[1] TRUE
> data = dbGetQuery(dbconn, "SELECT * FROM secretstuff");
> data
  id vault                       treasure occupied
1  1   687              Potter Family Vault        Y
2  2   713 Something wrapped in brown parchment      N
```

Figure 2-15. *The Executed Code*

It all has to do with how much data you're bringing down and what you want to do with it. If you have a large number of records, the first route is best as it will let you read in various "chunks" of data into your data frames. The dbSendQuery() function is also more flexible – you don't have to use a SELECT statement, you could use an insert, update, or drop statement to modify the database directly. In practical work though, dbGetQuery() will speed you up by allowing you to write cleaner, more concise code.

Speaking of cleaner and more concise code, it's a good time to note that those two things can often be at odds. You may have noticed that sometimes I place semicolons at the end of my code statements and sometimes not. The reason for this is that R can support putting multiple statements on the same line of code. The following two code blocks are equally valid:

```
x <- 2
y <- 3
```

or

```
x <- 2; y <- 3
```

This seems very handy, and it is – for simple code declarations. But imagine code that looks like this – again, equally valid:

```
library("RMySQL");data = dbGetQuery(dbConnect(MySQL(), user="pr4",
password="pr4", dbname="pr4-database", host="127.0.0.1", port=33306),
"SELECT * FROM secretstuff");data;
```

That line of code – yes, it's a single line – will work fine. But it can be extremely challenging to read and understand, especially when you're new to R. Eventually I believe every R user finds a comfortable level of code "conciseness," where their code is easy to read and also doesn't span dozens of unnecessary lines. When starting out, though, it is sometimes very useful to "unpack" code like this, placing it on multiple lines and executing parts of it sequentially instead of all at one time, in order to troubleshoot where errors might exist.

Now that we've looked at getting data out of a database, what about the situation where a database isn't an option – but the data is still online? Imagine a website that has reports of data, but it's all nicely formatted on HTML pages with pretty styling. How would we get that data then? By scraping it – of course!

Web Scraping Data

Web scraping is a very detailed topic that an entire book could be written about, so my goal in this section is to give you a quick use scenario, talk briefly about how to accomplish your task, and then give you some advice for playing around with it. You'll soon find that once you can scrape data off of a web page, you will find new and clever uses for such an ability to automate your life.

In brief, web scraping involves downloading the source HTML of a web page and parsing out exactly the data you're interested in. R has a number of tools available to help do this, and in this example, we'll use the rvest package. Imagine the following scenario: I need to get the officially published number of total faculty at my university. It just so happens that a website exists, maintained by the United States Department of Education, that has this information. It's the National Center for Education Statistics College Navigator which pulls its data from IPEDS (the Integrated Postsecondary Education Data System; See Figure 2-16). All higher education institutions that accept federal grant and loan money are required to report data to IPEDS, and while it is possible to download the IPEDS databases through Data.gov, let's imagine that I am familiar with College Navigator, and I want to scrape the data from there.

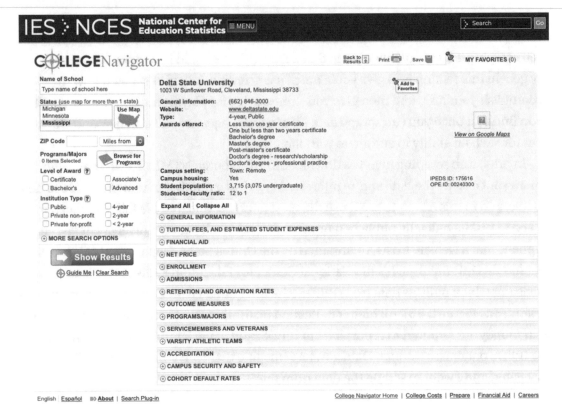

Figure 2-16. *The College Navigator Entry for Delta State University*

Pulling up my university in NCES, I can see that there are a ton of collapsed tables on the page. Expanding the first, I see the number I want – total faculty. (See Figure 2-17).

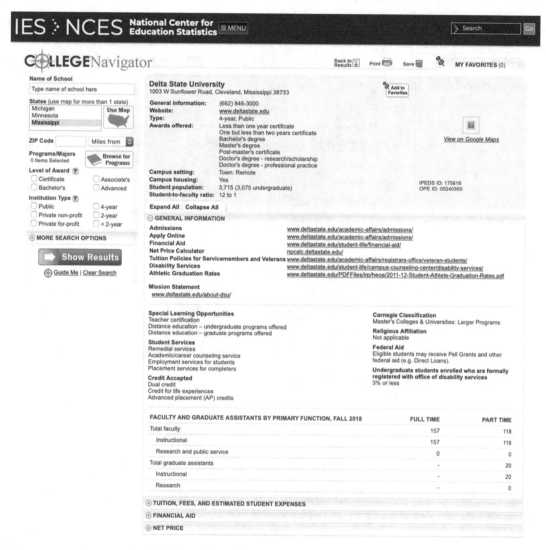

Figure 2-17. *Expanded View in NCES*

Well, from here I can see the number – 157 – and if I wanted to, I could just paste that number into my R script as I need it. But when that number changes, say if we hire someone new, I'm going to have to update it. And that's just going to add extra work for me in the future. Figure out how to scrape it once, and unless NCES changes their design layout, I should be good for a while. Also, imagine if I have 20 schools and I want to pull this number for all 20 – much easier to just collect a series of URLs and feed them into my R script vs. open each new page, expand the tab, and write down the number (also much less prone to typos!).

The first step is to figure out how the data is formatted in HTML. Using the "Inspect Element" command in my browser (Safari; other browsers have similar commands; See Figure 2-18 and Figure 2-19), I can see that it's an HTML table (`<td>`) inside a CSS class named `tabular`.

Figure 2-18. *Inspect Element Command*

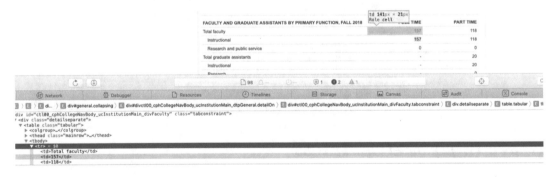

Figure 2-19. *Viewing the Attributes*

Now I know where it is, and I can begin to build my script in R. This script pulls in everything I need, producing the output below it:

```
install.packages("rvest");
library("rvest");
addr <- https://nces.ed.gov/collegenavigator/?s=MS&pg=2&id=175616
page <- read_html(addr);
nodes <- html_nodes(page,".tabular td");
totfaculty <- html_text(nodes)[2]
paste("The total number of faculty are",totfaculty);[5]
```

And the output of the script looks like this (See Figure 2-20).

---

[5]1–3.scraping.example.r

```
> install.packages("rvest");
also installing the dependencies 'sys', 'askpass', 'curl', 'jsonlite', 'mime', 'openssl', 'xml2', 'httr',
'selectr'

trying URL 'https://cloud.r-project.org/bin/macosx/el-capitan/contrib/3.6/sys_3.3.tgz'
Content type 'application/x-gzip' length 47231 bytes (46 KB)
==================================================
downloaded 46 KB

trying URL 'https://cloud.r-project.org/bin/macosx/el-capitan/contrib/3.6/askpass_1.1.tgz'
Content type 'application/x-gzip' length 21926 bytes (21 KB)
==================================================
downloaded 21 KB

trying URL 'https://cloud.r-project.org/bin/macosx/el-capitan/contrib/3.6/curl_4.3.tgz'
Content type 'application/x-gzip' length 741337 bytes (723 KB)
==================================================
downloaded 723 KB

trying URL 'https://cloud.r-project.org/bin/macosx/el-capitan/contrib/3.6/jsonlite_1.6.1.tgz'
Content type 'application/x-gzip' length 1120424 bytes (1.1 MB)
==================================================
downloaded 1.1 MB

trying URL 'https://cloud.r-project.org/bin/macosx/el-capitan/contrib/3.6/mime_0.9.tgz'
Content type 'application/x-gzip' length 35386 bytes (34 KB)
==================================================
downloaded 34 KB

trying URL 'https://cloud.r-project.org/bin/macosx/el-capitan/contrib/3.6/openssl_1.4.1.tgz'
Content type 'application/x-gzip' length 2690137 bytes (2.6 MB)
==================================================
downloaded 2.6 MB

trying URL 'https://cloud.r-project.org/bin/macosx/el-capitan/contrib/3.6/xml2_1.2.2.tgz'
Content type 'application/x-gzip' length 1102370 bytes (1.1 MB)
==================================================
downloaded 1.1 MB

trying URL 'https://cloud.r-project.org/bin/macosx/el-capitan/contrib/3.6/httr_1.4.1.tgz'
Content type 'application/x-gzip' length 492648 bytes (481 KB)
==================================================
downloaded 481 KB

trying URL 'https://cloud.r-project.org/bin/macosx/el-capitan/contrib/3.6/selectr_0.4-2.tgz'
Content type 'application/x-gzip' length 490483 bytes (478 KB)
==================================================
downloaded 478 KB

trying URL 'https://cloud.r-project.org/bin/macosx/el-capitan/contrib/3.6/rvest_0.3.5.tgz'
Content type 'application/x-gzip' length 662160 bytes (646 KB)
==================================================
downloaded 646 KB


The downloaded binary packages are in
    /var/folders/nt/z82_3xdd3m9fdg7623m3j69m0000gn/T//Rtmp3eOoVw/downloaded_packages
> library("rvest");
Loading required package: xml2
> addr <- "https://nces.ed.gov/collegenavigator/?s=MS&pg=2&id=175616"
> page <- read_html(addr);
> nodes <- html_nodes(page,".tabular td");
> totfaculty <- html_text(nodes)[2]
> paste("The total number of faculty are",totfaculty);
[1] "The total number of faculty are 157"
```

Figure 2-20. *Output of 1-3.scraping.example.r*

First off, you'll notice a ton of downloaded packages – remember that R packages can rely on each other, and in this case, rvest uses a lot of other packages to get its job done. The majority of the time these don't cause any issue, but it's important to remember this if you ever have a script stop working – it might be that one of the packages that it depends on isn't working right or loading properly.

Next, you'll see a line declaring the variable addr which is the URL of my institution in NCES. It's the address I'd paste into my browser's address bar in order to view it. Next are the page and nodes variables, the first of which downloads the HTML code from the page and the second breaks it down into components. We can see what these look like by typing their name (See Figure 2-21).

```
> page
{html_document}
<html xmlns="http://www.w3.org/1999/xhtml" lang="en" xml:lang="en">
[1] <head id="ctl00_hd">\n<meta http-equiv="Content-type" content="text/html;charset=UTF-8">\n<title>\r ...
[2] <body id="ctl00_bodyMain" onload="if(typeof imgPL=='function')imgPL();if(typeof sp=='function')sp() ...
> nodes
{xml_nodeset (554)}
 [1] <td>Total faculty</td>\n
 [2] <td>157</td>\n
 [3] <td>118</td>
 [4] <td style="padding-left:16px">Instructional</td>\n
 [5] <td>157</td>\n
 [6] <td>118</td>
 [7] <td style="padding-left:16px">Research and public service</td>\n
 [8] <td>0</td>\n
 [9] <td>0</td>
[10] <td>Total graduate assistants</td>\n
[11] <td>-</td>\n
[12] <td>20</td>
[13] <td style="padding-left:16px">Instructional</td>\n
[14] <td>-</td>\n
[15] <td>20</td>
[16] <td style="padding-left:16px">Research</td>\n
[17] <td>-</td>\n
[18] <td>0</td>
[19] <td scope="row">Tuition and fees</td>\n
[20] <td>$6,418</td>\n
...
```

Figure 2-21. *The Output of the Page and Nodes Variables*

By examining the nodes variable, I can see that the line I want is in element 2 of the node. From there, all I need to do is use the html_text() function to clean it up (by stripping off the HTML code) and store it in a variable, totfaculty. I can then do whatever I want with it, and in this case, I'm pasting it into my output, letting the person running the script know what the value was.

Obviously, I can expand this example however I like. I could run the code on multiple page addresses and download the total faculty for a variety of other schools and then build a table of them. I could also further explore the page and grab other elements, like the University's name:

```
header <- html_nodes(page, ".headerlg");
name <- html_text(header);
paste("The total number of faculty at",name,"is",totfaculty);
```

Once you start scraping, you can really get carried away with all the data you can grab. Combine that with reading from databases, flat files, and scripts themselves, and you can quickly build up a little data arsenal in your R console. So once it's all there, what are you going to do with it? Probably at some point you'll want to save it to use later. Let's talk about that in the next section.

Saving R Data

As you work with R, you create a bunch of objects. You can see those objects anytime by using the ls() command. After the previous examples, these were the objects left in my workspace (See Figure 2-22).

```
> ls()
 [1] "addr"        "data"        "database"    "dbconn"      "header"      "name"        "nodes"
 [8] "page"        "password"    "results"     "totfaculty"  "username"
```

Figure 2-22. *Objects in My Workspace*

Some of those objects are pretty small – just a username or an HTML page. But others are quite large – data, for example, is a data frame from my secretstuff table. If I close R, I'll get a message asking what I want to do with the items on my workspace, specifically asking if I want to save my workspace "image" (See Figure 2-23).

Figure 2-23. *Workspace Save Prompt*

What exactly does this mean? Well, it means that the next time I open R, I'll see a message that my Workspace and History have been restored. Now if I type ls() again, everything is just as it was when I left (See Figure 2-24).

```
R version 3.6.2 (2019-12-12) -- "Dark and Stormy Night"
Copyright (C) 2019 The R Foundation for Statistical Computing
Platform: x86_64-apple-darwin15.6.0 (64-bit)

R is free software and comes with ABSOLUTELY NO WARRANTY.
You are welcome to redistribute it under certain conditions.
Type 'license()' or 'licence()' for distribution details.

  Natural language support but running in an English locale

R is a collaborative project with many contributors.
Type 'contributors()' for more information and
'citation()' on how to cite R or R packages in publications.

Type 'demo()' for some demos, 'help()' for on-line help, or
'help.start()' for an HTML browser interface to help.
Type 'q()' to quit R.

[R.app GUI 1.70 (7735) x86_64-apple-darwin15.6.0]

[Workspace restored from /Users/jon/.RData]
[History restored from /Users/jon/.Rapp.history]

> ls()
 [1] "addr"       "data"       "database"   "dbconn"     "header"     "name"      "nodes"
 [8] "page"       "password"   "results"    "totfaculty" "username"
 ~ |
```

Figure 2-24. *Workspace Restored*

This is great, as long as I'm still working on the same things that I was working on before. But what if I want to work on a different set of data, or files, or projects? Then I'll need to work with my "workspace" a bit more by directly saving, clearing, and restoring it. I can use the following commands:

Command	What It Does	Example
`getwd()` and `setwd()`	Gets or sets the working directory – the path on your computer that R will look for files to read and will write files if not given a full directory path	`getwd(); setwd ("/Users/jon/ Downloads")`
`history()`	Views previous command history	`history (max.show=Inf`
`savehistory()` and `loadhistory()`	Saves and loads history from a file	`savehistory ("myhistoryfile")`
`save.image()`	Saves everything in your workspace (e.g., all objects) to an image	`save.image ("mywork.RData")`
`load()`	Loads an image into R's workspace	`load ("mywork.RData")`

You'll notice that, sometimes, individuals distribute their RData file vs. another format because it provides a full view of the workspace – which can be helpful if you have multiple datasets loaded or specially written functions to analyze data. If you don't want to write everything to an RData format, you can also use `saveRDS()` to save a single item, such as `saveRDS(data, file = "thedata.rds")`, reading it in with `readRDS("thedata.rds")`. Thus, to save and distribute your data, all you might need to provide to someone is the RData and R script file, which typically has the ending `.r` as we've seen thus far.

If your friend isn't an R user though, and you've been unable to convert her to the language yet, then I suppose you can also save in other applications.

Saving to Another Application

R has a number of Import/Export options to help move data wherever you need it to be. Here are a few options, and some of the commands or packages you could explore:

Other Format	Options
Excel or spreadsheet	Use commands such as `write.csv()` or `write.xlsx()` from the `openxlsx` package.
Database	Use query functions in packages such as RMySQL or RODBC to connect up to the database and push the data.
Word or word processors	This one is a little trickier. Packages such as R2wd work, but only on Windows. The package ReporteRs is an option, but requires Java to run. If possible, simply use the HTML format options listed as follows.
HTML format	Using RMarkdown and packages such as `knitr`, one can create dynamic HTML content easily within R, exporting it in prettier formats than spreadsheets. We'll discuss this more in future chapters.

We've come a long way in this chapter – from typing in all of our R data to bringing it in through web scraping and databases. We're now ready for our first project – launching a web-based survey, getting the data into R, analyzing it, and becoming a sales or marketing superstar!

## CHAPTER 3

Project 1: Launching, Analyzing, and Reporting a Survey Using R and LimeSurvey

When I was a graduate student, a former student who had gone into industry came back to visit us a year post-graduation. He was working for a company in marketing, a rare departure from the bulk of our comrades who had gone into academia. Talking with him, I asked what the biggest difference was. He smiled and told me of a meeting he'd recently been in with the sales team. They were very happy that sales were up that month compared to last month. He asked "What is the standard deviation of monthly sales?" They looked at him perplexed, until one of them asked "Is that important?"

Anyone who has taken a statistics course knows the answer – the actual average is hard to place without the standard deviation, which is an estimate of how far any given score is typically located away from the mean. If Month A has you earning $500 in sales, and Month B has you at $600, that sounds good. Find out that the standard deviation is $125, and all of a sudden there really hasn't been too big of a difference between A and B.

In many ways, businesses thrive on data; however, getting it and interpreting it can be a challenging task. In this chapter, I'm going to give you a real-world scenario: a market research project. I'll show you how to collect the data, analyze the data, and report the data, all using open source software. Along the way, I'll give a bit of a dose on survey research and data analysis that, while not intended to replace research

© Jon Westfall 2020
J. Westfall, *Practical R 4*, https://doi.org/10.1007/978-1-4842-5946-7_3

methodology courses or statistics courses, does come from a professor who regularly teaches them. My goal is to give you enough to start exploring, and if you find that you need more information, I can give you some references on that as well! Let's get started.

The Project: A Customer Satisfaction Survey Regarding a New Product

Our scenario is simple: you work for a company who has just rolled out a new product. You want to know how people like the product and are specifically interested in a few key demographic groups – gender, age, and a few targeted questions to help you identify preferences your customers already have. To top it off, your boss specifically wants to know the exact right combination – should you target older men? Younger women? Computer geeks? Or people enamored with the "Cat yelling at a woman" meme that was so popular in late 2019? Or all of those mentioned?

We'll walk through how to accomplish the preceding scenario in the quickest way possible while also exploring a few new open source tools that will aid us: LimeSurvey, and later, RStudio. Let's start with the former!

Introducing LimeSurvey

Almost 2 decades ago, in 2003, an open source software project named PHPSurveyor was first released by programmer Jason Cleeland on SourceForge.net. In a time before widespread adoption of platforms such as Qualtrics (est. 2002) and SurveyMonkey (est. 1999), most of the survey data that was collected on the Internet came from custom-written software, likely HTML Forms pages that had been strung together and coded to write to a database back end. I recall a programming project I was hired to do in 2005 that was simply that – a survey. Today with SurveyMonkey having a free tier and Google Forms an option, it's easy to get basic data from large groups of people with low cost; however, features such as conditional branching, modifiable templates, and closed access surveys (e.g., invite-only) can be difficult to achieve without paying a premium – unless you know about PHPSurveyor's current name: LimeSurvey.

LimeSurvey offers a number of premium features that make it an essential tool in any researcher-on-a-budget's toolkit. These include

- The ability to branch respondents to different questions based on previous answers (e.g., a question early on can ask if the person smokes, and if yes, later they can be shown questions regarding their smoking habits).

- The ability to fully customize the look and feel of the survey using pre-defined templates.

- A closed access/token option, which allows you to send personalized invitations to respondents, with a one-time access code that allows them to take the survey.

- A panel integration feature that lets you keep and reuse a group of respondents allowing you to send out multiple surveys and track responses across all of them. Essentially, you could use this to build a robust user profile of your customers or constituents.

- Programmatic options to embed previous answers into subsequent questions, randomize the order of various questions, and fully import or export previous surveys.

- Multi-user access, allowing an entire organization to use LimeSurvey without worry of one group interfering with another.

All of this is offered free through the self-hosted Community Edition of LimeSurvey. Those who find the following steps a bit daunting and would rather pay for a hosted service can look into LimeSurvey Pro, which has various tiers available depending on how many responses you plan to collect.

Assuming you're a bit tech-savvy and you want to run LimeSurvey on your own server or cloud storage provider, I'll outline the steps as follows to get you up and running. Then, we'll build a sample survey.

Installing LimeSurvey on a LAMP

Installing LimeSurvey follows the same basic method as any other open source server-based application described as "LAMP" or "LAMP stack." If you already know what that means, you'll be up and running fairly quickly. If you do not, I'll give you the basic road map. First, you'll want to head over to the LimeSurvey homepage (Figure 3-1) and click HOST YOURSELF. This will take you to the Community Edition download screen (Figure 3-2).

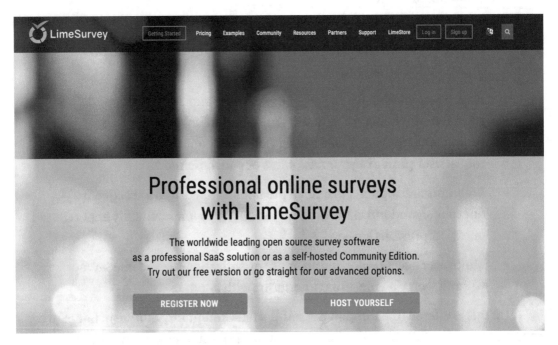

Figure 3-1. *The LimeSurvey Homepage*

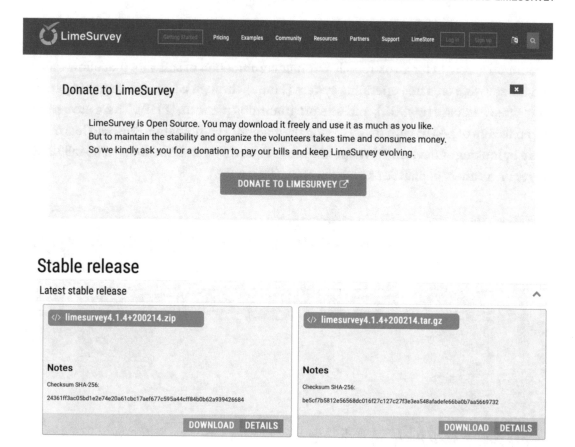

Figure 3-2. *The Stable Release of LimeSurvey Community Edition*

If you already have a server or cloud storage bucket that you can install the software into, you can download the latest stable version in whatever format you prefer. I tend to simply use wget on Linux to download the latest stable gzipped version, which I can then unpack (Figure 3-3).

External links [edit]

- Install a LAMP server on Ubuntu Linux
- Install a LAMP server on Debian GNU/Linux
- Install a LAMP server on SUSE Linux
- Install a LAMP server on Amazon AWS
- Install a LAMP server on CentOS 5.x.

Figure 3-3. *Downloading LimeSurvey in a Linux Terminal*

Now we need to talk a little bit about server options. LimeSurvey runs as a LAMP application, with LAMP standing for **Linux**, **Apache**, **MySQL** (or **MariaDB**), and **P**HP. It's a common acronym for an extremely popular combination of software that allows you to run the software on a free operating system (Linux), through a free web server (Apache) with a free database (MySQL), and free programming platform (PHP). There are several dozen flavors of LAMP, with many having their favorite combination. You can learn more by looking at the LAMP Wikipedia entry (Figure 3-4) and find links to install LAMP server on a variety of platforms at the bottom (Figure 3-5).

Figure 3-4. *LAMP Entry on Wikipedia*

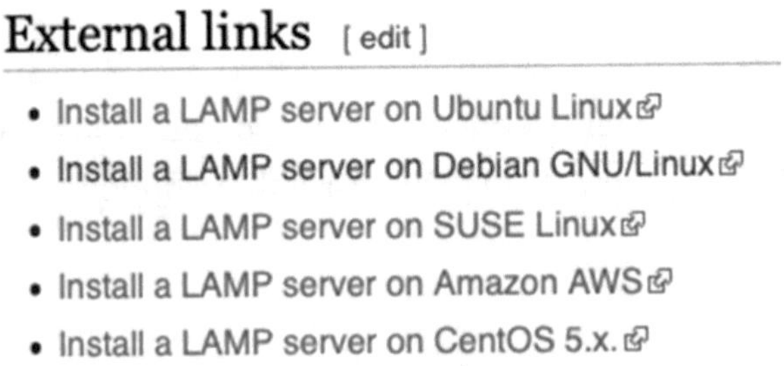

External links   [edit]

- Install a LAMP server on Ubuntu Linux⊡
- Install a LAMP server on Debian GNU/Linux⊡
- Install a LAMP server on SUSE Linux⊡
- Install a LAMP server on Amazon AWS⊡
- Install a LAMP server on CentOS 5.x.⊡

Figure 3-5. *Links to Install a LAMP Server*

If you are more familiar with cloud applications, you can install LimeSurvey on a cloud platform such as Amazon Web Services or Microsoft's Azure. You'll need a server instance to house the files and serve them and a database to write to. Various blog posts and tutorials exist that can walk you through your platform and installation.

If you simply want to test out LimeSurvey on your own computer, I've used XAMPP (Figure 3-6) for many years on Windows and Mac computers. It's a simple one-stop download that will get your computer set up with the essential elements quickly. It's meant for development work and is a great place to try out LimeSurvey before buying a virtual server or cloud computing service. In a small environment, such as a corporate office, you might even be able to use it to run surveys on a secured intranet, within your own work group.

Figure 3-6. *The XAMPP Homepage*

However you decide to house or serve your files, you'll run through a pretty basic installation process. Once the files are unpacked, navigating to them (by going to the web address associated with where you placed them, e.g., `http://localhost`) will launch the LimeSurvey installation. It will ask you a series of questions regarding how to configure LimeSurvey, as well as connection details for your database. Once you've got your system up and running, you can navigate to the LimeSurvey login page at `/admin` (Figure 3-7), logging in with the username and password you set during installation (Figure 3-8).

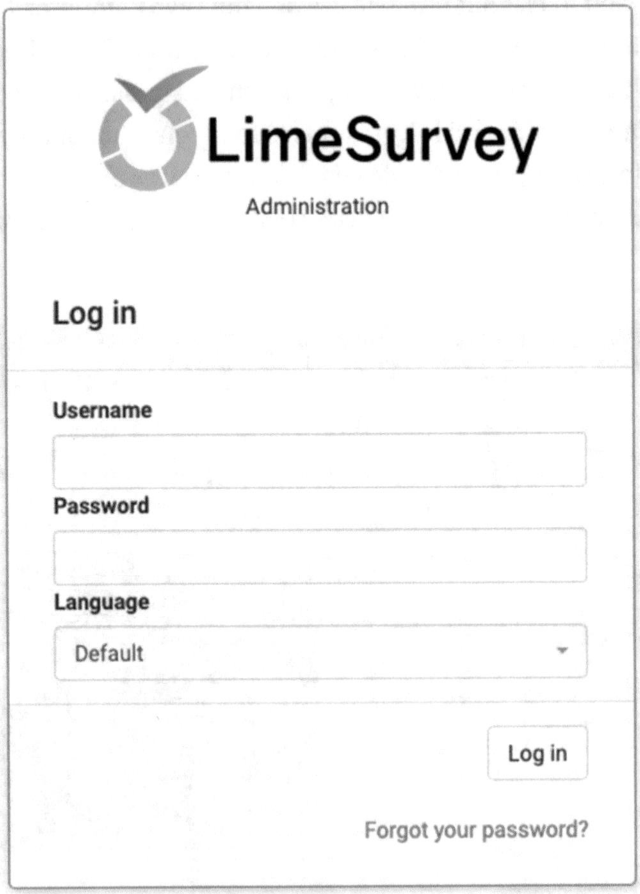

Figure 3-7. *The Login Screen for LimeSurvey, at /admin*

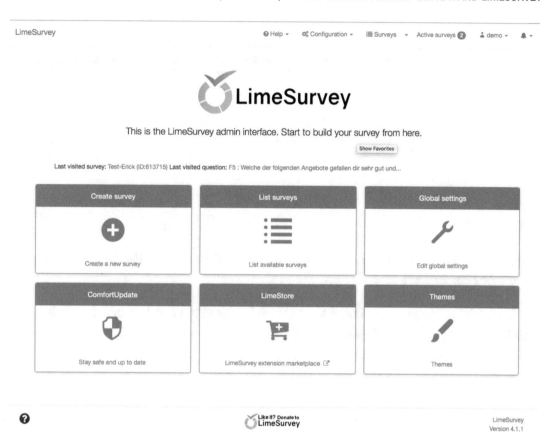

Figure 3-8. *The LimeSurvey Admin Homepage*

It's important to note that earlier versions of LimeSurvey do differ slightly in their layout, and local administrators can customize this screen as well. In Figure 3-9, we see a slightly earlier version that you'll see is subtly different than the version in Figure 3-7. Regardless of version, the same basic operations exist. They just might be slightly bigger or smaller, depending on browser size and customizations.

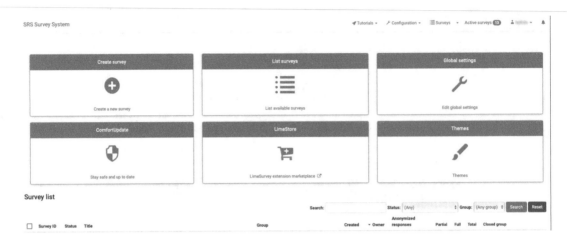

Figure 3-9. *The LimeSurvey Admin Homepage of an Earlier Version, Showing the Create Survey Button*

Once you've logged in, it's time to start building your survey. You can do this by clicking the "Create Survey" button that we saw in Figures 3-7 and 3-9. You'll be taken to the Create New Survey screen (Figure 3-10).

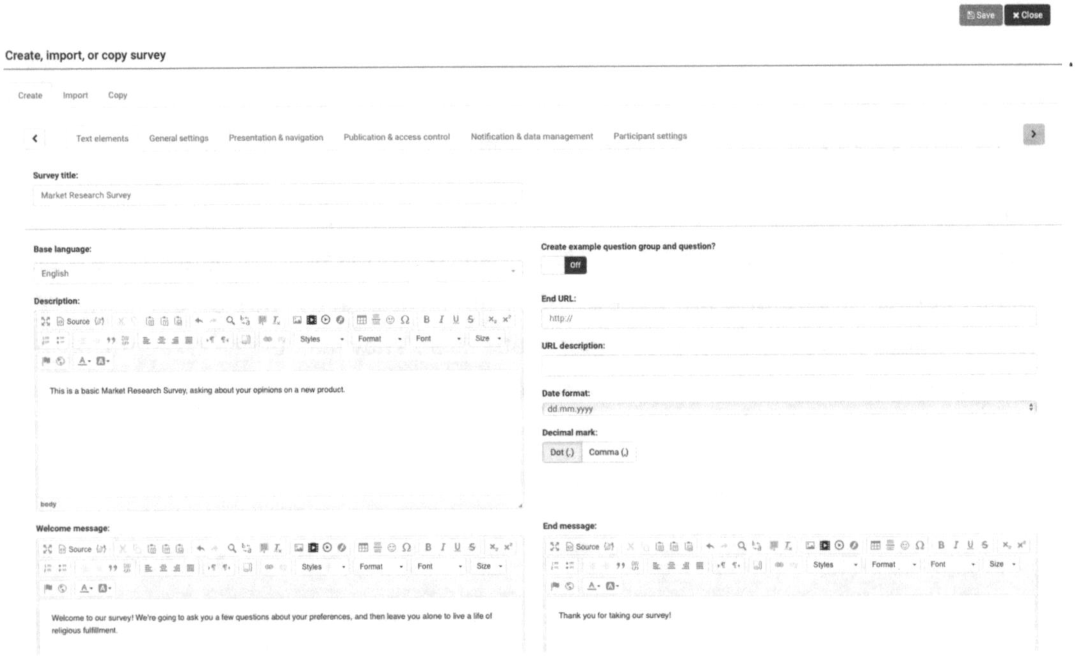

Figure 3-10. *The Create New Survey Screen*

I've filled in the basic information required to create a new survey in Figure 3-10, and once I hit Save, I'll get a screen confirming that the new survey has been saved in the system (Figure 3-11).

Figure 3-11. *The Saved New Survey*

You'll notice on the Saved New Survey screen that you have all of the basic information you entered as well as a few new entries. Most notably is the survey URL that is listed. This is the address you'll give to people whom you'd like to take your survey. You'll see that it indicates the language the survey is written in. LimeSurvey allows you to have multiple languages available for any survey, which can be useful if you work with a bilingual population or have customers around the world.

At the top left, you'll see a slider button labeled "Settings/Structure" (Figure 3-12). The Settings options are visible in Figure 3-11; they include

- General settings for how the survey is to be run.

- Text elements to customize the name of the survey, description, welcome text, and end message.

- Data policy settings that determine how participants will be informed regarding their data usage.

- Theme options to customize the look of the survey.

- Presentation to customize how many questions should be displayed or grouped.

- Participant settings to customize the length of the secure token string, as well as the anonymized response options.

- Notification & data.

- Publication & access – should the survey be listed publicly, should it be open or closed access, and should respondents have to enter a CAPTCHA code to register for it or access it?

In the second section of the menu are settings related to the specific items in the survey vs. settings. These include

- The option to list all questions in the survey.

- The option to list all question groups in the survey.

- An option to view responses currently collected.

- An option to view the panel of respondents invited to participate in the survey, which also allows you to add new respondents or remove access to respondents who haven't participated yet.

- Statistics and Quotas that can be viewed or set, respectively.

- An assessment feature that can be used to automatically score options in a survey. Think "Buzzfeed quiz" – you can set up LimeSurvey to ask a series of questions and then report a result to the respondent.

- Survey permissions which allow multiple users to work on the survey.

- Email templates that control how invitation, reminder, and notification emails are written.

- Panel integration which lets you control options related to respondents from this survey being added to a central respondent database.

- Resources such as images and files that are needed for the survey.

- And finally, any plugins you've installed that modify the survey.

There is a lot to explore in LimeSurvey, and for our demonstration, we'll simply add a few question groups and questions. We'll then launch the survey and collect responses. I'd encourage you to explore the options yourself, as there are tons of features that are very specialized but might be exactly what you need for your scenario.

To get started on our survey, I'm going to click the Settings/Structure slider to Structure, and the screen changes to what you see in Figure 3-13.

Figure 3-12. *The Settings/Structure Slider*

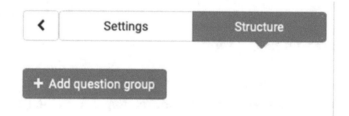

Figure 3-13. *Changing to Structure, the Add question group Button*

You'll notice an Add question group button at the top. Questions must live within specific question groups, which can be useful to help break up the survey into logical parts. I'm going to click Add question group and fill out the information on the screen in Figure 3-14.

Figure 3-14. *The Add question group Screen*

Filling out the required information, I've clicked "Save and add question" in the upper right. This takes me to the screen in Figure 3-15, which lets me enter information in for my first question. In this case, I'd like to ask about the person's gender.

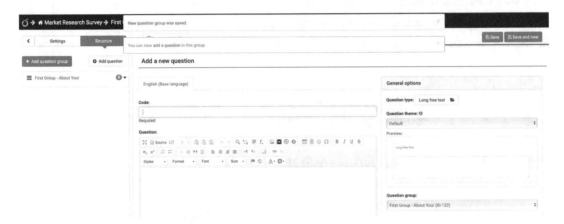

Figure 3-15. *Adding a New Question*

LimeSurvey supports a number of different question types, depending on how you'd like respondents to answer your question. You might want them to pick from a pre-determined set of items (list) or give ratings on a variety of items (array) or be able to select multiple options (multiple choice). Clicking the Question type button (which initially reads as "Long free text") gives you a selector that shows multiple question types and gives an example of what they look like to the respondent. In Figure 3-16, I've found the "Gender" option under "Mask questions" and selected it.

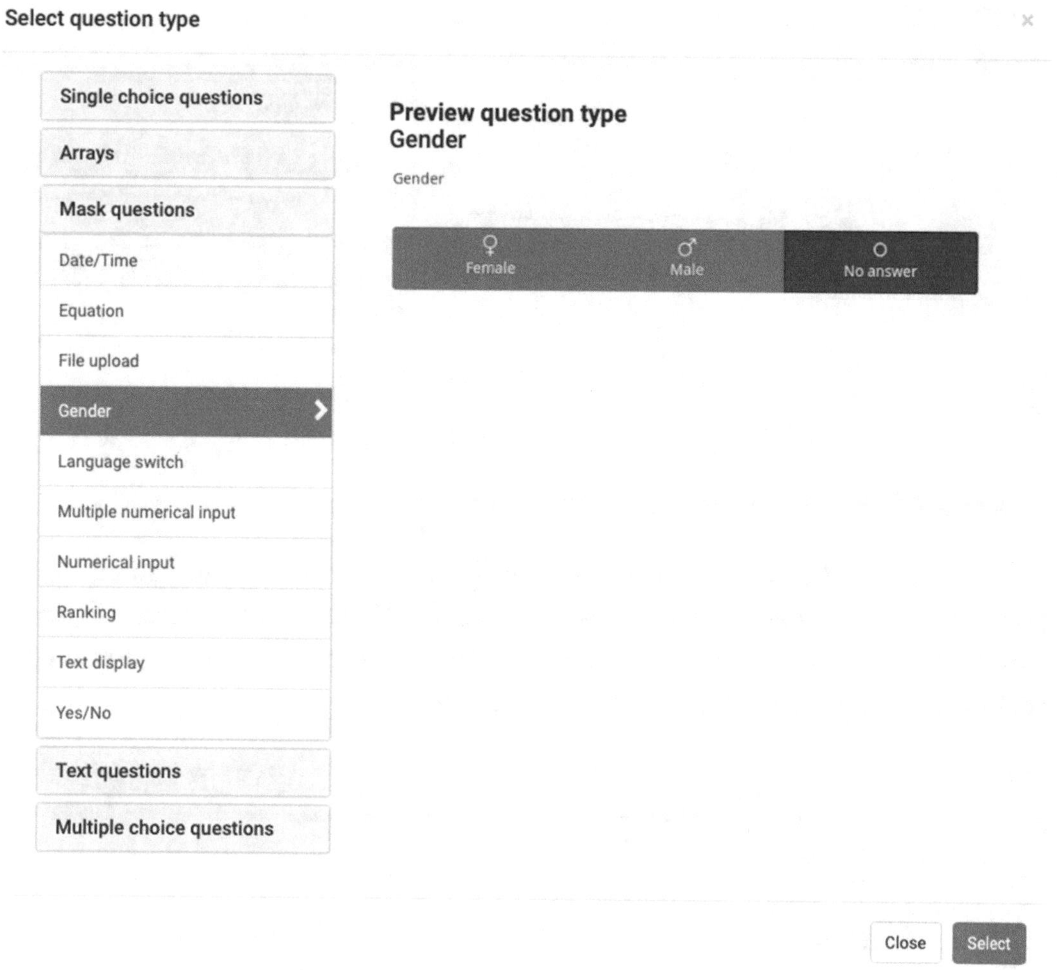

Figure 3-16. *Question Type Selection, Showing Gender*

Once I hit "Select", the Add a new question screen changes to have the gender option preview (Figure 3-17).

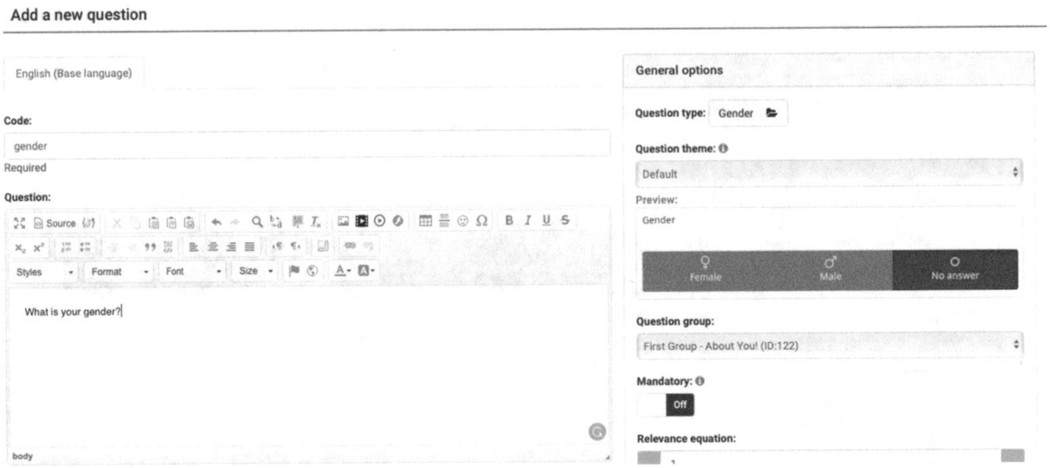

Figure 3-17. *Values for the Gender Question*

Hitting "Save", I get an overview screen that shows the question information (Figure 3-18). It also has a series of Preview buttons at the top – one to preview the survey, one to preview the question group, and one to preview the specific question. I've clicked "Preview Survey" and see the result in Figure 3-19.

Figure 3-18. *The Saved Gender Question*

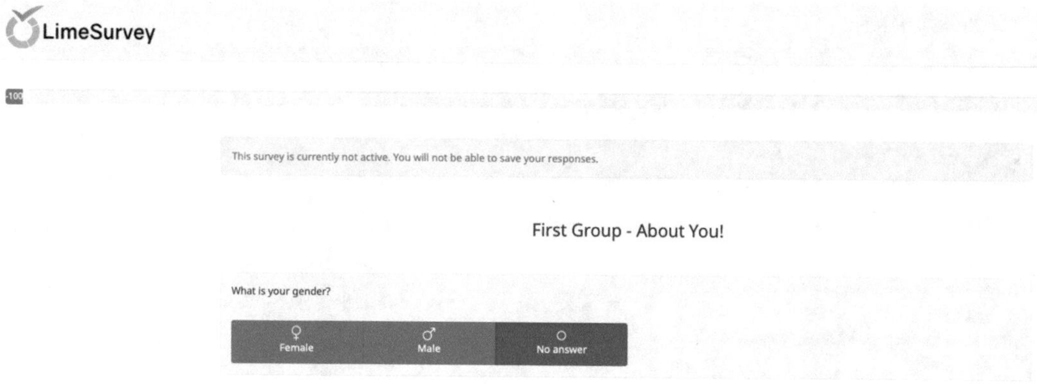

Figure 3-19. *A Preview of the Gender Question*

OK, now we're making progress! I have my first question group and my first question inside of it. Let's add a few more questions. I'll start by choosing Add a new question again and then creating an Age question (Figure 3-20). I'll then change the question type to Numerical input, which will require the user to enter a number (Figure 3-21). Finally I'll make sure people answer my question by changing the slider for Mandatory to Yes (Figure 3-22).

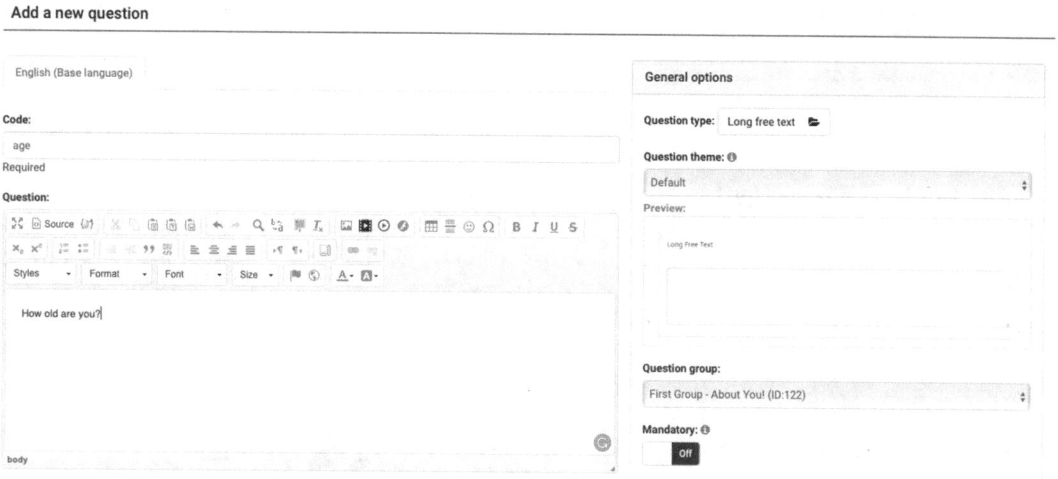

Figure 3-20. *The Age Question*

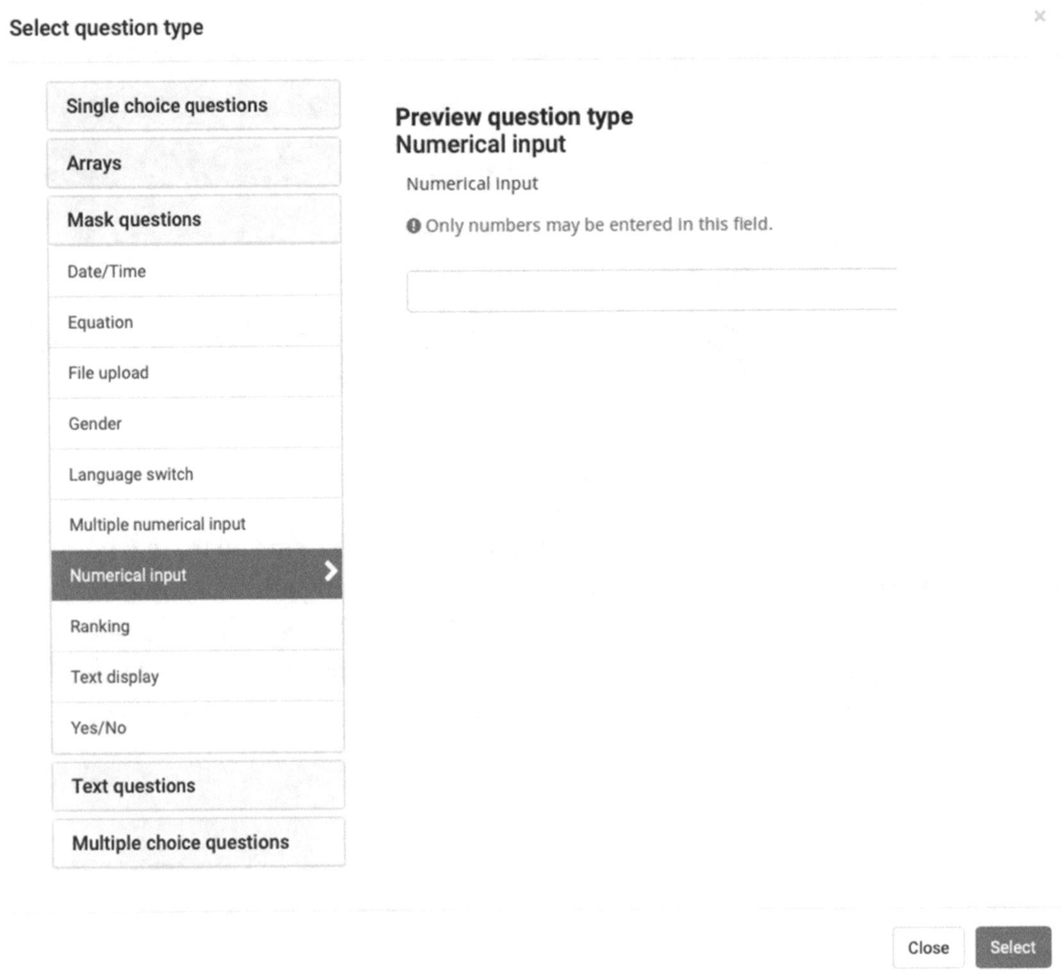

Select question type   ✕

Single choice questions	
Arrays	
Mask questions	
Date/Time	
Equation	
File upload	
Gender	
Language switch	
Multiple numerical input	
Numerical input	**›**
Ranking	
Text display	
Yes/No	
Text questions	
Multiple choice questions	

Preview question type
Numerical input

Numerical Input

ⓘ Only numbers may be entered in this field.

                                                    Close   Select

Figure 3-21. *A Numerical Input Question Type*

Mandatory: ⓘ

On

Figure 3-22. *Making a Question Mandatory by Changing the Slider*

Once we've collected these two pieces, we have some demographics that might be useful in our sales operation. However, what if we have some very targeted questions that might not apply to everyone? We can use a Multiple choice question type that lets individuals choose all of the options that apply to them. We start by adding a new question and changing the question type to Multiple choice (Figure 3-23).

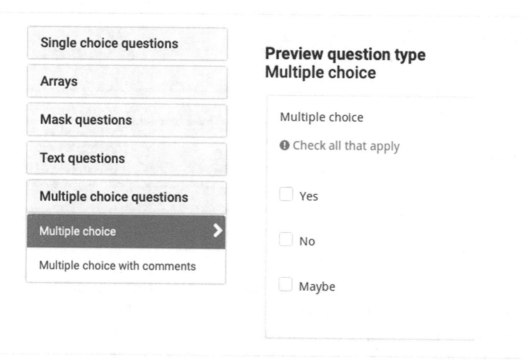

Figure 3-23. *A Multiple choice Question*

Filling in the required information and saving, you'll see a saved question screen as follows. But notice, in Figure 3-24, that it shows a warning telling us that we'll need to add subquestions. Clicking that warning takes us to the screen in Figure 3-25 where we can add our subquestions or answer options.

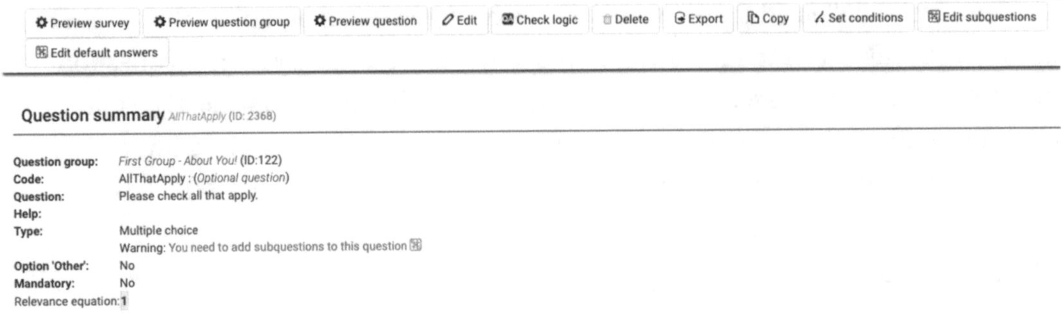

Figure 3-24. *The All That Apply Question*

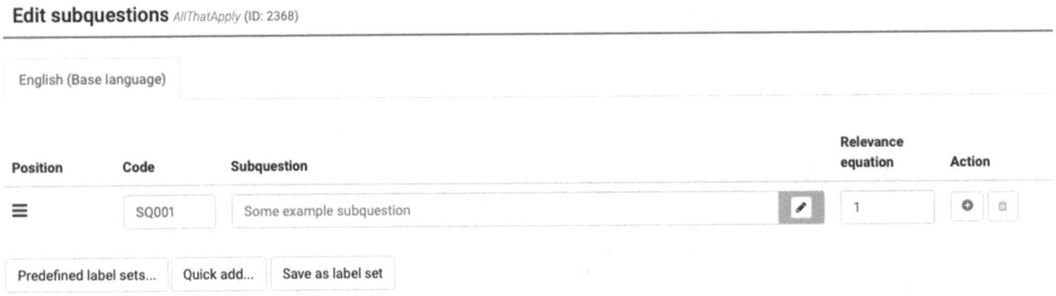

Figure 3-25. *Adding Answer Options*

This screen lets us create a short code to represent each subquestion and then enter the text that we'd like. If you've got one or two options, it's not too big of a deal to add them manually by clicking the green plus arrow next to the last option to insert a new one. I've done that twice to get the screen to look like it does in Figure 3-26.

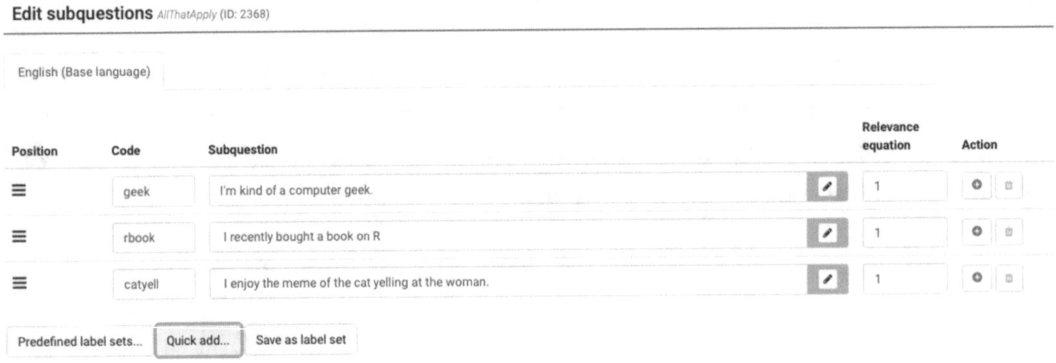

Figure 3-26. *The Completed Answer Options for Our Survey*

Once I save that, it's time to add the final question – one that asks the survey respondent to rate our new product. I'm going to add a new question group just for this purpose and add a new question inside of it. The question type is a list, under Single Choice Questions. Similar to the Multiple choice question type, once I save it, I'm going to have to add responses, in this case, a number between 1 and 10. I could go through and hit the green plus arrow nine times to get all ten options entered, but instead I'll use the Quick Add Label screen shown in Figure 3-27. By entering the code for each label and the label itself (the same thing for this question), I can quickly create the question's options without a lot of clicking. Figure 3-28 shows the answer options screen after I chose "Replace" in the previous figure. Figure 3-29 shows me the completed rating question.

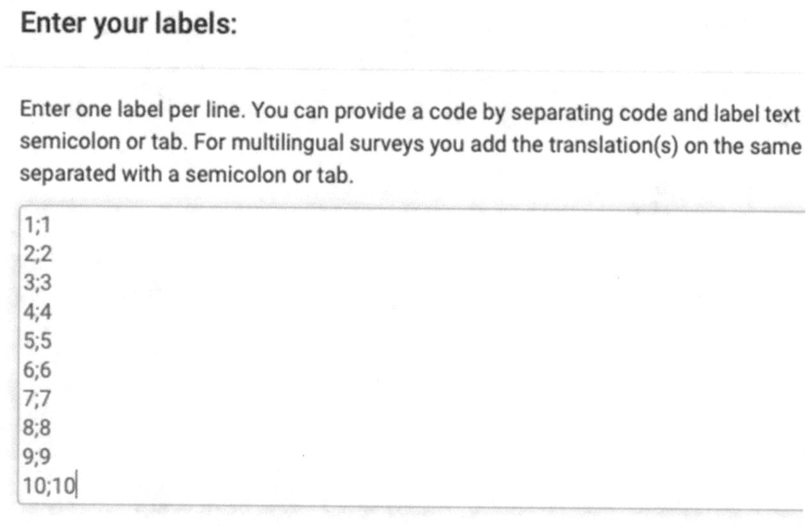

Enter your labels:

Enter one label per line. You can provide a code by separating code and label text semicolon or tab. For multilingual surveys you add the translation(s) on the same separated with a semicolon or tab.

```
1;1
2;2
3;3
4;4
5;5
6;6
7;7
8;8
9;9
10;10
```

Figure 3-27. *The Quick Add Label Screen*

Edit answer options enjoy (ID: 2373)

English (Base language)

Position	Code	Answer options	Actions
≡	1	1	✎ ⊕ 🗑
≡	2	2	✎ ⊕ 🗑
≡	3	3	✎ ⊕ 🗑
≡	4	4	✎ ⊕ 🗑
≡	5	5	✎ ⊕ 🗑
≡	6	6	✎ ⊕ 🗑
≡	7	7	✎ ⊕ 🗑
≡	8	8	✎ ⊕ 🗑
≡	9	9	✎ ⊕ 🗑
≡	10	10	✎ ⊕ 🗑

Figure 3-28. *The Labels Added Through Quick Add*

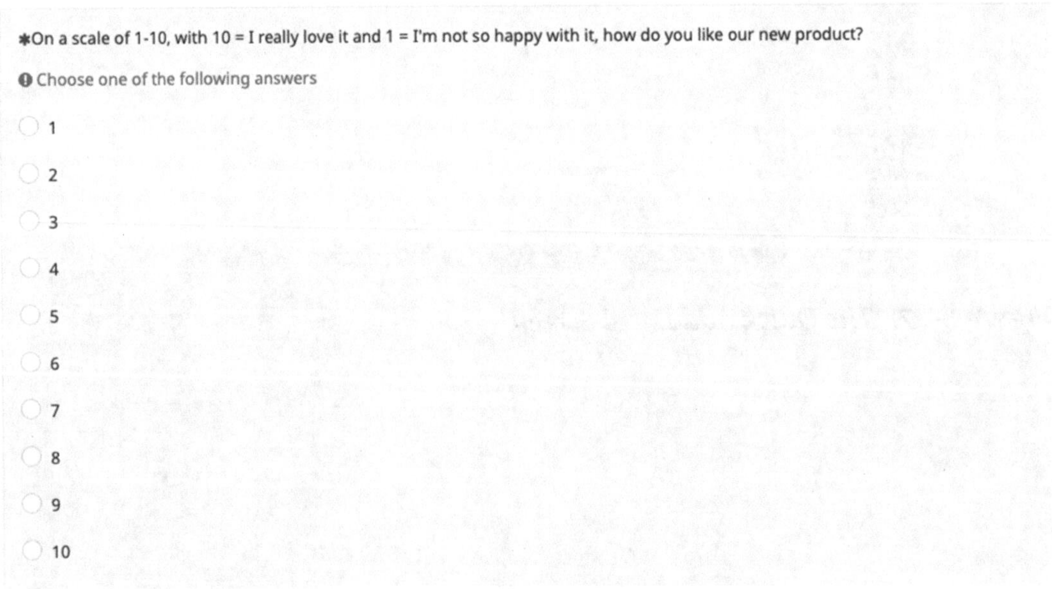

✱On a scale of 1-10, with 10 = I really love it and 1 = I'm not so happy with it, how do you like our new product?

ⓘ Choose one of the following answers

○ 1

○ 2

○ 3

○ 4

○ 5

○ 6

○ 7

○ 8

○ 9

○ 10

Figure 3-29. *A Preview of the Overall Rating Question*

I now have my completed survey! If you are following along and want to check mine to yours, you can import my completed survey by creating a new survey in LimeSurvey and choosing the Import tab and importing the file `limesurvey_survey_167537.lss` that's included in the code package for this chapter.

Choosing to preview the survey, I see the screen shown in Figure 3-30. Note that it's warning me that the survey is not yet active. As an administrator, I can go through and test out everything in the survey, but no data will actually be saved. That's fine for now; let's just make sure the survey looks OK.

Figure 3-30. *A Preview of the Survey Start Page*

OK, we're past the first page, let's look at the second. It's shown in Figure 3-31. I wonder what happens if I don't fill out that required age question.

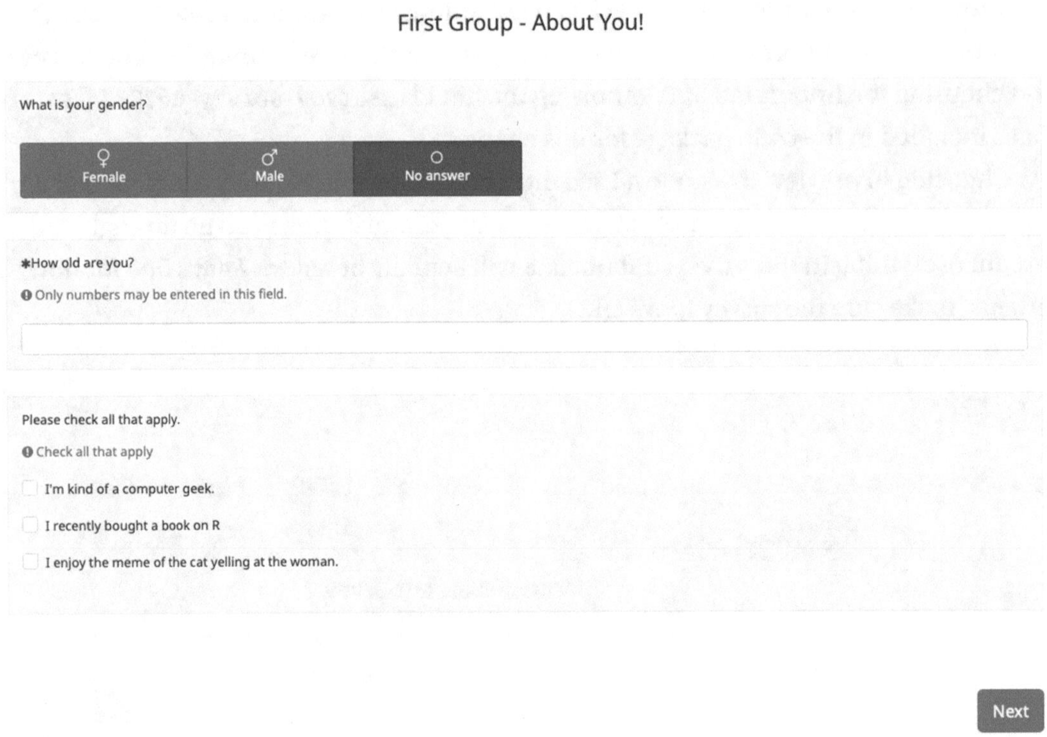

First Group - About You!

What is your gender?

| ♀ Female | ♂ Male | ○ No answer |

**How old are you?

ⓘ Only numbers may be entered in this field.

Please check all that apply.

ⓘ Check all that apply

☐ I'm kind of a computer geek.

☐ I recently bought a book on R

☐ I enjoy the meme of the cat yelling at the woman.

Next

Figure 3-31. *A Preview of the Survey's First Section*

Turns out that missing that red asterisk that shows me the question is required does have repercussions. If I submit the page without anything in that box, I get the error in Figure 3-32. Going back to the page, I now have a warning text on the question, helping me see what I missed (see Figure 3-33).

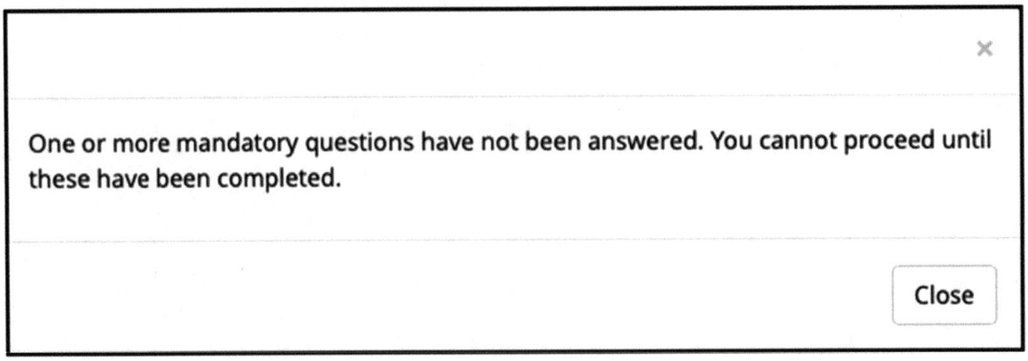

×

One or more mandatory questions have not been answered. You cannot proceed until these have been completed.

Close

Figure 3-32. *A warning if mandatory questions aren't answered*

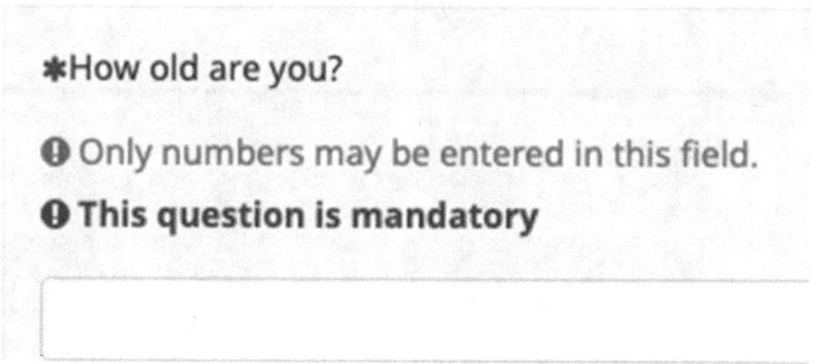

✳How old are you?

❶ Only numbers may be entered in this field.

❶ **This question is mandatory**

Figure 3-33. *The Warning Text visible after not submitting a required question*

Moving along, I can see the last section of the survey in Figure 3-34 and finally the end message, along with another warning that the survey is not active in Figure 3-35.

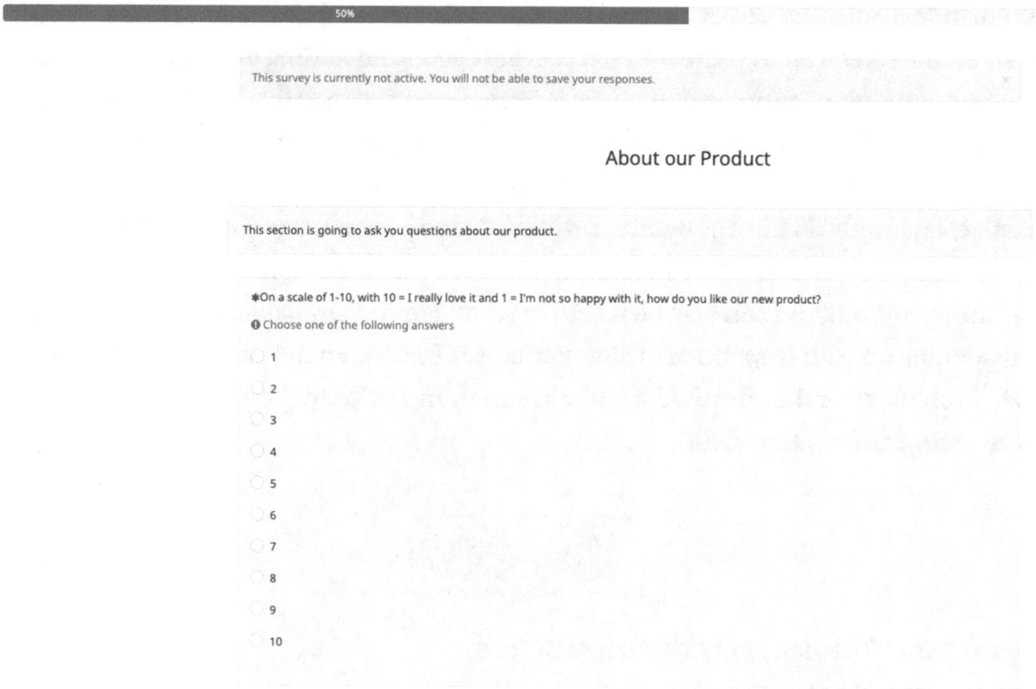

Figure 3-34. *A Preview of the Survey's Second Section*

Figure 3-35. *A Warning That the Survey Is Not Active*

If I'm happy with the survey, it's time to activate! Activating the survey by clicking the green "Activate this survey" button (shown in Figure 3-36) does a few things. First, as noted on the screen (see Figure 3-37), it prevents you from adding or deleting question groups, questions, or subquestions. This is because once you activate, a new database table is created for your survey, and the structure of that table depends on how many questions are defined. You also will see options for saving additional information. In practice, I typically do not anonymize responses, and I turn everything else to "Yes" – the more information I have, the easier it is to troubleshoot later if something goes wrong. The timing information can also be useful to view later if you suspect something strange is happening on your respondent's end. Perhaps they opened the survey and then left for several minutes? Or they finished a 50-item survey in 1 minute. That might let you know it's not completely honest data!

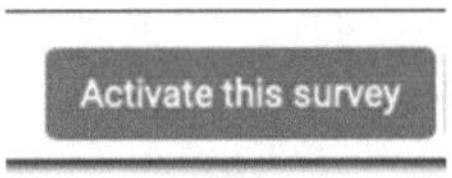

Activate this survey

Figure 3-36. *The Activate this survey Button*

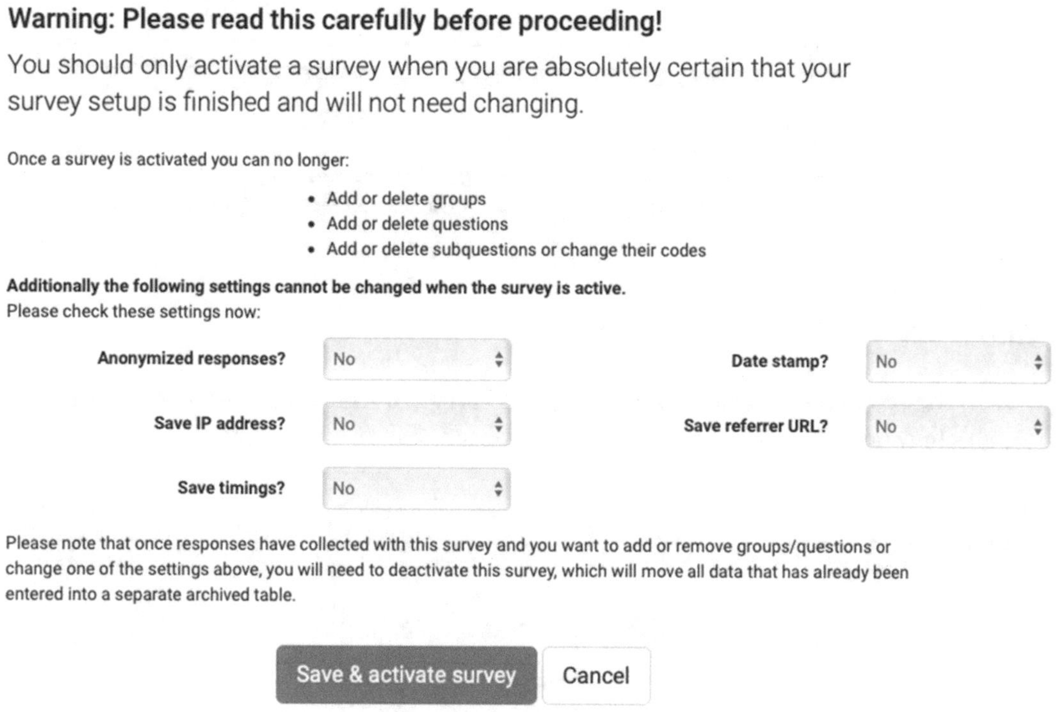

Warning: Please read this carefully before proceeding!

You should only activate a survey when you are absolutely certain that your survey setup is finished and will not need changing.

Once a survey is activated you can no longer:

- Add or delete groups
- Add or delete questions
- Add or delete subquestions or change their codes

Additionally the following settings cannot be changed when the survey is active.
Please check these settings now:

Anonymized responses?	No ⬍	Date stamp?	No ⬍
Save IP address?	No ⬍	Save referrer URL?	No ⬍
Save timings?	No ⬍		

Please note that once responses have collected with this survey and you want to add or remove groups/questions or change one of the settings above, you will need to deactivate this survey, which will move all data that has already been entered into a separate archived table.

Save & activate survey   Cancel

Figure 3-37. *The Activation Options Screen*

Choosing "Save & activate survey", you're next given a page (Figure 3-38) that asks if you want to switch to closed access mode. In open access mode, the default, anyone with the web link to the survey can take it. This is especially useful if you want to blast it out over social media or get many people to take it that might not be known to you already. However, if you need to track who is taking your survey, then you'll want the closed access mode. In this mode, a survey respondent must have a "token" or access code that will let them into the survey. You can track which tokens have been used, you can modify them to expire at a certain time, and you can create new ones as needed. If you use the built-in respondent functions in LimeSurvey, you can even have LimeSurvey create tokens and email them to your participants directly from the application. In our case, we won't enable this feature – but it might be something you'd want to look at later!

Activate survey (167537)

Survey has been activated. Results table has been successfully created.

This survey is now active, and responses can be recorded.

Open-access mode: No invitation code is needed to complete the survey.
You can switch to the closed-access mode by initialising a survey participants table by using the button below.

Switch to closed-access mode   No, thanks.

Figure 3-38. *The Closed Survey Option*

Now that you've activated your survey, you can go to the survey link and see a similar screen to before (Figure 3-39) but without the warnings.

Figure 3-39. *The Activated Survey Start Screen*

Once someone takes your survey, you will find the tallies in the Response summary screen start to fill up (Figure 3-40). However, even with my taking the survey five times (Figure 3-41), I suspect that won't be enough data for us. I've gone into the data file (that you can view in our book's data download) and added more fictional data, so we have something to analyze later.

| Summary | Display responses | Data entry | Statistics | Export ▾ | Import ▾ | View saved but not submitted responses | Batch deletion |

Response summary

Full responses	1
Incomplete responses	0
Total responses	1

Figure 3-40. *The Response Tallies*

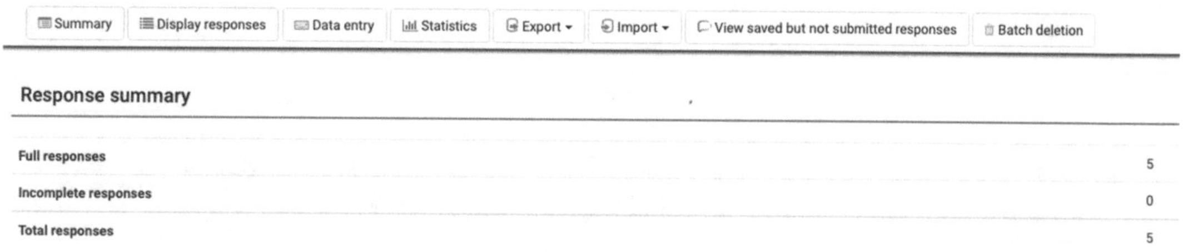

| Summary | Display responses | Data entry | Statistics | Export ▾ | Import ▾ | View saved but not submitted responses | Batch deletion |

Response summary

Full responses	5
Incomplete responses	0
Total responses	5

Figure 3-41. *Adding a Few More Responses – but They Still Won't Be Enough!*

Once all of your data is collected, you'll want to see what you've found. There are two ways to do this, broadly, in LimeSurvey. The first is to use the built-in statistics export options (Figure 3-42) which allow you to view your statistics on the Web (Figure 3-43) or in a PDF report that you can download (Figures 3-44, 3-45, 3-46, and 3-47). You'll see that LimeSurvey can visualize and display the data not only in table format but also graphically. This can be very nice to use when presenting your data to a team. It's also live data, so if the survey is still open, you could use this screen to grab a daily snapshot to see if sentiment changes over time.

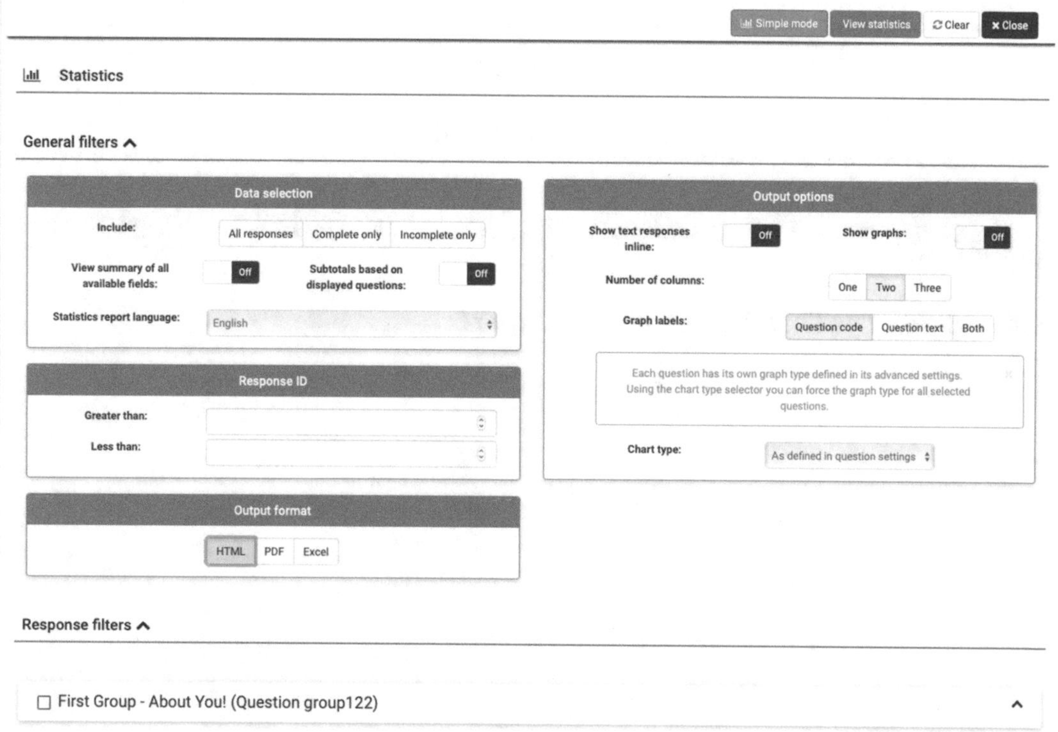

Figure 3-42. *The Statistics Export Options*

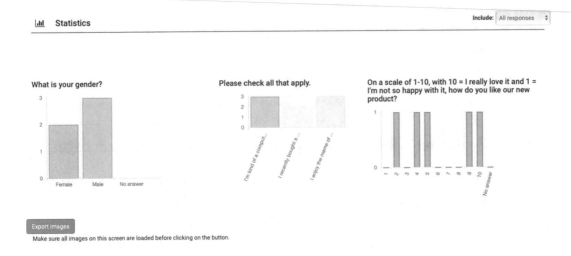

Figure 3-43. *An Example of the Statistics on the Web*

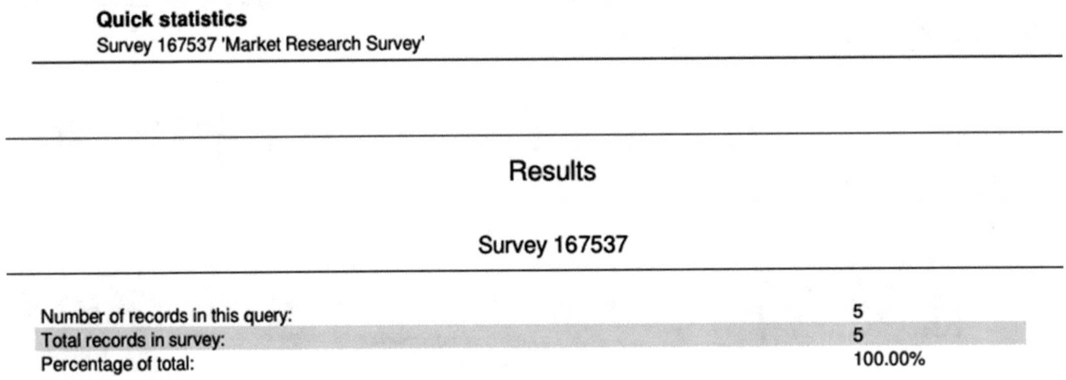

Quick statistics
Survey 167537 'Market Research Survey'

Results

Survey 167537

Number of records in this query:	5
Total records in survey:	5
Percentage of total:	100.00%

Figure 3-44. *The First Page of the PDF Export*

Quick statistics

Survey 167537 'Market Research Survey'

Summary for age

How old are you?

Calculation	Result
Count	5
Sum	154.000000
Standard deviation	9.5
Average	30.8
Minimum	20.000000
1st quartile (Q1)	21
2nd quartile (Median)	29
3rd quartile (Q3)	41.5
Maximum	45.000000

Null values are ignored in calculations
Q1 and Q3 calculated using minitab method

Figure 3-45. *The Quick Statistics for the Age Question*

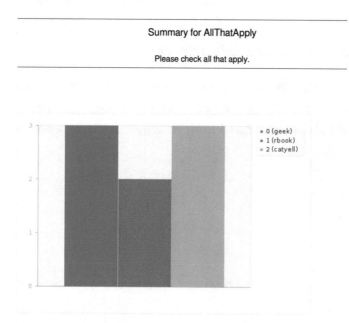

Figure 3-46. *Summary of the Check All That Apply Question*

Summary for enjoy

On a scale of 1-10, with 10 = I really love it and 1 = I'm not so happy with it, how do you like our new product?

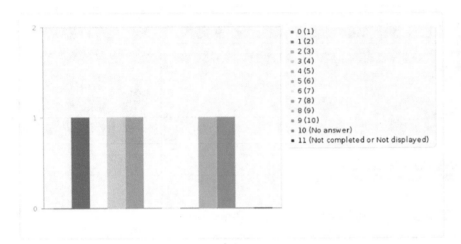

Figure 3-47. *Summary of the Product Enjoyment Question*

You can also view the raw responses in LimeSurvey directly using the Survey responses option under the Responses and statistics menu. If you've got a small dataset, this can be very useful (e.g., perhaps during testing) to see if there are any anomalies in data recording.

Responses and statistics

| | Summary | | Display responses | | Data entry | | Statistics | | Export ▾ | | Import ▾ | | View saved but not submitted responses | | Batch deletion |

Survey responses

Display mode: Extended Compact

		id	seed	lastpage	completed	startlanguage	gender What is your gender?	age How old are you?
☐					All ⬍			
☐	▦ ▭ ✎ ▭	1	273890634	2	✓	en	Male [M]	38
☐	▦ ▭ ✎ ▭	2	1062884957	2	✓	en	Male [M]	20
☐	▦ ▭ ✎ ▭	3	1240659597	2	✓	en	Female [F]	22
☐	▦ ▭ ✎ ▭	4	1061617602	2	✓	en	Male [M]	45
☐	▦ ▭ ✎ ▭	5	913213161	2	✓	en	Female [F]	29

Selected response(s)... ▴   ▥

Displaying 1-5 of 5 result(s). 10 ⬍ rows per page

Figure 3-48. *Listing of Responses in LimeSurvey*

However, if we're going to really get to the heart of the data, we're going to need the data in a format that's easy for R to work with. For that, we'll use the Export menu off of the Responses and statistics area (Figure 3-49). Two of the built-in options (Figure 3-50) reference R. The first (Figure 3-51) is the R Syntax file – this will have LimeSurvey generate an R script that correctly loads the data in and then maps the responses onto the question codes. You can customize how it does this mapping using the "Headings" options on the right of Figure 3-50.

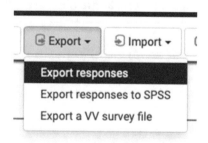

Figure 3-49. *The Export Menu Option*

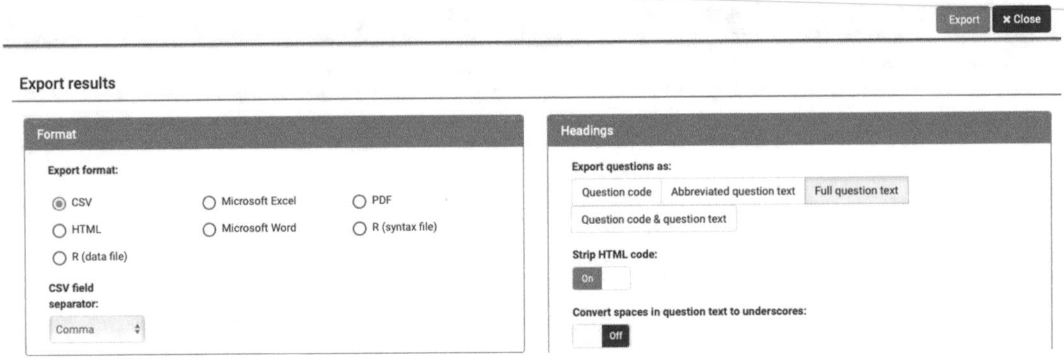

Figure 3-50. *The Export Results Screen*

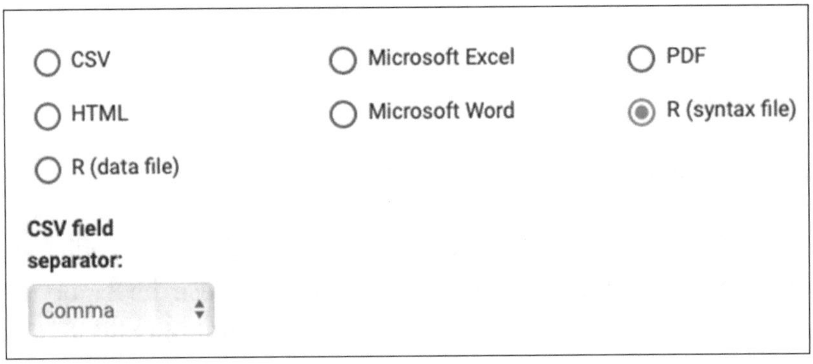

Figure 3-51. *Choosing the R syntax file*

Finally, after you've customized and download the R syntax file, you'll need to download the R data file. This export is actually very similar to the CSV option that LimeSurvey provides. However, it will format the column names and codes to be easier for R to parse.

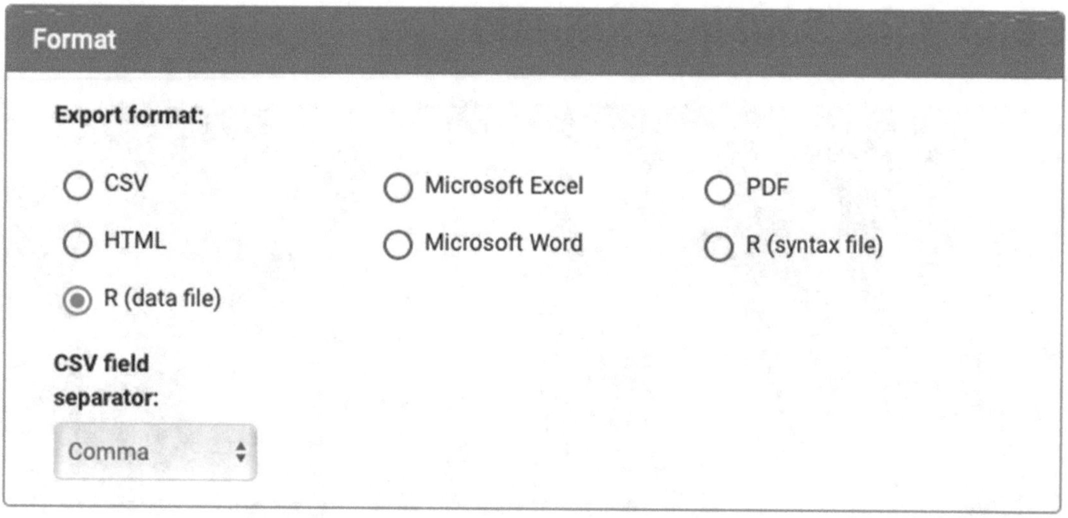

Figure 3-52. *Choosing the R data file*

On your computer, after export, you should have two files – the R script (with .R as the file extension) and the data (with .csv as the extension).

At this point, we could fire up R, load in the script, and have it load our data. However, you'll quickly notice that the basic R application on Windows, Mac, and Linux leaves a lot to be desired, as I mentioned earlier. Now is a great time to introduce RStudio – a product I briefly mentioned in Chapter 1. RStudio is an open source integrated development environment (IDE) for R. Installing it after you've already installed R on a machine allows you to have a much more comfortable place to work, placing many of your regularly used options and commands in an easy-to-find location. In the next section, I'll walk you through downloading and installing RStudio and creating a new project that you can use to house the data files from the preceding example. For the remainder of the book, whenever we're working in R, we'll be working in RStudio. This will also help us in areas of cross-platform compatibility, since the menu options won't be radically different!

Getting the Data into RStudio

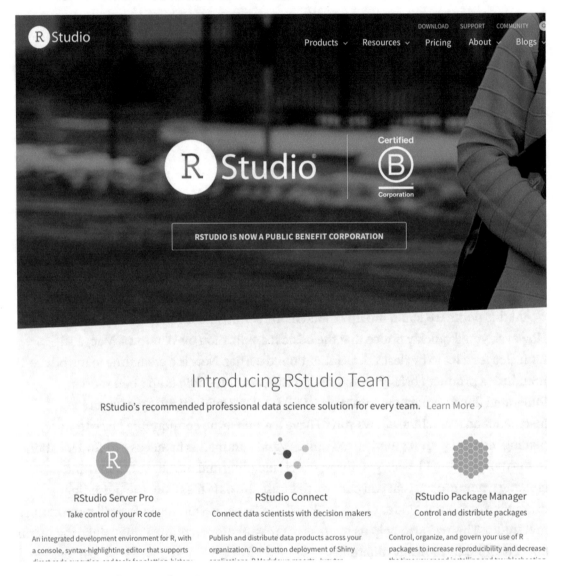

Figure 3-53. *The RStudio Homepage*

As I've mentioned earlier, when I began working with R, there weren't too many options for how you ran R. The basic R clients for Windows, Mac, and Linux were available, and some third-party IDEs could integrate with them, but none were too spectacular in their implementation. Some, such as R Commander, tried to emulate a point-and-click interface that would let you run statistical tests by selecting the appropriate GUI menu command. Others, such as JGR (Java GUI for R, pronounced "Jaguar"), tried to create a prettier interface by adding functionality that the core interface lacked. It wasn't until RStudio was released that we had an open source, cohesive, integrated development environment that was designed with R specifically in mind. Introducing support for basic necessities, such as projects that you could switch easily between, and advanced features such as an integration with output package `knitr`, RStudio is the IDE that I use the majority of the time. Let's go ahead and download it by first heading to the RStudio homepage at `https://rstudio.com` (Figure 3-54).

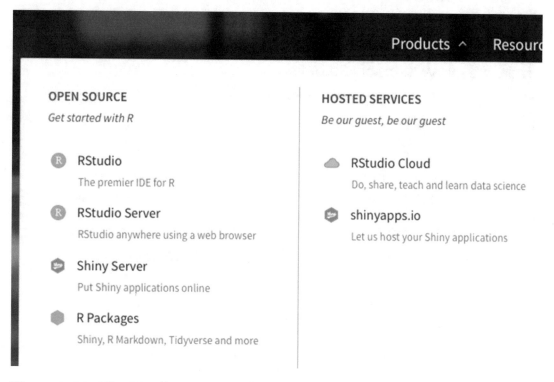

Figure 3-54. *The RStudio Products Page*

The homepage can be a bit overwhelming, but you'll want to find the Download option in the upper right to be taken to the downloads for RStudio Desktop. We'll cover some of the other RStudio software offerings, such as RStudio Server and Shiny later in the book. Once you choose download, you'll be taken to a screen (Figures 3-55, 3-56, and 3-57) to choose between RStudio Desktop and RStudio Server. Click "Download" for RStudio Desktop Open Source License, which is free.

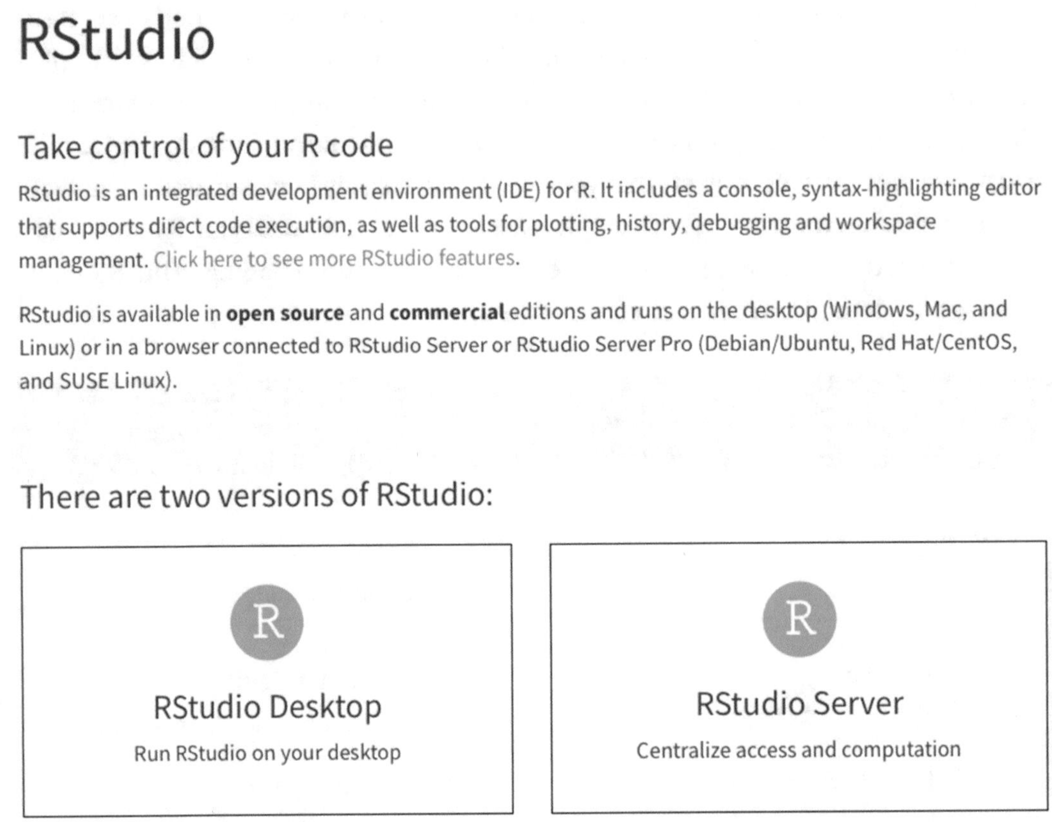

RStudio

Take control of your R code

RStudio is an integrated development environment (IDE) for R. It includes a console, syntax-highlighting editor that supports direct code execution, as well as tools for plotting, history, debugging and workspace management. Click here to see more RStudio features.

RStudio is available in **open source** and **commercial** editions and runs on the desktop (Windows, Mac, and Linux) or in a browser connected to RStudio Server or RStudio Server Pro (Debian/Ubuntu, Red Hat/CentOS, and SUSE Linux).

There are two versions of RStudio:

RStudio Desktop

Run RStudio on your desktop

RStudio Server

Centralize access and computation

Figure 3-55. *Choice between RStudio Desktop and RStudio Server*

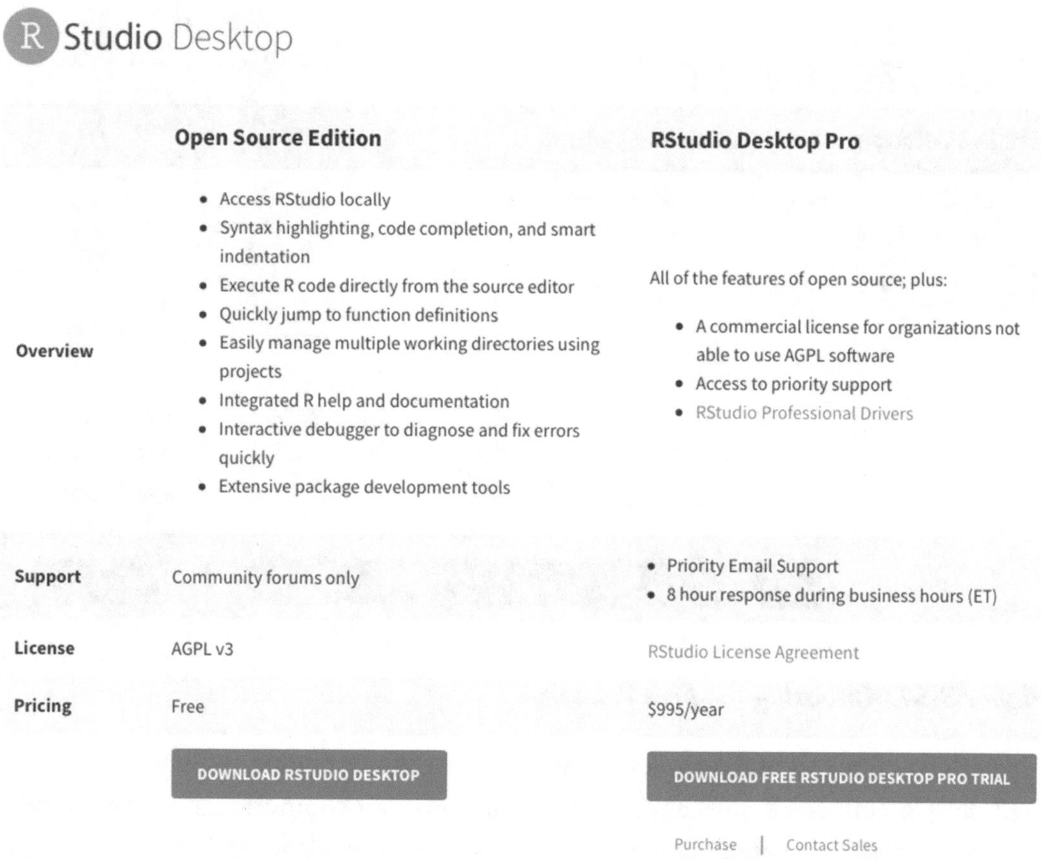

R Studio Desktop

	Open Source Edition	RStudio Desktop Pro
Overview	• Access RStudio locally • Syntax highlighting, code completion, and smart indentation • Execute R code directly from the source editor • Quickly jump to function definitions • Easily manage multiple working directories using projects • Integrated R help and documentation • Interactive debugger to diagnose and fix errors quickly • Extensive package development tools	All of the features of open source; plus: • A commercial license for organizations not able to use AGPL software • Access to priority support • RStudio Professional Drivers
Support	Community forums only	• Priority Email Support • 8 hour response during business hours (ET)
License	AGPL v3	RStudio License Agreement
Pricing	Free	$995/year
	DOWNLOAD RSTUDIO DESKTOP	DOWNLOAD FREE RSTUDIO DESKTOP PRO TRIAL Purchase | Contact Sales

Figure 3-56. *Open Source Edition versus Pro*

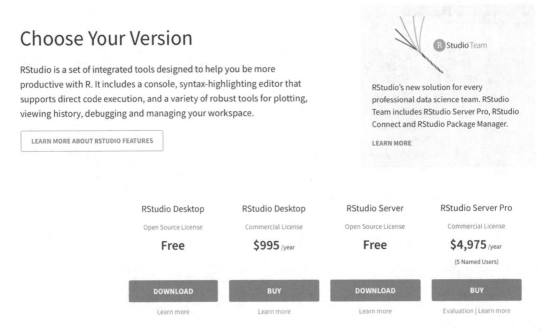

Figure 3-57. *Choosing the Free Version*

Next, you'll see several download options for various operating systems. It's important to note that R must already be installed on your computer before you install RStudio. Choose the version for your operating system, download, and install it like any other program. See Figure 3-58.

RStudio Desktop 1.2.5033 - Release Notes

1. Install R.   RStudio requires R 3.0.1+.

2. Download RStudio Desktop.   Recommended for your system:

Requires macOS 10.12+ (64-bit)

All Installers

Linux users may need to import RStudio's public code-signing key prior to installation, depending on the operating system's security policy.

RStudio 1.2 requires a 64-bit operating system. If you are on a 32 bit system, you can use an older version of RStudio.

OS	Download	Size	SHA-256
Windows 10/8/7	⬇ RStudio-1.2.5033.exe	149.83 MB	7fd3bc1b
macOS 10.12+	⬇ RStudio-1.2.5033.dmg	126.89 MB	b67c9875
Ubuntu 14/Debian 8	⬇ rstudio-1.2.5033-amd64.deb	96.18 MB	89dc2e22
Ubuntu 16	⬇ rstudio-1.2.5033-amd64.deb	104.14 MB	a1591ed7
Ubuntu 18/Debian 10	⬇ rstudio-1.2.5033-amd64.deb	105.21 MB	08eaa295
Fedora 19/Red Hat 7	⬇ rstudio-1.2.5033-x86_64.rpm	120.23 MB	38cf43c6
Fedora 28/Red Hat 8	⬇ rstudio-1.2.5033-x86_64.rpm	120.87 MB	452bc0d0
Debian 9	⬇ rstudio-1.2.5033-amd64.deb	105.45 MB	27c59722
SLES/OpenSUSE 12	⬇ rstudio-1.2.5033-x86_64.rpm	98.87 MB	9c1e200c
OpenSUSE 15	⬇ rstudio-1.2.5033-x86_64.rpm	106.91 MB	98fd2258

Figure 3-58. *Download Options and Installers for RStudio Desktop*

Once you have RStudio downloaded and installed, launching it will bring you to a screen broken out into three areas: an R console on the left, taking up the entire left hand side; a set of tabs in the upper right for environment, history, and connections; and a set of tabs in the lower right for Files, Plots, Packages, Help, and a Viewer. Let's start by creating a new project. Choose "New Project" from the File menu (Figure 3-59) and choose where you would like to save the project from the screen in Figure 3-60. I tend to keep all of my projects in their own directory, so I choose "New Directory".

101

Figure 3-59. *The New Project Option from the File Menu*

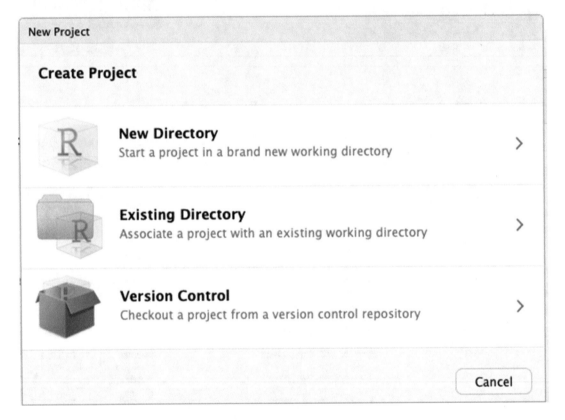

Figure 3-60. *Creating a New Project*

Next, you'll receive a screen with a few ponderous options (Figure 3-61). While we'll choose "New Project", let's outline what the others are:

- R Package: A special version of a project that lets you build your own package file. Helpful if you're creating functions you'd like to share with others.

- Shiny Web Application: Shiny is RStudio's environment for serving web applications, which allows you to create web applications that are responsive to different data. We'll see examples of a Shiny Web App later in this book.

- R Package using…: Depending on what you plan on putting in your package, you may need to compile the code using different compilers. This allows you to select the compiler you'd like.

As mentioned, continue with "New Project".

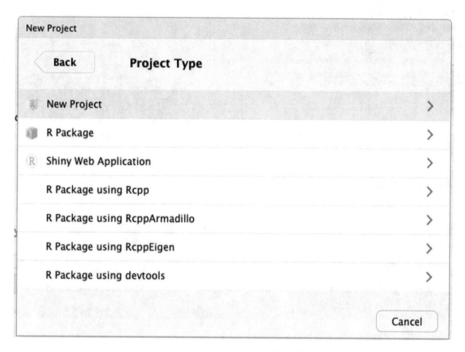

Figure 3-61. *Continuing to Choose a New Project*

With a new project created (I called mine "market-research-survey"), you'll be taken to the RStudio interface. Note that the only file in the new directory is an Rproj file, which contains information allowing RStudio to set up the project environment. It's probably useful to move the two R output files from LimeSurvey into the same directory, which I've done. You can see them now appear in the directory window in Figure 3-63.

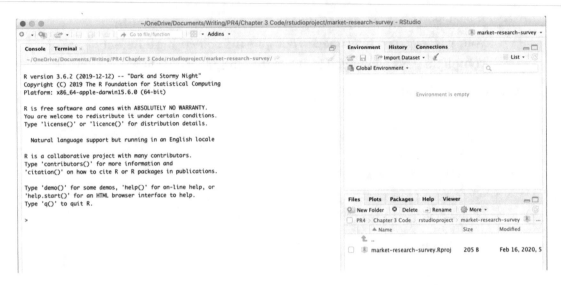

Figure 3-62. *Basic Layout of a New Project*

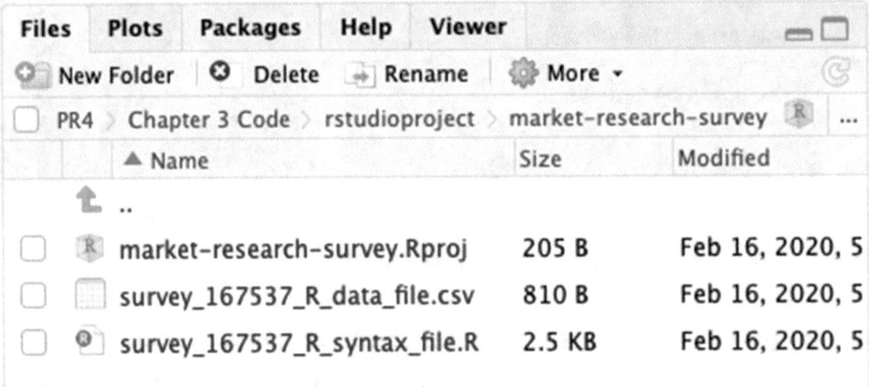

Files	Plots	Packages	Help	Viewer		

PR4 > Chapter 3 Code > rstudioproject > market-research-survey

▲ Name	Size	Modified
..		
market-research-survey.Rproj	205 B	Feb 16, 2020, 5
survey_167537_R_data_file.csv	810 B	Feb 16, 2020, 5
survey_167537_R_syntax_file.R	2.5 KB	Feb 16, 2020, 5

Figure 3-63. *The Files Area after Moving the Data and Syntax File into the Directory*

Clicking the R syntax file that LimeSurvey wrote, you'll see it open in a color-coded script window (Figure 3-64) and the entire screen resizes to put the R syntax file in the upper left, moving the console window to the lower left instead of the entire left-hand pane (Figure 3-65). You can, of course, change these layouts if you prefer them to be different.

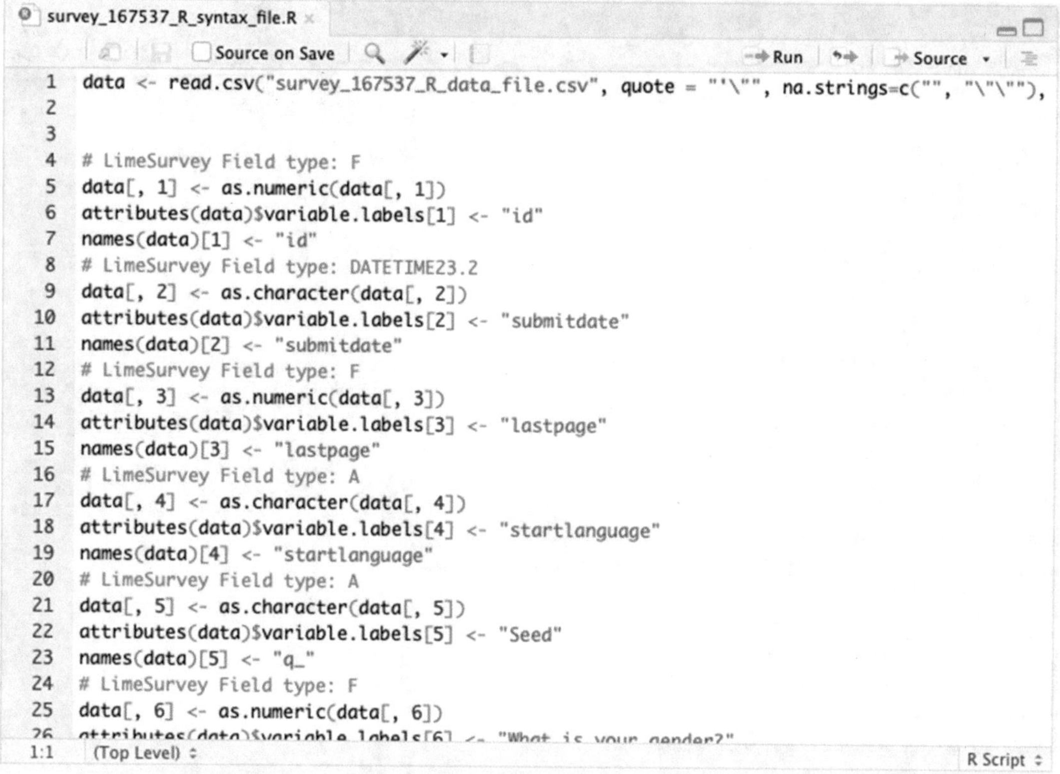

```
survey_167537_R_syntax_file.R ×                                                              ▢
        🗐 🖫  ☐ Source on Save   🔍 🪄 ▾  ▯              ⇥ Run  ↩⇥  ⇥ Source  ▾  ≛
   1   data <- read.csv("survey_167537_R_data_file.csv", quote = "'\"", na.strings=c("", "\"\""),
   2
   3
   4   # LimeSurvey Field type: F
   5   data[, 1] <- as.numeric(data[, 1])
   6   attributes(data)$variable.labels[1] <- "id"
   7   names(data)[1] <- "id"
   8   # LimeSurvey Field type: DATETIME23.2
   9   data[, 2] <- as.character(data[, 2])
  10   attributes(data)$variable.labels[2] <- "submitdate"
  11   names(data)[2] <- "submitdate"
  12   # LimeSurvey Field type: F
  13   data[, 3] <- as.numeric(data[, 3])
  14   attributes(data)$variable.labels[3] <- "lastpage"
  15   names(data)[3] <- "lastpage"
  16   # LimeSurvey Field type: A
  17   data[, 4] <- as.character(data[, 4])
  18   attributes(data)$variable.labels[4] <- "startlanguage"
  19   names(data)[4] <- "startlanguage"
  20   # LimeSurvey Field type: A
  21   data[, 5] <- as.character(data[, 5])
  22   attributes(data)$variable.labels[5] <- "Seed"
  23   names(data)[5] <- "q_"
  24   # LimeSurvey Field type: F
  25   data[, 6] <- as.numeric(data[, 6])
  26   attributes(data)$variable.labels[6] <- "What is your gender?"
 1:1   (Top Level) �↕                                                            R Script ↕
```

Figure 3-64. *The R Syntax Downloaded from LimeSurvey*

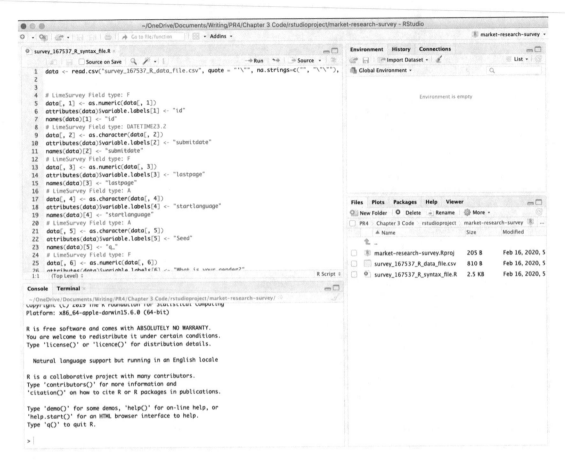

Figure 3-65. *The Entire Screen with R Syntax Open*

Now that we have the script open, let's click the "Source" button in the upper right (Figure 3-66). This will tell R to run the entire R script. You could also select all of the lines of code and choose Cmd+Enter on a Mac or Ctrl+Enter on a PC to accomplish the same task.

Figure 3-66. *The Source Button*

Once the script has been executed, the data is loaded into its own variable, aptly named `data` although you could modify the script to call it whatever you like. Once you've loaded the data, you can view it by typing `data` to show everything or `head(data)` to show the first six lines (see Figure 3-67).

```
> data
  id           submitdate lastpage startlanguage        q_ gender age AllThatApply_geek
1  1 1980-01-01 00:00:00        2            en  273890634   Male  38               Yes
2  2 1980-01-01 00:00:00        2            en 1062884957   Male  20               Yes
3  3 1980-01-01 00:00:00        2            en 1240659597 Female  22               Yes
4  4 1980-01-01 00:00:00        2            en 1061617602   Male  45      Not selected
5  5 1980-01-01 00:00:00        2            en  913213161 Female  29      Not selected
  AllThatApply_rbook AllThatApply_catyell enjoy
1       Not selected                  Yes    10
2       Not selected         Not selected     2
3                Yes                  Yes     5
4       Not selected                  Yes     9
5                Yes         Not selected     4
>
```

Figure 3-67. *Showing the Data*

We now have the data loaded into RStudio, and we can work with it in the confines
of our project. If you were to exit RStudio, it would ask if you'd like to save the workspace,
similar to how R normally works; however, now that becomes a bit more useful since you
can easily see what's sitting in that workspace in the "Environment" window in the upper
right. I'd encourage you to explore the RStudio interface a bit more now to understand
how it's laid out. Once you've gotten comfortable, move on to the next section where
we will mine our data a tad, talk about how to use some of RStudio's features, and
understand exactly what predicts our customer's satisfaction!

Getting Advanced: Linear Regression

In a data analytics sense, there are two sorts of people: those who think there might be
a relationship between data and those who are pretty sure there is a direction and how
to use that direction (I'd normally say the second type are those who know there is a
relationship, but if a statistician were to read that, they'd probably feel it was too strong!).
One way that we can be pretty confident of a relationship is to use a tool called linear
regression. But first, let's back up and discuss possible ways to analyze a survey.

First, understanding your data is key, especially to make sure there are no errors
in coding or reading of it. In this case, R and LimeSurvey are your friends – the data is
directly entered by the user, and so there is no situation for you, as the researcher, to
make a typo or error in coding: a major advantage of an electronic survey vs. paper.
Second, one might find the exploratory analysis information that LimeSurvey provides
above (in the form of its built-in statistics section) to be very useful in understanding

how the data fits. The data here is generated for the following examples, and in the real world, it's likely you'll have many more variables to consider as you plan your analysis. Most high school math sequences discuss, at some point, probabilities, means, and standard deviations. Those, along with frequencies, give you an idea of what possible relationships you might have in your data.

In this section, we're going to assume that you've already reviewed your data and that you've decided to use an advanced technique, linear regression. In Chapter 2, I explained that there are also a host of diagnostics and assumptions you'll want to check before you use such a tool. My point in using it here is not to suggest that it's a cure-all for any statistical analysis – it's merely to show it in an applied context, giving you one possible way to analyze the data. With those caveats mentioned, I'll give you a quick version of what linear regression is in this section and how it works. For now, know that the output you see in Figure 3-68 will have some meaning by the end of this chapter. Avoid the temptation to freak out at the numbers, and trust me!

```
> fit2 <- lm(enjoy ~ age + AllThatApply_geek + AllThatApply_rbook + AllThatApply_catyell * gender,data=data);
> summary(fit2)

Call:
lm(formula = enjoy ~ age + AllThatApply_geek + AllThatApply_rbook +
    AllThatApply_catyell * gender, data = data)

Residuals:
    Min      1Q  Median      3Q     Max
-3.9167 -0.4143  0.0833  0.4287  2.7299

Coefficients:
                                            Estimate Std. Error t value Pr(>|t|)
(Intercept)                                 -4.37828    1.47716  -2.964  0.00454 **
age                                          0.42250    0.06563   6.438 3.62e-08 ***
AllThatApply_geekNot selected               -4.11934    0.68186  -6.041 1.56e-07 ***
AllThatApply_rbookNot selected              -0.02883    0.48346  -0.060  0.95267
AllThatApply_catyellNot selected            -0.16907    0.62496  -0.271  0.78781
genderMale                                  -2.07167    1.01096  -2.049  0.04541 *
AllThatApply_catyellNot selected:genderMale  0.46801    1.37554   0.340  0.73502
---
Signif. codes:  0 '***' 0.001 '**' 0.01 '*' 0.05 '.' 0.1 ' ' 1

Residual standard error: 1.08 on 53 degrees of freedom
Multiple R-squared:  0.8845,    Adjusted R-squared:  0.8714
F-statistic: 67.62 on 6 and 53 DF,  p-value: < 2.2e-16
```

Figure 3-68. *An Example Linear Model*

Before we can get into how we run and read the output in Figure 3-68, we need to do a bit of data housekeeping. The first thing I recommend doing is taking a look at the R syntax script to learn some useful interface tricks in RStudio. If you look at the top of the script, on Line 1, you'll see the code that loads the survey data file into a variable named data. One thing I like to do is add a setwd() command at the top – this will make sure that R is always looking in the directory we intend it to look. While RStudio defaults your working directory to the directory your project file lives in, sometimes it is useful to look elsewhere, and setwd() ensures you come back to where you intend. Adding the setwd() in Figure 3-70, you'll see that the interface has changed – the title of the file now has an asterisk (*) at the end of it, which tells us the file has unsaved changes. A quick Cmd+S or Ctrl+S will save the file, and the file name will change back to normal (Figure 3-71).

```
survey_167537_R_syntax_file.R
   Source on Save    Q    ⚡ ▾                                  → Run    ↪    Source  ▾
1  data <- read.csv("survey_167537_R_data_file.csv", quote = "'\"", na.strings=c("", "\"\""),
2
3
4  # LimeSurvey Field type: F
5  data[ 1] <- as.numeric(data[ 1])
```

Figure 3-69. *The Syntax File without a Setwd Command*

```
survey_167537_R_syntax_file.R* ×
   Source on Save    Q    ⚡ ▾                                  → Run    ↪    Source  ▾
1  setwd("~/OneDrive/Documents/Writing/PR4/Chapter 3 Code/rstudioproject/market-research-surve
2  data <- read.csv("survey_167537_R_data_file.csv", quote = "'\"", na.strings=c("", "\"\""),
3
4
5  # LimeSurvey Field type: F
```

Figure 3-70. *Adding the Setwd Command*

Figure 3-71. *The filename changes back to black without an asterisk after save*

Moving over to the Environment tab on the right, you'll see that right now we have one item loaded – the survey data that we've named data – this screen lets us save and load an R workspace image through the file folder and save icon and also lets us clear out the entire environment by using the broom icon (Figure 3-72). It can be very useful to use this tab whenever we're adding or removing lines of data from our data file, since it lets us easily see the number of observations. If we're doing an operation we think will remove variables (columns) or observations (rows), we can keep an eye on this output to make sure we aren't going in the opposite (or no) direction.

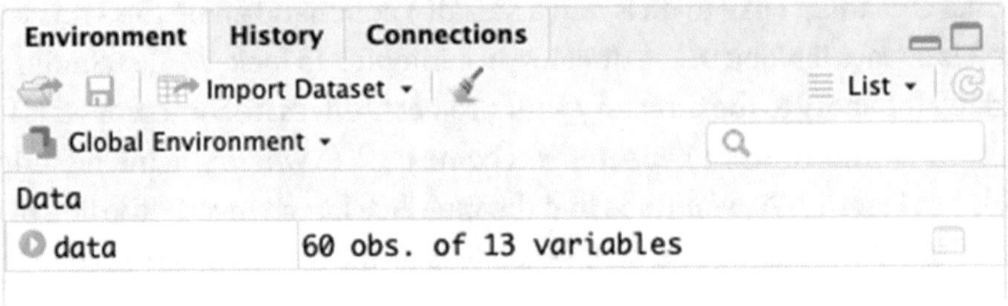

Figure 3-72. *The Data Frame in the Environment Window*

Take a moment to click the data object and it will load the data viewer, showing you the observations and variables (Figure 3-73). If you scroll over, you'll find a variable after enjoy named `X.with.10...I.really.love.it.and....i.m.not.so.happy.with.it` – what is that?!? Turns out that the R syntax script is only human (well, programmed by a human) – in this case, the variables didn't exactly line up, leading there to be a few empty variables (as evidenced by the NA lines) at the end of the data file. To remove those last two columns, we use the following line of code (Line 56): `data <- data[,1:11]` which tells R to reassign the data variable to a subset of the current data variable, namely, to include all of the observations (as evidenced by nothing between the [and the comma), and then the first 11 variables (the 1:11 portion). Variables 12 and 13, the data that didn't really exist, get dropped. This is also how you might go about cutting down a dataset – if you only wanted the first five observations, you could write the statement `data <- data[1:5,]`.

	id	submitdate	lastpage	startlanguage	q_	gender	age	All
	id	submitdate	lastpage	startlanguage	Seed	What is your gender?	How old are you?	[I'm
1	1	1/1/80 0:00	2	en	273890634	Male	38	Yes
2	2	1/1/80 0:00	2	en	1062884957	Male	20	Yes
3	3	1/1/80 0:00	2	en	1240659597	Female	22	Yes
4	4	1/1/80 0:00	2	en	1061617602	Male	45	Not
5	5	1/1/80 0:00	2	en	913213161	Female	29	Not
6	6	1/1/80 0:00	2	en	273890634	Male	38	Yes
7	7	1/1/80 0:00	2	en	1062884957	Male	20	Yes
8	8	1/1/80 0:00	2	en	1240659597	Female	22	Yes
9	9	1/1/80 0:00	2	en	1061617602	Male	45	Not
10	10	1/1/80 0:00	2	en	913213161	Female	29	Not
11	11	1/1/80 0:00	2	en	273890634	Male	38	Yes
12	12	1/1/80 0:00	2	en	1062884957	Male	20	Yes
13	13	1/1/80 0:00	2	en	1240659597	Female	22	Yes
14	14	1/1/80 0:00	2	en	1061617602	Male	45	Not
15	15	1/1/80 0:00	2	en	913213161	Female	29	Not
16	16	1/1/80 0:00	2	en	273890634	Male	38	Yes
17	17	1/1/80 0:00	2	en	1062884957	Male	20	Yes

Showing 1 to 17 of 60 entries

Figure 3-73. *Clicking the Data Frame opens the Data Viewer*

enjoy	X.with.10...I.really.love.it.and.1...I.m.not.so.happy.with.it	X
On a scale of 1–10, with 10 = I really love it and 1 = I'm no...		
10	NA	N
2	NA	N
5	NA	N

Figure 3-74. *Seeing Extra Columns at the End*

Now that we have the last two empty variables gone, let's do a bit more digging into our data. First, we're going to install a new package – psych – while there are plenty of ways to look at statistics in R, some are prettier than others. One of my favorite functions is the describe() function in the psych package. Loading the package in on Line 58 and then running it on Line 59, we see the output in Figure 3-75. It shows us summary statistics, such as the mean and standard deviation, for each of our variables. Some of these really don't make much sense (a mean of gender?), but others are meaningful, such as age and the enjoyment rating.

```
> library("psych");
> describe(data);
                     vars  n       mean           sd       median       trimmed
id                      1 60       30.5        17.46         30.5         30.50
submitdate*             2 60        NaN           NA           NA           NaN
lastpage                3 60        2.0         0.00          2.0          2.00
startlanguage*          4 60        NaN           NA           NA           NaN
q_*                     5 60 910453190.2 337591237.96 1061617602.0 948747708.88
gender*                 6 60        1.6         0.49          2.0          1.62
age                     7 60       30.8         9.58         29.0         30.38
AllThatApply_geek*      8 60        1.4         0.49          1.0          1.38
AllThatApply_rbook*     9 60        1.6         0.49          2.0          1.62
AllThatApply_catyell*  10 60        1.4         0.49          1.0          1.38
enjoy*                 11 60        6.0         3.06          5.0          6.00
```

Figure 3-75. *The describe() Function from the psych Library*

This brings us to an interesting topic: errors. You'll notice that after you run that command (describe(data)), you receive the errors in Figure 3-76. Briefly, R is telling us that some of the data wasn't coded in a way that let us run the command properly (Errors 1 and 2) and that others just don't apply to the statistics we tried to run (Errors 3–76). My advice with R errors tends to always be the same: Google is your friend. R's errors are not always the most user-friendly, and when it comes to some packages, the authors of the package don't always state things in clear ways when they throw an error. You might need to search the exact error string to find situations where others have had the same issue and to receive guidance. Asking fellow R users can also be useful.

```
Warning messages:
1: In describe(data) : NAs introduced by coercion
2: In describe(data) : NAs introduced by coercion
3: In FUN(newX[, i], ...) : no non-missing arguments to min; returning Inf
4: In FUN(newX[, i], ...) : no non-missing arguments to min; returning Inf
5: In FUN(newX[, i], ...) :
  no non-missing arguments to max; returning -Inf
6: In FUN(newX[, i], ...) :
  no non-missing arguments to max; returning -Inf
```

Figure 3-76. *Many Errors Trying to Use the describe() Function with the Entire Dataset*

Another interesting observation comes from comparing Figures 3-75 and Figure 3-77 – you'll notice that a lot more information is in Figure 3-77. That's because I resized my console window and took a larger screenshot. R doesn't always have the proper dimensions in text for items, so there are times when making your console window larger or smaller can really help you see the big picture, as it were.

```
> describe(data);
                     vars  n        mean            sd       median      trimmed         mad       min         max        range  skew kurtosis          se
id                      1 60        30.5         17.46         30.5        30.50       22.24         1          60          59  0.00   -1.26        2.25
submitdate*             2 60         NaN            NA           NA          NaN          NA       Inf        -Inf        -Inf   NaN     NA          NA
lastpage                3 60         2.0          0.00          2.0         2.00        0.00         2           2           0  NaN     NaN        0.00
startlanguage*          4 60         NaN            NA           NA          NaN          NA       Inf        -Inf        -Inf   NaN     NA          NA
q_*                     5 60 910453190.2 337591237.96 1061617602.0 948747708.88 220024424.23 273890634 1240659597  966768963 -1.12   -0.27 43582841.41
gender*                 6 60         1.6          0.49          2.0         1.62        0.00         1           2           1 -0.40   -1.87        0.06
age                     7 60        30.8          9.58         29.0        30.38       13.34        20          45          25  0.29   -1.50        1.24
AllThatApply_geek*      8 60         1.4          0.49          1.0         1.38        0.00         1           2           1  0.40   -1.87        0.06
AllThatApply_rbook*     9 60         1.6          0.49          2.0         1.62        0.00         1           2           1 -0.40   -1.87        0.06
AllThatApply_catyell*  10 60         1.4          0.49          1.0         1.38        0.00         1           2           1  0.40   -1.87        0.06
enjoy*                 11 60         6.0          3.06          5.0         6.00        4.45         2          10           8  0.13   -1.61        0.39
```

Figure 3-77. *Expanding the View to See the Entire Output*

Returning to the output, remember how I said that some of those variables really don't lend themselves to means and standard deviations? Those include the gender and "Check All That Apply" questions. For those, I really would like to know either the number of people that choose each option or the percentage of people that chose that option. I can do that pretty easy in R using the table() function. In Figure 3-78, I've nested table() inside of prop.table() – reading from the outside in, it starts by pulling a variable, data$gender, for example, and asking for a table of responses. This will give me the raw counts. Counts are useful in some times and places (e.g., Sesame Street), but most of the time people find percentages to be more easily understood. That's why I put the prop.table() function around the table. This tells R to give me the proportions in each response category. As we can see, it's much easier to tell someone "Yes, 60% of respondents were male" or "40% have recently bought a book on R" vs. the raw numbers.

```
> prop.table(table(data$gender));

Female   Male
   0.4    0.6
> prop.table(table(data$AllThatApply_geek));

        Yes Not selected
        0.6          0.4
> prop.table(table(data$AllThatApply_rbook));

        Yes Not selected
        0.4          0.6
> prop.table(table(data$AllThatApply_catyell));

        Yes Not selected
        0.6          0.4
```

Figure 3-78. *Proportion Tables for Categorical Variables*

Now let's talk about what this section claimed to de-mystify: linear regression. To do this, I'm going to ask that you recall your first or second algebra class, where you learned the equation of a line. Remember that a line can be plotted by knowing the *slope* and the *y-intercept* – this is often written algebraically as **y=mx+b** with *m* standing in for slope and *b* standing in for the y-intercept.

If we have a line that has multiple slopes, it will rock the line up or down across the Y axis, in essence finding a sweet spot between the multiple slopes. Linear regression is, statistically, a process to determine the equation of a line. Feed it a bunch of Xs and Ys, and it will figure out the y-intercept and various slopes for each X.

We write this equation out in our R script on Line 66, which reads `fit <- lm(enjoy ~ gender + age + AllThatApply_geek + AllThatApply_rbook + AllThatApply_catyell, data=data)` – let's break that down a bit:

- `fit` is the name of a new object we're going to create in R to store the calculation.

- `lm()` is a function to plot a linear regression model.

- `enjoy` is the variable we want to predict (sometimes called our outcome variable). In this case, our boss wants to know what predicts satisfaction, so that's what we need to solve for.

- `~` instead of an equal sign indicates that we are estimating the result, since with sample data, we'll never know for sure.

- gender, age, AllThatApply_geek, AllThatApply_rbook, and
  AllThatApply_catyell are the predictor variables (also sometimes
  called the criterion variables). These are the X inputs that we want
  the linear model to calculate slopes for.

- data=data tells R to feed data from our dataset named data into the
  model. If our dataset had been named something else, for example,
  surveydata, this line would have read data=surveydata).

Now that you know what the line of code does, let's run it and get a warning
(see Figure 3-79).

```
> fit <- lm(enjoy ~ gender + age + AllThatApply_geek + AllThatApply_rbook + AllThatApply_catyell,data=data);
Warning messages:
1: In model.response(mf, "numeric") :
  using type = "numeric" with a factor response will be ignored
2: In Ops.factor(y, z$residuals) : '-' not meaningful for factors
```

Figure 3-79. *Warnings Running a Linear Model*

Turns out that we have a few issues we need to fix before we can run the linear
model. Looking at the structure of the data using the str() command (Figure 3-80), we
can see that we have a bit of a problem – our outcome variable, enjoy, is a factor, not a
number. R wants to predict a linear model, which means Y has to be a number.

```
> str(data)
'data.frame':    60 obs. of  11 variables:
 $ id                   : num  1 2 3 4 5 6 7 8 9 10 ...
 $ submitdate           : chr  "1/1/80 0:00" "1/1/80 0:00" "1/1/80 0:00" "1/1/80 0:00" ...
 $ lastpage             : num  2 2 2 2 2 2 2 2 2 ...
 $ startlanguage        : chr  "en" "en" "en" "en" ...
 $ q_                   : chr  "273890634" "1062884957" "1240659597" "1061617602" ...
 $ gender               : Factor w/ 2 levels "Female","Male": 2 2 1 2 1 2 2 1 2 1 ...
 $ age                  : num  38 20 22 45 29 38 20 22 45 29 ...
 $ AllThatApply_geek    : Factor w/ 2 levels "Yes","Not selected": 1 1 1 2 2 1 1 1 2 2 ...
 $ AllThatApply_rbook   : Factor w/ 2 levels "Yes","Not selected": 2 2 1 2 1 2 2 1 2 1 ...
 $ AllThatApply_catyell: Factor w/ 2 levels "Yes","Not selected": 1 2 1 1 2 1 2 1 1 2 ...
 $ enjoy                : Factor w/ 10 levels "1","2","3","4",..: 10 2 5 9 4 10 2 5 9 4 ...
```

Figure 3-80. *Looking at the Structure of the Data*

R can fix this problem by casting the data from one structure to another, in this
case using the as.numeric() function. One word of warning though – casting factors to
numbers can be tricky. Remember that factors depend on a reference level. R tries to

choose reasonable reference levels, so if the factor values are "1", "2", "3"... "10", it chooses the lowest, 1. However, if R chose wrong, or someone specifically defined the levels differently, we can run into issues.

Let's look at this in a short example. In Figure 3-81, I've first listed the enjoy data, and we can see each observation of the variable listed in order. I then ran the same command within the as.numeric() function. The numbers match the levels perfectly. I then reassigned data$enjoy to the numeric version of data$enjoy instead of the factor version. Running data$enjoy again shows that the data is now a number, not a factor (we know this because we don't see a "Levels" line).

```
> data$enjoy
 [1] 10 2 5  9  4  10 2 5  9  4  10 2 5  9  4  10 2 5  9  4  10 2 5  9  4  10 2 5  9  4  10 2 5  9  4  10 2 5  9  4  10 2 5  9  4  10 2 5  9  4
[51] 10 2 5  9  4  10 2 5  9  4
Levels: 1 2 3 4 5 6 7 8 9 10
> as.numeric(data$enjoy)
 [1] 10  2 5 9 4 10  2 5 9 4 10  2 5 9 4 10  2 5 9 4 10  2 5 9 4 10  2 5 9 4 10  2 5 9 4 10  2 5 9 4 10  2 5 9 4 10  2 5 9 4
[51] 10  2 5 9 4 10  2 5 9 4
> data$enjoy <- as.numeric(data$enjoy);
> data$enjoy
 [1] 10  2 5 9 4 10  2 5 9 4 10  2 5 9 4 10  2 5 9 4 10  2 5 9 4 10  2 5 9 4 10  2 5 9 4 10  2 5 9 4 10  2 5 9 4 10  2 5 9 4
[51] 10  2 5 9 4 10  2 5 9 4
```

Figure 3-81. *Recoding a Factor into a Numeric Response*

But what if something went wrong? Well, in Figure 3-82, I've created that scenario. It starts the same, but the second line of code I enter re-orders the levels so that 10 is the first level. Now we can see that if I do the exact same thing I did earlier, a 10 has become a 1, a 2 has become a 3, a 5 has become a 6, and a 9 has become a 10. Mass chaos! The moral of the story: Always test out your casting before you make it permanent to verify that you don't trash your data accidentally.

```
> data$enjoy
 [1] 10 2 5  9  4  10 2 5  9  4  10 2 5  9  4  10 2 5  9  4  10 2 5  9  4  10 2 5  9  4  10 2 5  9  4  10 2 5  9  4  10 2 5  9  4  10 2 5  9  4
[51] 10 2 5  9  4  10 2 5  9  4
Levels: 1 2 3 4 5 6 7 8 9 10
> data$enjoy <- relevel(data$enjoy,10)
> data$enjoy
 [1] 10 2 5  9  4  10 2 5  9  4  10 2 5  9  4  10 2 5  9  4  10 2 5  9  4  10 2 5  9  4  10 2 5  9  4  10 2 5  9  4  10 2 5  9  4  10 2 5  9  4
[51] 10 2 5  9  4  10 2 5  9  4
Levels: 10 1 2 3 4 5 6 7 8 9
> as.numeric(data$enjoy);
 [1]  1  3  6 10  5  1 3  6 10  5  1 3  6 10  5  1 3  6 10  5  1 3  6 10  5  1 3  6 10  5  1 3  6 10  5  1 3  6 10  5  1 3  6 10  5  1 3  6 10  5
[51]  1  3  6 10  5  1 3  6 10  5
```

Figure 3-82. *Recoding Gone Wrong*

Moving on, I'll now run a data cast from factor to numeric and then the linear model. You can see the output in Figure 3-83.

```
> data$enjoy <- as.numeric(data$enjoy);
> fit <- lm(enjoy ~ gender + age + AllThatApply_geek + AllThatApply_rbook + AllThatApply_catyell,data=data);
> |
```

Figure 3-83. *The Linear Model Equation and Code*

Or rather the lack of output. Nothing comes out. Turns out that's what we want – nothing coming out tells us that R did not find an error in our code, and it simply executed what we asked for. To actually see the output, we need to ask R to show us the output using the summary() function. Executing summary(fit) gives us the output in Figure 3-84.

```
> summary(fit);

Call:
lm(formula = enjoy ~ gender + age + AllThatApply_geek + AllThatApply_rbook +
    AllThatApply_catyell, data = data)

Residuals:
      Min         1Q     Median         3Q        Max
-3.247e-15 -1.256e-15 -4.644e-16  0.000e+00  1.635e-14

Coefficients: (1 not defined because of singularities)
                                Estimate Std. Error    t value Pr(>|t|)
(Intercept)                   -4.778e+00  3.548e-15 -1.346e+15   <2e-16 ***
genderMale                    -2.111e+00  1.563e-15 -1.351e+15   <2e-16 ***
age                            4.444e-01  1.421e-16  3.128e+15   <2e-16 ***
AllThatApply_geekNot selected -4.111e+00  2.129e-15 -1.931e+15   <2e-16 ***
AllThatApply_rbookNot selected        NA         NA         NA       NA
AllThatApply_catyellNot selected -6.942e-16 1.809e-15 -3.840e-01   0.703
---
Signif. codes:  0 '***' 0.001 '**' 0.01 '*' 0.05 '.' 0.1 ' ' 1

Residual standard error: 3.133e-15 on 55 degrees of freedom
Multiple R-squared:      1,     Adjusted R-squared:      1
F-statistic: 1.406e+31 on 4 and 55 DF,  p-value: < 2.2e-16

Warning message:
In summary.lm(fit) : essentially perfect fit: summary may be unreliable
```

Figure 3-84. *Summary of the Model, Showing Perfect Fit*

Something looks a little off here – and indeed, R tells us as much in the Warning message at the bottom: *essentially perfect fit* – what does that mean? It means that the data we have is suspiciously non-variable. And this is to be expected – because I basically copy and pasted the data ten times to create this dataset. R was not fooled – it figured out that the data wouldn't be expected to be this perfect and told us as much.

Perhaps I can make R happy by adding in a bit of variation to the dataset. Opening up the dataset in Excel, I purposefully added a few values that were not consistent with the trends reported in R. Now running the same command gives me different output and no error (Figure 3-85).

```
> summary(fit);

Call:
lm(formula = enjoy ~ gender + age + AllThatApply_geek + AllThatApply_rbook +
    AllThatApply_catyell, data = data)

Residuals:
    Min      1Q  Median      3Q     Max
-3.8926 -0.3950  0.1074  0.4140  2.7509

Coefficients:
                                  Estimate Std. Error t value Pr(>|t|)
(Intercept)                       -4.02638    1.04595  -3.849 0.000315 ***
genderMale                        -1.79318    0.58844  -3.047 0.003569 **
age                                0.40541    0.04190   9.676 2.16e-13 ***
AllThatApply_geekNot selected     -4.05739    0.65170  -6.226 7.39e-08 ***
AllThatApply_rbookNot selected     0.02854    0.44937   0.064 0.949589
AllThatApply_catyellNot selected  -0.06808    0.54546  -0.125 0.901135
---
Signif. codes:  0 '***' 0.001 '**' 0.01 '*' 0.05 '.' 0.1 ' ' 1

Residual standard error: 1.071 on 54 degrees of freedom
Multiple R-squared:  0.8842,     Adjusted R-squared:  0.8735
F-statistic: 82.47 on 5 and 54 DF,  p-value: < 2.2e-16
```

Figure 3-85. *Summary of the Model After Additional Variation Added*

Let's talk about that output now that we can see all of it. First, R reminds us what equation we were attempting to estimate. Second, it lists the Residuals – which is a measure of error. The residuals tell us how far away our predicted line is from the actual line in our data. The lower the residual, the better the data fits both the estimated and actual line.

Next, we see the coefficients of the equation. Let's walk through each one:

- (Intercept) is the y-intercept, the point at which our line crosses the Y axis if all Xs were at 0 or baseline.

- genderMale refers to the change in the line that accounts for a change in Gender from the reference level, female, to another level, Male. We can interpret this value to mean that Males enjoyed our product, on average, 1.79 more on the rating of 1–10 than females. Guess we want to target men!

- age refers to the change in enjoyment for each year of additional age. With a coefficient of 0.40, this means that for every 1 year older someone gets, their enjoyment rating goes up by 0.40.

- AllThatApply_geekNot works the same way the gender line worked – those who were not a geek enjoyed the product, on average, –4.06 less than those who were geeks.

- The last two lines also work the same way; however, you'll notice that the p-value in the far right column is above 0.05. Typically, this means we don't recognize it as a significant predictor, and thus we don't interpret it. The first four lines all are below 0.05 and are significant predictors.

At the bottom, we get some summary information about the model, including standard error, and percentage of variance accounted for. Finally, we get an overall ANOVA omnibus test of differences, showing that the model does have predictive validity.

If we would like, we can also examine different means by group to verify our findings. For example, in Figure 3-86, I've used the tapply() function to calculate a mean based upon gender. I can see that men do indeed have higher enjoyment ratings. The second example of tapply() makes me also wonder if perhaps men and women differ in enjoyment based upon if they like or dislike the meme – it certainly seems like men who liked the meme had the highest enjoyment and had a larger margin of difference between them than females. I can test this by slightly tweaking the estimated model. Instead of having all of my factors tested for a main effect, I can specifically look for interactions between that meme and gender. The model shown in Figure 3-87 does exactly that.

```
> # Example of using tapply to get the mean of enjoy by gender
> tapply(data$enjoy,data$gender,mean);
Female    Male
  4.25    6.75
> # Example of using tapply to get the mean of enjoy by gender and by AllThatApply_catyell
> tapply(data$enjoy,list(data$gender,data$AllThatApply_catyell),mean);
             Yes Not selected
Female 4.916667        3.583333
Male   8.720000        2.272727
```

Figure 3-86. *Using tapply to get means by group*

```
> summary(fit2)

Call:
lm(formula = enjoy ~ age + AllThatApply_geek + AllThatApply_rbook +
    AllThatApply_catyell * gender, data = data)

Residuals:
    Min      1Q  Median      3Q     Max
-3.9167 -0.4143  0.0833  0.4287  2.7299

Coefficients:
                                        Estimate Std. Error t value Pr(>|t|)
(Intercept)                             -4.37828    1.47716  -2.964  0.00454 **
age                                      0.42250    0.06563   6.438 3.62e-08 ***
AllThatApply_geekNot selected           -4.11934    0.68186  -6.041 1.56e-07 ***
AllThatApply_rbookNot selected          -0.02883    0.48346  -0.060  0.95267
AllThatApply_catyellNot selected        -0.16907    0.62496  -0.271  0.78781
genderMale                              -2.07167    1.01096  -2.049  0.04541 *
AllThatApply_catyellNot selected:genderMale  0.46801    1.37554   0.340  0.73502
---
Signif. codes:  0 '***' 0.001 '**' 0.01 '*' 0.05 '.' 0.1 ' ' 1

Residual standard error: 1.08 on 53 degrees of freedom
Multiple R-squared:  0.8845,    Adjusted R-squared:  0.8714
F-statistic: 67.62 on 6 and 53 DF,  p-value: < 2.2e-16
```

Figure 3-87. *The linear model with an interaction component*

In this model, we see the combination of gender and the cat meme, the very last line, and find that there is not a significant difference (the p-value is above 0.05). So while that difference looked really large in Figure 3-86, it wasn't so large that it was statistically significant.

In this chapter, we've covered a lot of ground – we've set up a survey instrument, collected data, analyzed that data, and have reached a point that we can make a conclusion: in our example, we'd like to target our marketing at male computer geeks! In the next chapter, we'll continue this by digging deeper into human behavior, before we pivot outward in Chapter 5 to discuss R in other parts of our daily life. But before we go, let's answer the question that started us off – who do we target in our marketing? Apparently, we target somewhat older males who classify themselves as geeks. Sounds like whatever this product is, I'm the prime market for it!

CHAPTER 4

Project 2: Advanced Statistical Analysis Using R and MouselabWEB

Imagine the following scenario: you're lying in bed, sick. While you know it's a bad idea, you wonder if perhaps you should engage in a little at-home diagnosing, and you head over to your search engine of choice. You plug in your symptoms and get taken to a page that has way too many advertisements – all you want is information, yet everywhere you look you see adds for amazing cure-alls and nonsense likely conspiracy theories. It's almost as if the person laying the page out knew where you would be most likely to look and purposefully put all of the information you needed somewhere else.

And it's actually possible they did. For many years, technology such as eye tracking has helped market researchers figure out where people are gazing, and they can then use that information for good or evil. Eye trackers, the combination of hardware and software that monitor gaze and fixation, can cost between $7000 and $30,000, depending on the model, and thus aren't within the budgets of most of us. However, in this chapter, I'll introduce a piece of software that can do much the same function, albeit less automatically and less unobtrusively. By the end of it, you'll have a working example that helps you understand the order that people look at information, which pieces of information they review most, and what they eventually decide based off of that information. We'll also discuss the concept of R Packages and "future-proofing" your code at the end of the chapter, because nothing is worse than writing a great piece of code only to have it die in less than a year because of something out of your control!

© Jon Westfall 2020
J. Westfall, *Practical R 4*, https://doi.org/10.1007/978-1-4842-5946-7_4

Introducing MouselabWEB

MouselabWEB is an open source tool that enables researchers (or anyone else) to monitor how people take in information and then use it to make a decision. As you can see in the example at the bottom of Figure 4-1, it does this by having boxes of information covered until the mouse rolls over them (as I did in Figure 4-2). The basic premise is that individuals will use the information they find in the boxes to learn about the choice they want to make. They will then refer to the boxes as needed to make their decision.

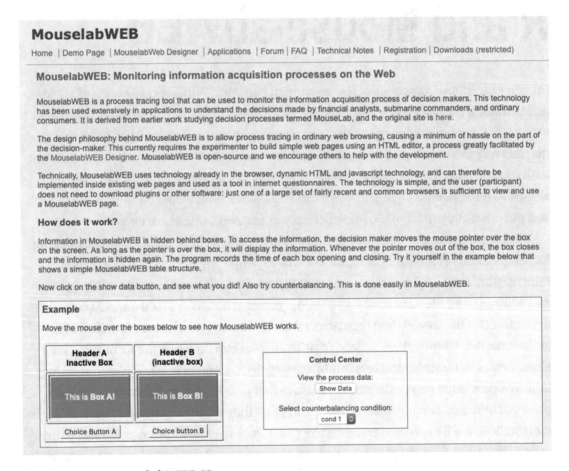

Figure 4-1. *MouselabWEB Homepage*

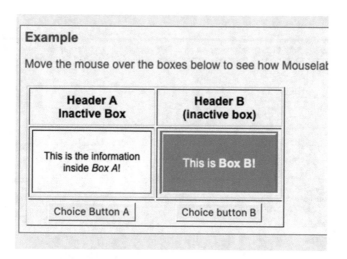

Figure 4-2. *Mousing over a Box to view it's content*

One could imagine a few scenarios for this:

- Choosing which car to buy, with boxes labeled for color, engine size, price, insurance premium, and average maintenance cost

- Choosing a college major, with boxes labeled for job opportunities, required number of courses, average cost of tuition, and occupational outlook

- Choosing where to eat lunch with co-workers, with boxes labeled for "have we recently eaten there?", "are they fast?", and "are they pricey?"

Basically, any time you have a choice to make, you can construct a MouselabWEB page that will list the attributes of the various options and then allow the user to select an option. While the user is "mousing around" the page, opening and closing boxes, the software is tracking a number of things.

To see this in action, I'm going to go to the MouselabWEB Demo Page and do the demo experiment. I'll put in my name as "Jon-PR4" and Condition number 1 (Figure 4-3). The first page (Figure 4-4) asks me to review information inside each box and then match up the professor with the subject they teach. A simple information search. The second page (Figure 4-5) gives me choices of two cameras to buy, with information on each, and allows me to pick one (measuring my preferences). The final page (Figure 4-6) simply asks me to rate how difficult the decision regarding the camera was.

Demo Page

The best way to get an impression of the possibilities of MouselabWEB is to have a look at the demo pages, which will walk you through some mock-up experimental pages. The demo is based on the walkthrough section of the manual, which actually will show you how you can generate these demo pages yourself.

Try it out

The demo experiment consists of three pages.

Page 1: Introduction screen with practice page for MouselabWEB boxes

Page 2: Camera example, showing all the important features of a mouselabWEB (complex counterbalancing, headers, choice buttons)

Page 3: Page without mouselabWEB structure, presenting just a scale.

Below, you can enter a subject name and condition number to test the MouselabWEB pages. Enter a name you can recognize later, as you will be able to look back at your own data later using the Datalyser. Note that this example has 8 counterbalancing conditions (orders), so depending on the condition number given, you will see one of these 8 orders. The number does not have to be between 0 and 7; any positive whole number will work (e.g., 10 will give you condition 3).

Subject name:	Jon-PR4
Condition number:	1
Start demo	

Figure 4-3. *Choosing a Name and Condition Number for the MouselabWEB Demo*

Introduction: Practice with boxes

In this questionnaire, you will be asked to make choices between several alternatives.

The attributes of these products will be hidden behind boxes. You can look at the attributes by moving the mouse pointer into the box. The box will open and you can see the information, until you move the mouse out of the box again.

The following practice task is designed to help you become familiar with moving the mouse over and out of the boxes. Behind the boxes are three courses, taught by different professors. Look at the information in the boxes and answer the question below.

| Box 1 | Box 2 | Box 3 |

What class does Professor Smith teach?

○ Spanish
○ Marketing
○ Philosophy
| Next Page |

Figure 4-4. *The first demo page - searching for the subject Professor Smith teaches*

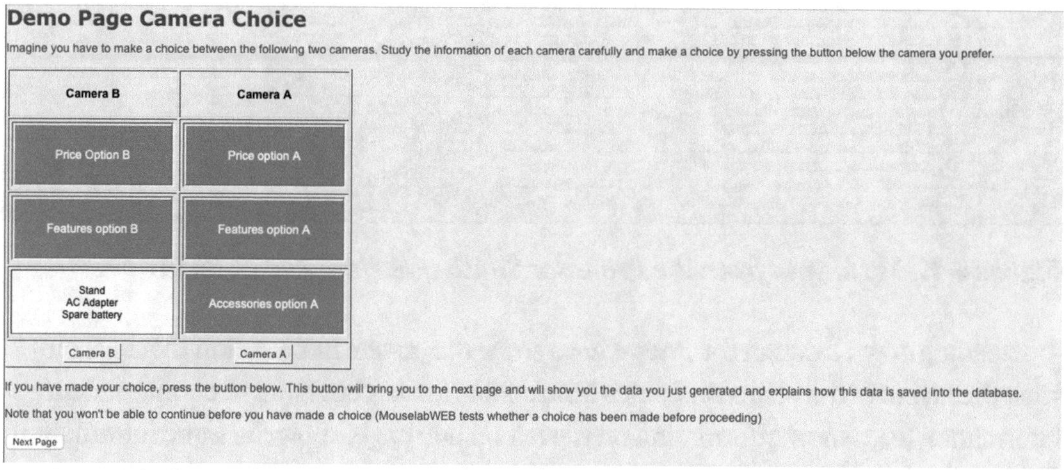

Figure 4-5. *The second demo page - Choosing a camera*

Figure 4-6. *The final demo page, asking about the difficulty of the camera question*

Once I've finished the demo, I can use the MouselabWEB Datalyser screen to view or export my demo data. In Figure 4-7, you can see the output from the first page of the demo. The data is set up in a "long" format, which means that each action has its own line. We'll discuss "long" and "wide" data formats a bit later in this chapter, principally how to convert one from the other. For now, we'll walk through this line by line.

The first line lists my participant number (12656), the section I was on (intro), and my name (Jon-PR4). The next three columns show my IP address, the condition number I was in (1), and the date and time that I ran the demo. The interesting stuff begins in the next column, which shows that the page finished loading the body 22 milliseconds after the page was requested. MouselabWEB needs to know this so it can figure out how long you might have been looking at the page before ever interacting with it.

12656	intro	Jon-PR4	160.		1		2020-03-13 14:58:17	onload	body	body		22	Philosophy
12656	intro	Jon-PR4	160.		1		2020-03-13 14:58:17	subject	header	1		25	Philosophy
12656	intro	Jon-PR4	160.		1		2020-03-13 14:58:17	order	col	0_1_2		25	Philosophy
12656	intro	Jon-PR4	160.		1		2020-03-13 14:58:17	order	row	0		25	Philosophy
12656	intro	Jon-PR4	160.		1		2020-03-13 14:58:17	events	open_close	0_0		25	Philosophy
12656	intro	Jon-PR4	160.		1		2020-03-13 14:58:17	mouseover	a0	Professor Marx Spanish		2800	Philosophy
12656	intro	Jon-PR4	160.		1		2020-03-13 14:58:17	mouseout	a0			5186	Philosophy
12656	intro	Jon-PR4	160.		1		2020-03-13 14:58:17	mouseover	a1	Professor Jones Marketing		5195	Philosophy
12656	intro	Jon-PR4	160.		1		2020-03-13 14:58:17	mouseout	a1			6984	Philosophy
12656	intro	Jon-PR4	160.		1		2020-03-13 14:58:17	mouseover	a2	Professor Smith Philosophy		6984	Philosophy
12656	intro	Jon-PR4	160.		1		2020-03-13 14:58:17	mouseout	a2			9313	Philosophy
12656	intro	Jon-PR4	160.		1		2020-03-13 14:58:17	submit	submit	submit		11245	Philosophy

Figure 4-7. *My output from the Professor Smith question seen in Figure 4-4*

Reading down through the lines, I have some diagnostic information that tells me what the layout of the boxes was, since MouselabWEB can be set up to counterbalance information (e.g., show information on the left on one page, show the same information on the right the next time the page is loaded – useful to determine if it's the information that's driving the decision or where it is placed). We know that, in some cases, humans have a right- or left-ward bias, or are more sensitive to the first or last pieces of information they are shown (a primacy or recency effect, respectively). This makes the counterbalance feature especially useful to guard against these biases. Returning to the output, reading the mouseover events, you can see that I first opened box a0, with Professor Marx's information inside. I opened the box at 2800 milliseconds after the page loaded (2.8 seconds) and closed it at 5186 milliseconds, meaning I looked at it for about 2.3 seconds. I then opened up Professor Jones's box, looked at it for just under 2 seconds, and then opened up Professor Smith's box, looking at it for just over 2 seconds. Finally, after 11254 milliseconds on the page, I submitted the demo, with Philosophy as my choice for what Professor Smith taught.

As you can probably imagine, the amount of data one could generate from these studies can be massive. Thankfully, the creators of MouselabWEB provided not only a tool to create the pages (the MouselabWEB Designer that we'll see in the next section) but also a tool to export the data (the MouselabWEB Datalyser). With those in mind, let's create our own example and settle an age-old debate: to be (a cat person) or not to be (a cat person).

Our Example: Pro- or Anti-Cat

Our example here is a bit fanciful, but a good teaching tool. Imagine that you're interviewing potential roommates and you need to know how well they'd do with your cat, Mr. Flufkins. In order to do this, you'll have them walk through a very simple set of pro- and anti-cat facts and then see what they choose. Along the way, you're curious if they look at any one fact more than another and in what order they look at the facts. You figure you might be able to use this information to co-write a book with Mr. Flufkins on how to identify "cat people" vs. everybody else.

In order to do this, we're going to use the MouselabWEB Designer. MouselabWEB can be downloaded free of charge after a quick registration of your email account (so that you can get periodic updates and information on bug fixes, the "owners" of MouselabWEB are academic researchers, they don't have any desire to sell your information). You can download the full package or just the designer portion. Eventually, you'll need to host the full package on a web server of some sort, so I'd recommend downloading everything.

It's a bit outside the scope of this book to discuss how to set up a LAMP stack (Linux, Apache, MySQL, PHP); however, know that you'll need such a setup going to host your MouselabWEB pages, specifically with PHP 5. PHP 7 has removed the mysql_ functions in PHP for the newer MySQL commands and thus broke compatibility with MouselabWEB. The quick steps that you'll need to do to install MouselabWEB on your LAMP server are

1. Upload the software to your server.

2. Create a MySQL database for it to store data in.

3. Modify the mlwebdb.inc.php file to have the proper username, password, and database table for your database.

Once you've done that, you should be able to test out MouselabWEB by running the designer. It's a separate download, so you may want to put it in its own directory below your root website URL (e.g., http://mywebsite.org/designer). Loading it up, you should see a screen similar to Figure 4-8.

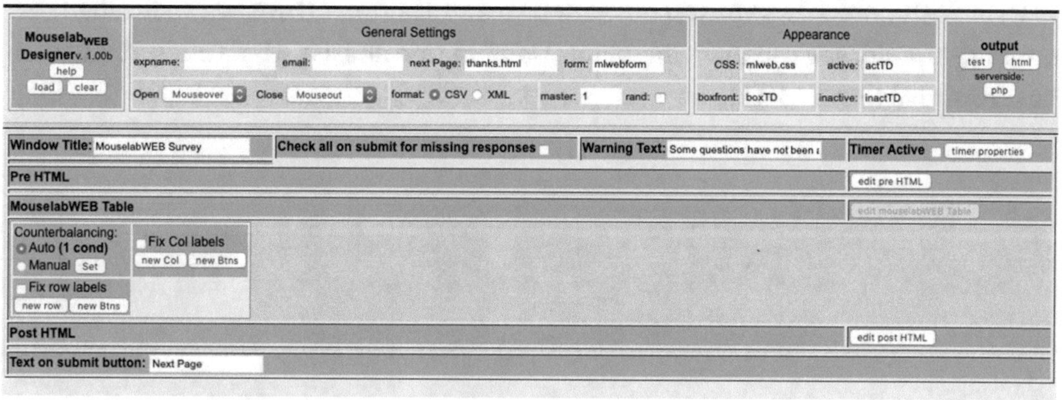

Figure 4-8. *The MouselabWEB Designer*

The interface is pretty easy to understand – you can add new rows and columns by pressing the "new row" or "new Col" button. If you'd like to add buttons to make a choice, you can do that by pressing the "new Btns" button and can then choose push buttons or radio options. In Figure 4-9, I've put in all of our information for our pro- or anti-cat test.

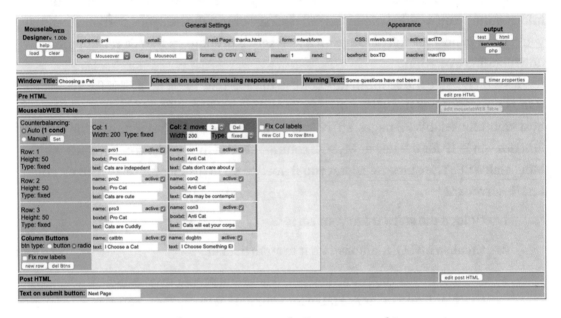

Figure 4-9. *Designer with our Cat Example Programmed in*

You'll notice that in the upper right there is an "Output" section. This lets you download the HTML or PHP version of the page, as well as test the entire page from within the designer interface. Pressing the "test" button brings up a screen similar to Figure 4-10, which lets you test out your boxes and buttons. Once you've finished mousing around, you can press the "Show Data" button and see what your script would have recorded (Figure 4-11).

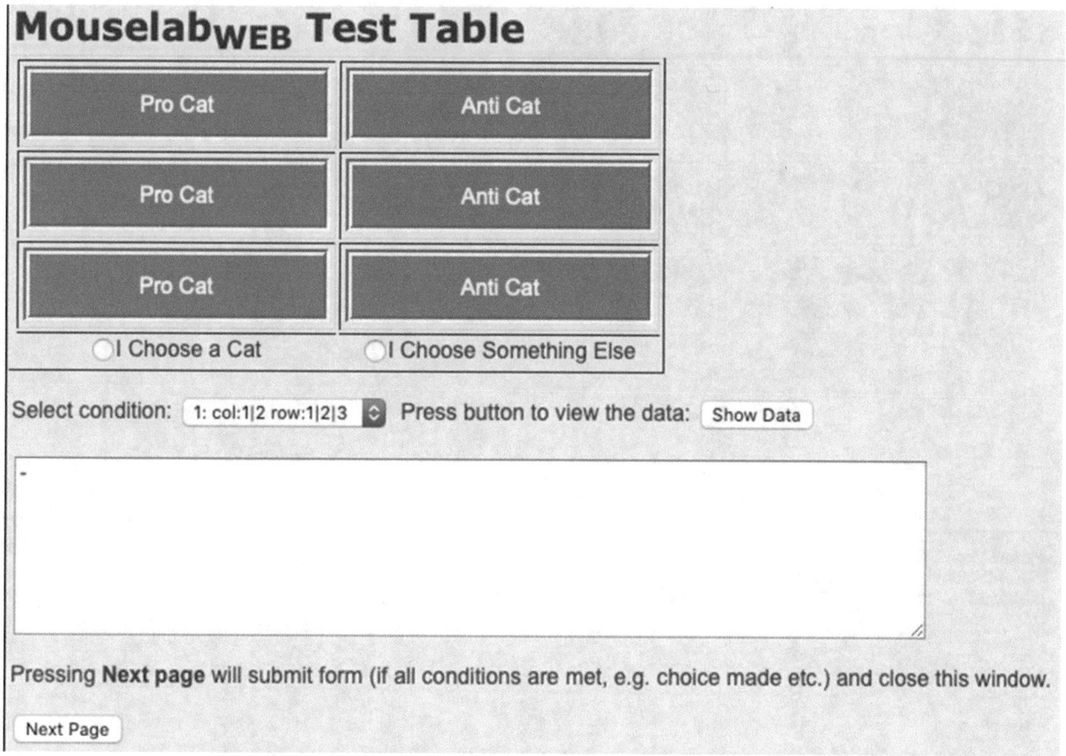

Figure 4-10. *Pressing the "test" button to show the Test Table*

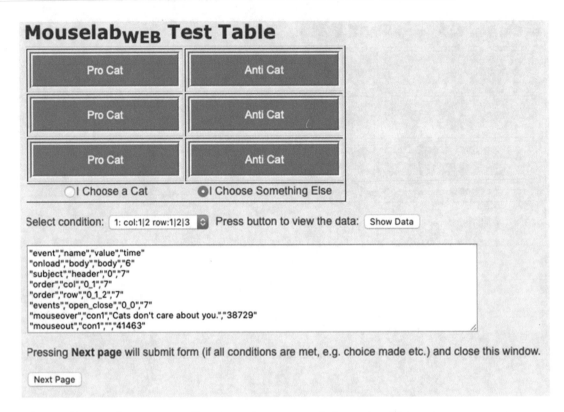

Figure 4-11. *The output after mousing around the test table*

Finally, once you're all done, you can press the php button to get the PHP output (Figure 4-12) that you can then customize and save to your web server.

Output template for PHP

Save the following text as **pr4.php**. FTP the file to an PHP enabled webserver, in the folder where the php-package is installed. Whenever this page is called with two additional attributes, e.g. pr4.php?subject= [subjectname]&condnum=[somenumber], it will save the data in a table called mlweb, using this [subjectname] as a subject identifier and counterbalancing on [condnum].

The following files should be in the same web-folder as this page, otherwise the page will not work correctly:

- The stylesheet as assigned in the designer: *mlweb.css*
- The mlweb javascript file: *mlweb.js*
- A transparent image named: *transp.gif*
- A *configured* file that links to the database: *mlwebdb.inc.php*
- The file that saves the data in the database: *save.php*
- The next page (nextURL: *thanks.html*) should exist.

All these files, including default stylesheets, are in the distribution package and would normally already be installed on the webserver. For installation and setting up the links to the database, see the manual.

```
<?php
if (isset($_GET['subject'])) {$subject=$_GET['subject'];}
 else {$subject="anonymous";}
if (isset($_GET['condnum'])) {$condnum=$_GET['condnum'];}
    else ($condnum=-1;}?><HTML>
<HEAD>
<TITLE>Choosing a Pet</TITLE>
<script language=javascript src="mlweb.js"></SCRIPT>
<link rel="stylesheet" href="mlweb.css" type="text/css">
</head>
```

close   download

Figure 4-12. *The PHP Output*

The PHP version is more minimal than the test version, since it doesn't need to show the data back to the participant. In Figures 4-13 and 4-14, we can see the output PHP being run, first with all the boxes closed and then with them open.

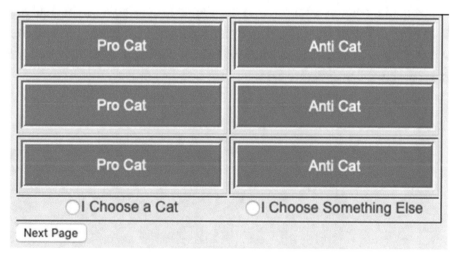

Figure 4-13. *Our completed table with all boxes closed*

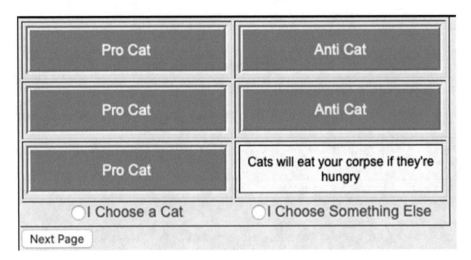

Figure 4-14. *Our completed table with a box open*

And that's about it – there are a lot of ways we could continue to customize, including piping a participant ID number in or counterbalancing the order, but for our simple page, we've got everything we need. Now we just need to interview roommates. And in my case, because I'm an overachiever, I interviewed 34 of them. It's time to download the data and crunch the numbers!

Downloading the Data

Downloading MouselabWEB data is most easily done through the Datalyser, a special PHP script created by the researchers who developed MouselabWEB that lets you get your data in a few different ways. The Datalyser is named "datalyser.php" and lives in the same directory as the other MouselabWEB files. Loading it up in your web browser, you'll get a screen similar to Figure 4-15.

MouselabWEB Datalyser

Part of MouselabWEB, version 1.00beta

This screen enables you to download data in CSV (comma separated values) format. This is a textfile format in which each field is enclosed in brackets (") and separated by commas. Such a file can be read by most statistical programs. If the **unpack events** box is checked, the program will unpack the process data (whether it is in XML or CSV format in the database) into a list of events.

The **download and process selected** button allows to download processed data that can be analyzed directly. It will delete acquisitions below the threshold, will calculate time and frequency columns for each box on the screen, and will summarize data in divisions.

Disclaimer: The processing module has not been checked extensively for the 1.00beta version! Check whether the output is consistent with the event files.

The **Show Table** button allows you to look at the data in one table, either unpacked or as is. The **Playback** allows for playback of participants in one of the experiments. This button wil open a new page in which you can select a participant from the list.

Password: For any action you do on this page, a password is required. Type the password before pressing a button. This prevents unauthorized users that browse to this page from actually reading your data!

Experiment name	Download	Show data	Play back
pr4	☑	Show Table	Replay
	sel all Reset sel Invert sel		
	download selected ☑ Unpack events		
Password: •••••	download and process selected		
	Threshold (ms) 200		
	divisions (1=all, 2=halfs ect.): 1		

Figure 4-15. *The Datalyser*

There are a few things to note about the Datalyser screen. The first is that all experiments that you run will be listed here, as it shows all experiments in the database. If you want to separate some of them out, you'll need to specify a different database in the `mlwebdb.inc.php` file that I mentioned earlier.

We've already seen an example of the "Show Table" command in Figure 4-7; however, the "Replay" command can be very useful when understanding how participants engaged with your boxes. Clicking it shows a screen similar to Figure 4-16. You can then choose any participant (Figure 4-17) and get the output of their session (Figure 4-18). This is very useful on a person-by-person basis.

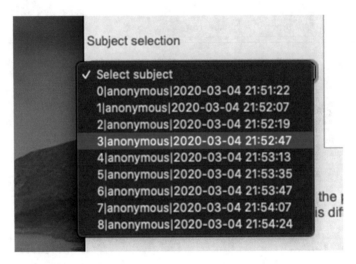

Playback for experiment: pr4

Process data of current subject

Subject selection

[Select subject ⇕]

[Playback Data]

Note: The Replay routine assumes that the php-file you want to replay has the same name as the experiment itself: pr4.php . You can change the name of the file on the replay page if it is different from the file name.

Figure 4-16. Playback of a Single Participant

Subject selection

✓ Select subject
0|anonymous|2020-03-04 21:51:22
1|anonymous|2020-03-04 21:52:07
2|anonymous|2020-03-04 21:52:19
3|anonymous|2020-03-04 21:52:47
4|anonymous|2020-03-04 21:53:13
5|anonymous|2020-03-04 21:53:35
6|anonymous|2020-03-04 21:53:47
7|anonymous|2020-03-04 21:54:07
8|anonymous|2020-03-04 21:54:24

Figure 4-17. Selecting which participant to playback

Process data of current subject

onload	| body	| body	| 6	
subject	| header	| 0	| 10	
order	| col	| 0_1	| 10	
order	| row	| 0_1_2	| 10	
events	| open_close	| 0_0	| 10	
mouseover	| pro3	| Cats are Cuddly	| 1587	
mouseout	| pro3	|	| 10046	
mouseover	| pro2	| Cats are cute	| 10080	
mouseout	| pro2	|	| 12172	
mouseover	| pro1	| Cats are indepedent	| 12195	

Figure 4-18. The output of the playback screen

136

However, it's not going to be as useful for us if we want to analyze everything. For that we'll need the data file. Pressing the "download selected" box will let you download the raw data, with just a bit of processing to unpack the events. You'll be taken to a screen similar to Figure 4-19 where you can download the CSV file that we'll import into R.

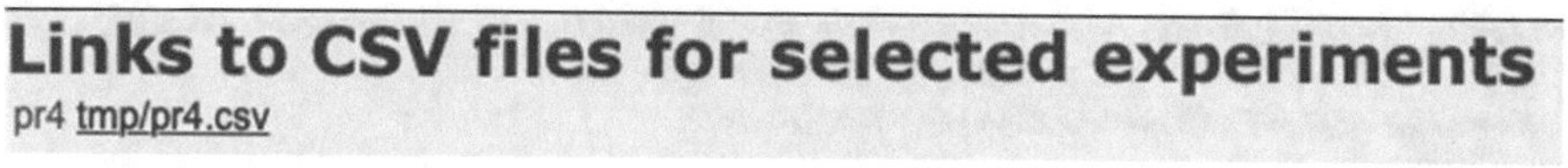

Links to CSV files for selected experiments

pr4 tmp/pr4.csv

Figure 4-19. *Links to the Raw Data File*

While the raw data is useful, the Datalyser has a great feature that allows you to process selected files into easier data to analyze, by removing any data below a threshold (200 milliseconds by default, so a quick "mouseover" that was unintentional will be removed) and by adding columns for how long time was spent on that particular box (as opposed to simply a timestamp in number of milliseconds since the page was loaded) and how many times that box was opened. Pressing the "download and process selected" box takes you to a page similar to Figure 4-20. It's this processed data file that we'll be using in R.

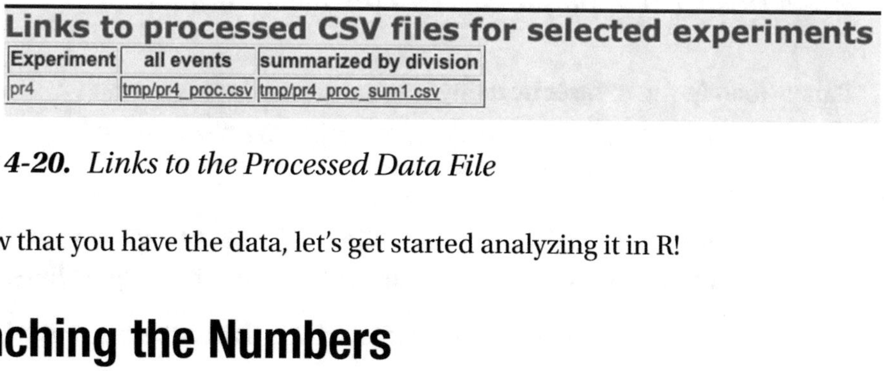

Links to processed CSV files for selected experiments

Experiment	all events	summarized by division
pr4	tmp/pr4_proc.csv	tmp/pr4_proc_sum1.csv

Figure 4-20. *Links to the Processed Data File*

Now that you have the data, let's get started analyzing it in R!

Crunching the Numbers

To understand what my 34 respondents did, I'm going to need to do a bit of analysis. To start

1. Open RStudio and create a new project (I named mine PR4MLWeb and you can open it in the code download for this book).

2. Move the processed data file (likely named *something*_proc.csv) into project directory.

3. Install the R packages that we'll be using by issuing the following command: `install.packages(c("lme4","lmerTest","psych"," reshape2"))`. You should get a result similar to Figure 4-21.

```
> install.packages(c("lme4", "lmerTest", "psych", "reshape2"))
trying URL 'https://cran.rstudio.com/bin/macosx/el-capitan/contrib/3.6/lme4_1.1-21.tgz'
Content type 'application/x-gzip' length 7809491 bytes (7.4 MB)
==================================================
downloaded 7.4 MB

trying URL 'https://cran.rstudio.com/bin/macosx/el-capitan/contrib/3.6/lmerTest_3.1-1.tgz'
Content type 'application/x-gzip' length 413697 bytes (404 KB)
==================================================
downloaded 404 KB

trying URL 'https://cran.rstudio.com/bin/macosx/el-capitan/contrib/3.6/psych_1.9.12.31.tgz'
Content type 'application/x-gzip' length 3801830 bytes (3.6 MB)
==================================================
downloaded 3.6 MB

trying URL 'https://cran.rstudio.com/bin/macosx/el-capitan/contrib/3.6/reshape2_1.4.3.tgz'
Content type 'application/x-gzip' length 307635 bytes (300 KB)
==================================================
downloaded 300 KB
```

Figure 4-21. *Installing multiple packages for this demonstration*

4. Finally load in the dataset by using the command `data <- read. csv(file="pr4example_proc.csv")`, replacing the filename with whatever your processed file is named.

We're now ready to start analyzing. We're going to first explore our data, then format our data as needed for our analyses, and then answer three important questions:

- Does the time spent viewing a box predict which choice the person will make?

- Do people open certain boxes later than others?

- Do cat lovers avoid looking at anti-cat information?

Viewing and Formatting

To start, I've executed the following code. For each line, I'll tell you the code, what it does, why I did it, and what the output looks like.

Code	What It Does	Why We're Doing It	Output Seen In
table (data$boxname)	Displays the data, breaking down by how many times people viewed each box	It's a good idea to look at your data in an easy-to-digest way. If we were to look at the data in our data viewer, we'd have 195 rows of data to view – much more than I can handle. But this lets me see at a glance if we have data across all options and if any were to look exceptionally high or low. If we had all 34 choose the catbtn, for example, I might wonder how honest everyone were being. Mr. Flufkins would be very skeptical.	Figure 4-22
by(data$boxtime, data$boxname, describe)	Gets descriptive statistics on the time spent in the box by box name	Think of this as a sanity check. This command lets us explore a bit more just to be sure our data is varied enough to be useful and doesn't have anything strange lurking in it. You'll notice that all of the button means are around 300–400 milliseconds – that's fine since it was the amount of time the mouse was over the button. Imagine though if all of the boxes were that way – we'd wonder if people were really reading the box content or not. Right now, it sorta looks like the pro2 box wasn't open very long. However, pro2 was the shortest text we had: "cats are cute", so it makes sense that people wouldn't be reading that very long. Again, we're just making sure that the numbers make sense.	Figure 4-23

(continued)

Code	What It Does	Why We're Doing It	Output Seen In
`data <- subset (data,event == "mouseout");`	Removes onclick events	The onclick events represent clicking the buttons at the bottom of the boxes. We don't need that information, so we remove it from the dataset.	Figure 4-24
`data$boxtime.c <- data$boxtime - mean (data$boxtime);`	"Centers" the variable boxtime by subtracting the average of all the boxtimes	In a regression analysis, we often want to center a variable so that the intercept term is meaningful. In this case, if we don't center, we're going to have an intercept set at 0. Since no one looks at a box for 0 seconds, it's easier to have the intercept set to the average boxtime. This will let us interpret our intercept term roughly as the average time a box is open.	Figure 4-24
`data$boxtime.c. scaled <- data$boxtime.c / 1000;`	Divides boxtime.c by 1000, converting milliseconds to seconds	This helps with our interpretation as well as keeping things a little easier to model.	Figure 4-24

```
> table(data$boxname)

catbtn   con1   con2   con3 dogbtn   pro1   pro2   pro3
    20     28     28     29     17     14     26     33
```

Figure 4-22. Table Output

```
> by(data$boxtime,data$boxname,describe)
data$boxname: catbtn
   vars  n  mean     sd median trimmed    mad min max range skew kurtosis    se
X1    1 20 365.8 119.27    330  357.31 111.19 188 685   497 0.78     0.28 26.67
-----------------------------------------------------------------------------------
data$boxname: con1
   vars  n    mean      sd median trimmed    mad min  max range skew kurtosis     se
X1    1 28 1146.39 1155.77  563.5  969.88 444.78 227 5658  5431 2.15      5.6 218.42
-----------------------------------------------------------------------------------
data$boxname: con2
   vars  n    mean     sd median trimmed    mad min  max range skew kurtosis  se
X1    1 28 1059.96 799.03    754     990 684.96 282 3094  2812 0.65    -0.73 151
-----------------------------------------------------------------------------------
data$boxname: con3
   vars  n    mean      sd median trimmed   mad min  max range skew kurtosis     se
X1    1 29 1680.83 2007.49    696  1359.8 732.4 202 9382  9180 2.11     4.96 372.78
-----------------------------------------------------------------------------------
data$boxname: dogbtn
   vars  n   mean    sd median trimmed   mad min max range skew kurtosis   se
X1    1 17 336.65 40.06    339  336.07 41.51 268 414   146 0.04     -1.1 9.72
-----------------------------------------------------------------------------------
data$boxname: pro1
   vars  n   mean     sd median trimmed    mad min  max range skew kurtosis     se
X1    1 14 915.21 740.82    495  852.08 416.61 214 2374  2160 0.57    -1.32 197.99
-----------------------------------------------------------------------------------
data$boxname: pro2
   vars  n   mean     sd median trimmed    mad min  max range skew kurtosis     se
X1    1 26 724.85 614.71    409  654.59 207.56 214 2082  1868    1    -0.74 120.56
-----------------------------------------------------------------------------------
data$boxname: pro3
   vars  n    mean      sd median trimmed     mad min  max range skew kurtosis     se
X1    1 33 2005.61 1862.72   1484  1779.7 1700.54 225 6456  6231 0.89    -0.49 324.26
```

Figure 4-23. *By output*

```
> data <- subset(data,event == "mouseout");
> data$boxtime.c <- data$boxtime - mean(data$boxtime);
> data$boxtime.c.scaled <- data$boxtime.c / 1000;
> |
```

Figure 4-24. *Subset output*

Now that we have our data ready, let's answer our questions!

Does the Time Spent Viewing a Box Predict Which Choice the Person Will Make?

To answer this question, we need to run a logistic regression. Whereas the technique we used in Chapters 2 and 3, linear regression, predicts continuous values (e.g., numbers), logistic regressions predict choices, and in this case, we need to predict the responses of someone choosing the Cat button. Logistic regression depends on many of the same assumptions that we need to check for linear, so if you're not familiar with the concept, please spend a few minutes with a stats textbook. In our case, we're going to predict choice by how long they spent inside each of the six boxes. The code to do that is

```
fit <- glmer(mlchoice=="catbtn" ~ (1|id) + boxtime.c.scaled %in%boxname,
data=data,family=binomial);
summary(fit);
```

The output is in Figure 4-25. Let's walk through it.

```
> fit <- glmer(mlchoice=="catbtn" ~ (1|id) + boxtime.c.scaled%in%boxname,data=data,family=binomial);
> summary(fit);
Generalized linear mixed model fit by maximum likelihood (Laplace Approximation) ['glmerMod']
 Family: binomial  ( logit )
Formula: mlchoice == "catbtn" ~ (1 | id) + boxtime.c.scaled %in% boxname
   Data: data

     AIC      BIC   logLik deviance df.resid
    58.7     83.2    -21.4     42.7      150

Scaled residuals:
      Min        1Q    Median        3Q       Max
-0.076399 -0.017674 -0.011366  0.001674  0.020061

Random effects:
 Groups Name        Variance Std.Dev.
 id     (Intercept) 3193     56.51
Number of obs: 158, groups:  id, 34

Fixed effects:
                             Estimate Std. Error z value Pr(>|z|)
(Intercept)                  12.59684    2.81698   4.472 7.76e-06 ***
boxtime.c.scaled:boxnamecon1  0.03926    2.96488   0.013 0.989436
boxtime.c.scaled:boxnamecon2 -0.82020    5.67681  -0.144 0.885119
boxtime.c.scaled:boxnamecon3 -2.79788    0.81766  -3.422 0.000622 ***
boxtime.c.scaled:boxnamepro1 -0.15245    7.27334  -0.021 0.983278
boxtime.c.scaled:boxnamepro2 -0.50999    5.37751  -0.095 0.924443
boxtime.c.scaled:boxnamepro3 -0.14406    1.17670  -0.122 0.902559
---
Signif. codes:  0 '***' 0.001 '**' 0.01 '*' 0.05 '.' 0.1 ' ' 1

Correlation of Fixed Effects:
                  (Intr) bxtm.c.scld:bxnmc1 bxtm.c.scld:bxnmc2 bxtm.c.scld:bxnmc3 bxtm.c.scld:bxnmp1 bxtm.c.scld:bxnmp2
bxtm.c.scld:bxnmc1 -0.035
bxtm.c.scld:bxnmc2  0.009  0.049
bxtm.c.scld:bxnmc3 -0.562  0.022              0.019
bxtm.c.scld:bxnmp1  0.030  0.027              0.064              0.001
bxtm.c.scld:bxnmp2  0.078  0.028              0.086             -0.005              0.062
bxtm.c.scld:bxnmp3 -0.266  0.015             -0.002              0.118             -0.006             -0.030
```

Figure 4-25. *The output of the logistic regression*

The first portion of the output gives us a reminder of the formula we used and how the model was fitted. It then gives us some regression diagnostics, such as

- AIC: The Akaike Information Criterion, a measure of prediction error. We'd use this if we were testing multiple models, by comparing the AICs and choosing whichever model had the highest AIC. Multiple models would be generated by having more variables – imagine also having demographic data on the individual, or previous behavioral data, and wondering if that all factors into their behavior here.

- BIC: The Bayesian Information Criterion, another measure used during model selection. In this case, if we were running multiple models, we'd want the lowest BIC.

- logLik: The Log-Likelihood, a model-fitting criterion that partially drives AIC.

- deviance: A measure of goodness of fit. The lower the better.

- df.resid: The residual degrees of freedom estimate in the model, which for our function (glmer) is the total random effects degrees of freedom. Degrees of freedom refer to the number of data points that are free to vary while still maintaining the integrity of the statistical test.

- Scaled Residuals: Whenever we draw a regression line, our data lives somewhere above or below it: After all, it is a line of best fit, but not a perfect line that goes through all of our data. The Residuals here tell us the distance off at the lowest end of the line, 25% of the line, 50% of the line, 75% of the line, and the highest. Numbers close to 0 are good, as they show there is not a lot of distance between where the regression line is and where the actual data are.

Now that we've gotten past that, we can look at the random effects group. Random effects refer to data that can have many possible levels, and we're interested in all of them. Fixed effects have a set number of levels, and we might only be interested in a few of them.

In our case, we've specified the ID variable as a grouping random effects variable. It turns out that some people are just faster readers than others, and this allows us to capture that essence of the participant apart from the rest of our data. Here R tells me that we had 158 observations over 34 groups (id numbers). The variance was 3193, with a standard deviation of 56.51. These numbers can be tricky to interpret, but it's worth noting that the standard deviation (56.51) is much, much larger than any of the fixed effects treatments below (which mostly range from 0 to 2). Therefore, we know that the individual person variance is a big deal – some people just look longer and boxes than others, and it doesn't affect what they do in terms of their information search, it's just a part of how they function as humans.

Finally, we get to the fixed effects. These tell us our estimates for how long people spent looking at each box when they ultimately decided to choose the cat option over something else. First, we notice that only two estimates are statistically significant (indicated by the asterisks next to them): the intercept (where the regression line crosses the Y axis) and the time spent in Con3 (the item that insinuated that cats will eat your corpse if they're hungry). We can interpret it that, on average, people spend about 12 seconds looking at boxes **overall**, and those that spend about 2.79 seconds **less** on Con3 are more likely to choose cat. Practically, the answer to our question is: yes, people who look at Con3 less than average, by about 2.7 seconds, are more likely to choose cat than others. Guess that argument against cats really holds a lot of sway for some. And sadly, in some cases, it's absolutely true.

Do People Open Certain Boxes Later Than Others?

One of the nice features that MouselabWEB includes is the counter variables it adds. The first box that someone opens gets a count of 1, the second a count of 2, and so on. Each line (see Figure 4-30) also lists the maxcount (how many boxes the person opened) and relcount – the counter divided by the maxcount. Looking at the top of our data, we can see that id 68 has a maxcount of 7 (they looked at seven boxes). The first box opened, con3, has a counter of 1, and a recount of .142, or 1 divided by 7. Based upon those values, we can determine if some boxes get opened before others, since we know where in the sequence a box was opened. To do this, you may decide to simply modify the preceding code something like this:

```
fit2 <- lmer(relcount ~ (1|id) + boxname,data=data);
summary(fit2);
```

If you do that, however, you'll get an error, as shown in Figure 4-26. This error is not all that useful – "boundary (singular) fit: see ?isSingular" – however, there are a few things we can do to troubleshoot it. The first is to run the command that it gives: ?isSingular. Running this code brings up the help menu entry in Figure 4-27. Admittedly, though, the explanation can be a little confusing to non-stats nerds. That's where your search engine of choice comes into play. It's worth noting that the R help files, as you can see in Figure 4-27, tend to be written targeted at someone who has a very comfortable knowledge of both programming and statistics. This is why the searching can be helpful as people typically re-explain it several times in different ways on forums such as Stack Overflow and Quora. After a little bit of searching around, we find our issue: the random effect term.

```
> fit2 <- lmer(relcount ~ (1|id) + boxname,data=data);
boundary (singular) fit: see ?isSingular
> summary(fit2);
```

Figure 4-26. *Help Entry for Error*

R: Test fitted model for (near) singularity ▾   Find in Topic

isSingular {lme4}   R Documentation

Test fitted model for (near) singularity

Description

Evaluates whether a fitted mixed model is singular, i.e. the parameters are on the boundary of the feasible parameter space: variances of one or more linear combinations of effects are (close to) zero.

Usage

```
isSingular(x, tol = 1e-05)
```

Arguments

x   a fitted merMod object (result of lmer or glmer)

tol   numerical tolerance for detecting singularity

Details

Complex mixed-effect models (i.e., those with a large number of variance-covariance parameters) frequently result in *singular* fits, i.e. estimated variance-covariance matrices with less than full rank. Less technically, this means that some "dimensions" of the variance-covariance matrix have been estimated as exactly zero. For scalar random effects such as intercept-only models, or 2-dimensional random effects such as intercept+slope models, singularity is relatively easy to detect because it leads to random-effect variance estimates of (nearly) zero, or estimates of correlations that are (almost) exactly -1 or 1. However, for more complex models (variance-covariance matrices of dimension >=3) singularity can be hard to detect; models can often be singular without any of their individual variances being close to zero or correlations being close to +/-1.

This function performs a simple test to determine whether any of the random effects covariance matrices of a fitted model are singular. The rePCA method provides more detail about the singularity pattern, showing the standard deviations of orthogonal variance components and the mapping from variance terms in the model to orthogonal components (i.e., eigenvector/rotation matrices).

While singular models are statistically well defined (it is theoretically sensible for the true maximum likelihood estimate to correspond to a singular fit), there are real concerns that (1) singular fits correspond to overfitted models that may have poor power; (2) chances of numerical problems and mis-convergence are higher for singular models (e.g. it may be computationally difficult to compute profile confidence intervals for such models); (3) standard inferential procedures such as Wald statistics and likelihood ratio tests may be inappropriate.

Figure 4-27. *The isSingular error*

Whereas we had multiple lines for each person in the first analysis, the variables for this question stay largely the same for each person – therein lies the problem – we were making this more complicated than it needed to be. Amending the code to a simple linear model without the random effects gives us nearly the exact same output, but without the error message.

Here's the revised code:

```
fit2 <- lm(relcount ~ boxname,data=data);
summary(fit2);
```

With the output in Figure 4-28, let's walk through it.

```
> fit2 <- lm(relcount ~ boxname,data=data);
> summary(fit2);

Call:
lm(formula = relcount ~ boxname, data = data)

Residuals:
     Min       1Q    Median       3Q      Max
-0.56388 -0.19403 -0.00144  0.20043  0.54636

Coefficients:
             Estimate Std. Error t value Pr(>|t|)
(Intercept)   0.41518    0.04550   9.125 4.11e-16 ***
boxnamecon2   0.03018    0.06435   0.469  0.63969
boxnamecon3   0.13347    0.06379   2.092  0.03807 *
boxnamepro1   0.05714    0.07881   0.725  0.46953
boxnamepro2   0.06059    0.06557   0.924  0.35699
boxnamepro3   0.18717    0.06186   3.026  0.00291 **
---
Signif. codes:  0 '***' 0.001 '**' 0.01 '*' 0.05 '.' 0.1 ' ' 1

Residual standard error: 0.2408 on 152 degrees of freedom
Multiple R-squared:  0.07605,   Adjusted R-squared:  0.04565
F-statistic: 2.502 on 5 and 152 DF,  p-value: 0.03292
```

Figure 4-28. *Output for our Second Question*

First, we see some familiar lines for residuals, and then we go straight into coefficients. In this model, we can think of coefficient correlations in a sense. As the relcount variable changes (the position that this box was opened, higher numbers mean later viewing), the output tells us there is a relationship between relcount and two boxes: con3 and pro3. Because the coefficients are positive, we can see that they move with relcount, so as relcount goes up, so does the likelihood that the box someone is looking at is con3 or pro3. This makes intuitive sense, those are the bottom most boxes. This is why MouselabWEB has a counterbalancing feature built in – because otherwise, a simple psychological effect of ordering might make us think pro3 and con3 were more important, since it appears people go back to them at the end. In reality, they might just be the last thing they view – a more parsimonious answer.

So answering our second question: yes, the boxes at the bottom (Pro3 and Con3) are more likely to be opened later in the decision-making session than the boxes at the top! Imagine how this finding might be useful in market research applications where you're curious what gets "the last word" as someone debates which option to choose.

Do Cat Lovers Avoid Looking at Anti-Cat Information?

Finally, we're going to look at an issue of avoidance: namely, are the cat lovers just avoiding the harsh facts about their feline friends? In order to analyze that question, we're going to need to get the data "massaged" into a slightly different format: from "long" data to "wide" data.

To understand what I mean, let's look at participant 68. Their data is in Figure 4-29, and we can see they have a line for each and every interaction they made on the page – six lines of data. However, to determine what boxes are being looked at the most for each person, I need their data to be all on its own line – something like the same data shown in Figure 4-30.

```
> subset(data,id==68)
  id   expname   subject   ip condnum choice   submitted       event roword colord evttype boxname boxin boxtime counter mlchoice relcount maxcount f_con3
1 68 pr4example anonymous NA      -1 catbtn 3/5/20 21:34 mouseout 0_1_2   0_1    0_0    con3  1573    1598       1   catbtn 0.1428571        7       1
2 68 pr4example anonymous NA      -1 catbtn 3/5/20 21:34 mouseout 0_1_2   0_1    0_0    con2  3193    1822       2   catbtn 0.2857143        7       0
3 68 pr4example anonymous NA      -1 catbtn 3/5/20 21:34 mouseout 0_1_2   0_1    0_0    con1  5038    1755       3   catbtn 0.4285714        7       0
4 68 pr4example anonymous NA      -1 catbtn 3/5/20 21:34 mouseout 0_1_2   0_1    0_0    pro1  6815    1676       4   catbtn 0.5714286        7       0
5 68 pr4example anonymous NA      -1 catbtn 3/5/20 21:34 mouseout 0_1_2   0_1    0_0    pro2  8514    1676       5   catbtn 0.7142857        7       0
6 68 pr4example anonymous NA      -1 catbtn 3/5/20 21:34 mouseout 0_1_2   0_1    0_0    pro3 10213    3465       6   catbtn 0.8571429        7       0
  f_con2 f_con1 f_pro1 f_pro2 f_pro3 f_catbtn f_dogbtn t_con3 t_con2 t_con1 t_pro1 t_pro2 t_pro3 t_catbtn t_dogbtn boxtime.c boxtime.c.scaled
1      0      0      0      0      0        0        0   1598      0      0      0      0      0        0        0  279.2278        0.2792278
2      1      0      0      0      0        0        0      0   1822      0      0      0      0        0        0  503.2278        0.5032278
3      0      1      0      0      0        0        0      0      0   1755      0      0      0        0        0  436.2278        0.4362278
4      0      0      1      0      0        0        0      0      0      0   1676      0      0        0        0  357.2278        0.3572278
5      0      0      0      1      0        0        0      0      0      0      0   1676      0        0        0  357.2278        0.3572278
6      0      0      0      0      1        0        0      0      0      0      0      0   3465        0        0 2146.2278        2.1462278
```

Figure 4-29. Long data for Participant 68

```
> subset(data_wide,id==68)
  id choice con1 con2 con3 pro1 pro2 pro3
1 68 catbtn    1    1    1    1    1    1
```

Figure 4-30. Wide data for Participant 68

Once the data is in "wide" format, all I need to do is run a logistic regression to predict if they're going to choose the cat button, and if they are avoiding the con information, I should see those choosing cat not even opening up those boxes. Mr. Flufkins wouldn't, that's for sure.

To do that, I need to add a new column to my data: `hit` – this simple variable gives a hit value of 1 to each row. If I wanted to do something fancier, I could always assign a higher value to certain boxes. This might be useful in a marketing context to "weight" more important information that impacts (or is proposed to impact) the viewer more so than the rest of the material. Next, after adding `hit`, I'm going to use a function from the `reshape2` package named `dcast()`. This function takes data in a long format and "casts" it to a wide format. The entire `reshape2` package provides a lot of useful functions that we will play more with in future chapters. For now, you can interpret the second line of the following code as telling `dcast()` to create a new data frame called `data_wide` from the existing data frame. On the left side of the tilde (~) are the columns that should remain constant on the line and on the right side are variables that should be counted for each person. The `value.var` parameter tells it to use the value in the `hit` variable we just created. In honesty, we could actually not use the `hit` step – `dcast()` defaults to counting the number of instances. But to be precise, and to discuss the option to weight values, I've included it here.

```
data$hit <- 1;
data_wide <- dcast(data,id + choice ~ boxname, value.var="hit");
```

Now our data looks a little different, as you can see in Figure 4-31.

```
> head(data_wide)
   id choice con1 con2 con3 pro1 pro2 pro3
1 68 catbtn    1    1    1    1    1    1
2 69 dogbtn    5    5    3    3    5    3
3 70 dogbtn    5    5    3    3    5    3
4 71 catbtn    0    0    0    0    1    1
5 72 catbtn    0    0    1    0    0    1
6 73 catbtn    0    0    0    0    0    1
```

Figure 4-31. *The data for the first 6 participants in wide format*

With the data in the right format, I can run a logistic regression using the following commands:

```
fit3 <- lm(choice=="catbtn" ~ con1 + con2 + con3 + pro1 + pro2 + pro3,
data=data_wide);
summary(fit3);
```

This provides the output in Figure 4-32.

```
> fit3 <- lm(choice=="catbtn" ~ con1 + con2 + con3 + pro1 + pro2 + pro3, data=data_wide);
> summary(fit3);

Call:
lm(formula = choice == "catbtn" ~ con1 + con2 + con3 + pro1 +
    pro2 + pro3, data = data_wide)

Residuals:
    Min      1Q  Median      3Q     Max
-0.90818 -0.31927  0.09182  0.15694  0.74943

Coefficients:
            Estimate Std. Error t value Pr(>|t|)
(Intercept)   0.6460     0.1634   3.954   0.0005 ***
con1          0.1265     0.2282   0.554   0.5840
con2         -0.1407     0.1881  -0.748   0.4611
con3         -0.3125     0.1758  -1.777   0.0868 .
pro1         -0.3159     0.3025  -1.044   0.3056
pro2          0.1257     0.1985   0.633   0.5322
pro3          0.2622     0.1495   1.754   0.0907 .
---
Signif. codes:  0 '***' 0.001 '**' 0.01 '*' 0.05 '.' 0.1 ' ' 1

Residual standard error: 0.4425 on 27 degrees of freedom
Multiple R-squared:  0.358,     Adjusted R-squared:  0.2153
F-statistic: 2.509 on 6 and 27 DF,  p-value: 0.04637
```

Figure 4-32. *Output of our third regression model*

This model shows us that there are marginally significant avoidance of con3 and marginally significant higher levels of pro3; however, both of these are at the 0.10 alpha level, and some statisticians will murder me for suggesting they're even possibly real effects (hopefully all of those people have dropped p-values all together at this point). The point is it certainly doesn't look to me like there is a strong relationship between the number of times you do (or don't) open a box and choosing the cat button or the something else button. It is interesting that the intercept is higher than 0.5 – this is encouraging since it shows people are at least likely to open each box. The value for the other button inverts this number – 0.354 – which means our friends who love other animals potentially are avoiding opening all boxes equally, compared to the cat lovers. Mr. Flufkins is planning a PR campaign as we speak to discuss how non-cat people aren't fair and balanced.

Conclusion

We've moved through a lot in this chapter, from thinking about how we'd track what information people use to actually tracking and analyzing it. And like LimeSurvey in Chapter 3, we've only scratched the surface of the features that MouselabWEB has – counterbalancing, embedding images, linking multiple pages together, and more can be accomplished. And, perhaps even more interesting is combining the two. Think about a scenario where LimeSurvey feeds into MouselabWEB or vice versa – you could not only collect information on what people think but also how they formed their opinion. Combine that with a little bit of knowledge about linear regression, and suddenly you're the office hero that makes sense of the data. There is one thing that can be a downer though – finding that the code you carefully crafted isn't working anymore. Let's talk about that briefly in the last section of our chapter.

Future-Proofing: R Packages

The greatest strength of R is that it's open source with literally thousands of people contributing to it. That same strength can be a weakness at times if you're not prepared for it.

When I wrote this chapter, I used four different libraries: lme4, lmerTest, psych, and reshape2. Each of those packages has a version number (for me, it was 1.1–21 for lme4, 3.1.1 for lmerTest, 1.9.12.31 for psych, and 1.4.3 for reshape2 – you can get the version of a package by using the sensibly named packageVersion() command). With each new version of a package, the maintainers add, edit, update, and remove elements to increase the overall quality of the package – whether that be to include new features or kill bugs in old features. And sometimes one man's bug is another man's treasure.

In 2013, the maintainers of lme4 realized that a function named mcmcsamp that had been used to generate a Markov Chain Monte Carlo sample wasn't always accurate. So they stopped using it, and certain output changed, namely, p-values were removed from linear regressions based on the Gaussian family. From a statistician's point of view, this was the correct thing to do. However, for those in other sciences, it caused an issue. For one, our scientific views are never (or should never be) based upon one or two tests. Scientific theories require a lot of evidence to support them. So in this situation, the lmer model with possible inaccuracy would only be a small piece of the larger puzzle. It's sensible to be cautious, but absurd when 99 signs are pointing one way, and we're going to doubt everything based upon one.

So the R community found another way to get those p-values, initially pvals.fnc() in the languageR package and then the lmerTest package that we used here. Today when I use those p-values, I know that they might not be 100% accurate (of course nothing in statistics is 100% accurate, it's all educated guesses), but I can present that to my reader or viewer as a caveat and be ready to address it.

However, what happens if you want to run your linear model *the day after* you update your package and find the p-values missing? There hasn't been time for others to write new code, and taking a side trip down construction of Markov Chain Monte Carlo samples is going to take quite a bit of time. The answer is simply build and load the previous version of the package.

To do this, you need to download the source of the version you'd like, compile it within R, and then load it. The first step is easy – downloading a file. In many cases, the old versions are on CRAN in the Archive section, or if you're paranoid, you might download the exact versions you used when you create a project and store them somewhere safe in case you need them later.

The second step can be a bit tricky depending on your computer. Linux and Mac computers tend to have the tools they need to compile code already installed; however, Windows machines sometimes lack these tools. If you run into errors compiling, you'll need to download complier software and install it.

Finally, the third step seems easy enough – load the newly built package using our regular commands. In the best possible world, the following code would download the very first version of lme4, build it, and install it:

```
url <- "https://cran.r-project.org/src/contrib/Archive/lme4/lme4_0.2-1.tar.gz"
install.packages(url, repos=NULL, type="source")
library("lme4")
```

But there's going to be two potential hiccups:

1. Telling R exactly what version to load can be tricky, with some people having multiple R installations on their machine just to keep certain versions of packages in a "snapshot" state.

2. Sometimes older versions of packages relied on features in another package that have since been changed or removed. For example, Package A may rely on something Package B did in 2009, but Package B removed that feature in 2014, so in 2020, loading the 2009 version of Package A won't work because you don't have the 2009 version of Package B. You can see where this can lead to a seemingly never-ending chase finding all of the previous versions you need.

Thankfully, this problem was something that the folks at Revolution Analytics thought about in 2014, before they were acquired by Microsoft, and they wrote a package named checkpoint. checkpoint is a clever package that allows you to pick a date in the past and install and use packages in R exactly as they were on that date. This is an easy way to ensure you can recreate and reproduce your analyses later, in the event that packages change. I might still suggest downloading specific versions of the package source code if it's vital to your operation, but tools like checkpoint should help you with your package version woes.

And there you have it, we've completed our foray into market research in both Chapter 3 and Chapter 4. But what if you aren't a market researcher? What if you just want to use R in your everyday life to help you with little tasks around the office? In the next section of the book, Chapters 5–7, we'll do exactly that!

CHAPTER 5

R in Everyday Life

A friend of mine tells the story of her serving on a budget committee many years ago. In the midst of making tough decisions about where to make cuts, the committee was provided with spreadsheets showing each office and how much money was assigned to each, plus a metric of return on investment. The idea was that the offices with high ROIs and low money would surely survive any cuts, but if you had the opposite – a ton of spending and not much to show for it – you were in trouble.

The irony of this process was that the spreadsheets were sorted in alphabetical order, not by either of the two columns that might be useful. My friend, being an Excel guru, sorted each one and re-sent them to the committee. The other committee members were enthusiastic, including the CFO. It wasn't until one day that the CFO realized one of his offices was at the top of the "high investment, low return" pile that he sheepishly asked her to stop sending her lists. That CFO wasn't around much longer.

How data is manipulated, sorted, and displayed is key to doing many of our jobs as professionals. And while we all know the Excel gurus that can point and click our data into shape with a flourish, we also know that this can take time and isn't very easy to re-train in someone new when the Excel guru moves on to bigger and better reports. What if we could script it – take the data and change it exactly the way we'd like and then report it? With R, all of that is possible. In this chapter, we'll look at several ways to format data, manipulate data, and finally report the data back out to software such as Microsoft Office. We'll also talk a bit about custom functions and show how you can use those to speed up your scripting.

Before we begin, a word about how this chapter is formatted: it's written in a "follow-along" style. The code snippets are small enough that I believe you will get a lot out of typing them in and executing them. I'll describe in text what results you should be seeing as you go along. This will help you become more comfortable with the environment and the operations we discuss! Let's begin!

© Jon Westfall 2020
J. Westfall, *Practical R 4*, https://doi.org/10.1007/978-1-4842-5946-7_5

Data Formatting

Sometimes data just isn't formatted in a usable way. Whether it's because we've scraped it off the Internet, or some well-meaning person has tried to make it "prettier" by adding information, numbers might not read as numbers, or information might be the reverse of what we want (e.g., names as Firstname Lastname vs. Lastname, Firstname). Additionally, we might want to trim our data to just the essentials or sort and filter our data in meaningful ways. We'll walk through all of these in this section.

String Manipulation

When we pull data into R, we often get "extra" pieces – spaces, text, or symbols we don't need. Imagine receiving a spreadsheet where someone has "helpfully" added "USD" after each price to indicate it's in dollars – or added "$" at the front. While visually useful, R won't be able to add the numbers like we'd like it to, as you can see in the following code:

```
x <- c("14.95 USD","25.62 USD","35.50 USD");
y <- c("14.95","25.62","35.50");
sum(as.numeric(y))
sum(as.numeric(x))
```

As you can see, the first sum works perfectly since it's summing the y variable, which R can easily see are numbers. However, x has all "USD" at the end. We can remove that with the substr() function, which takes a variable, starts at a certain point, and finishes at another point. substr(x,1,5) tells R to take each item and start at the first position and read until the fifth position. sum(as.numeric(substr(x,1,5))) will get us our sum of 76.07.

However, you might see a problem here – what if we have a three-digit amount? It will break the code because now we need to read until the sixth position, but only for that item. What we really need to do is strip off the last four characters, whatever those may be. We can do that with a little bit of logic – I first need to figure out how long each item is. Then I have to tell R to get to the position 4 back from the end. Thankfully, we have a function to determine how long an item is – nchar() will do it. Here's our modified code, with one item with three digits:

```
z <- c("14.95 USD","25.62 USD","35.50 USD","103.52 USD");
sum(as.numeric(substr(z,1, (nchar(z)-4))))
```

Looking at the z variable, we can see one item is over $100, yet we'll still get the correct sum (179.59) from these items. Also, for demonstration purposes, I've been nesting things within each other, but you can imagine a situation where you'd want to save those recoded variables so that they could be used later. In that case, you might do something like this:

```
a <- substr(z,1,(nchar(z)-4))
```

From the preceding examples, you can probably guess our code if someone has put in a leading $ in front of everything:

```
b <- c("$14.95", "$25.62","$35.50")
sum(as.numeric(substr(b,2,(nchar(b)))))
```

substr() is a very nice string function, but it's not the only one that R has. Here's a few others that are useful to know:

- toupper() and tolower() which convert from uppercase to lowercase.

- grep() and grepl() which search for patterns in strings, and in grep() case, it returns where they are. grepl() merely returns a TRUE or FALSE for each item, letting you know if the pattern was found.

- strsplit() which will split strings into smaller objects as needed.

- paste() which is one of the more versatile ways to add strings together, useful when displaying output in your script such as paste("The answer is ", b).

String processing could be its own book, and in fact there are several focused on it for different languages. In the end, most of the purpose-driven string modifications you're looking for will be well documented. For example, a quick search for "Switch last name first name R" provides a Stack Overflow listing for doing exactly that. Once you know the basic functions, you can also explore them further. And in practical purposes, imagine getting a report each week from a system that appends useless string information (such as "USD" or "beats per minute") and being able to simply run an R script to clean it up – much more useful than sitting in Excel and going row by row removing the extra characters.

Variable Magic

One other thing that is annoying to do in Excel that is much easier in R is working with data frames in terms of re-ordering or renaming variables within them or adding new ones. There are a few common tasks in the following table, with example code on how to accomplish them. We'll use the built-in `iris` data frame in the examples.

Task	Explanation	Code Example

Add a new variable.	It is accomplished by simply assigning a value to an unused variable name.	`head(iris)`
		`iris$newvar <- 0`
		`head(iris)`

Rename a variable.	You could simply add a new variable with the name you'd like, assigning the old variable to it. Or you can modify the `names` variable directly. The example does the latter.	`names(iris)`
		`names(iris)[1]`
		`<- "Renamed.Length"`
		`names(iris)`

Re-order variables.	Re-order the data frame by reassigning it with the order of variables you'd like. Iris has six columns (including my `newvar` column I created earlier). The following code puts `newer` at the start, the rest in their same order.	`head(iris)`
		`iris <- iris[,`
		`c(6, 1, 2, 3, 4, 5)]`
		`head(iris)`

Remove a variable.	Removing a variable can be done by index. In this example, we'll remove the `newvar` variable I created.	`iris <- iris[, -1]` `head(iris)`
Remove cases.	Sometimes we want to remove rows of data (cases); we can do that in the same way as we removed a variable in the last example, just before the comma. This takes out rows 1–3 in the `iris` dataset.	`iris <- iris[-(1:3),]` `head(iris)`
Duplicate cases.	In some situations, you may want to duplicate a case. The following code duplicates row 150. Note: If you've removed the first three rows, you'll end up with a last row of NAs here, because they are missing. Play around with your code and the `nrow()` function to see if you can adapt your code to compensate!	`rbind(iris,iris[150,])`

You'll notice that the last command used the rbind() function. rbind() is a row bind – it adds new rows to an already existing dataset. cbind() does the same for columns. These are easy commands to use if you have data in the order you want, but they can get you in trouble if you don't have the data formatted properly to start with (R will complain about this as well – it won't easily bind row if the number of columns doesn't match, or bind columns if the number of rows doesn't match). Another function, merge(), exists that can help you add two datasets together that aren't perfectly matched up. We'll use merge() later in the book.

Now that we've seen how to do some basic manipulations, let's move on to the next area: sorting and filtering!

Sorting and Filtering

We've already seen a few ways to filter data in R earlier when we discussed removing rows or columns. But what if we want to write code that's a little more readable instead of using index numbers? And how would we sort the entire data frames based on given values? We'll continue to use the iris dataset and do some simple operations on it:

- What if I want to sort the dataset by Sepal.Length from lowest to highest value? iris <- iris[order(iris$Sepal.Length),]

- What about descending order? Just put a negative sign before the column: iris <- iris[order(-iris$Sepal.Length),]

- What about multiple items? Add them in the argument:
  iris <- iris[order(-iris$Sepal.Length,iris$Sepal.Width),]

It's important to note that sorting could be used to get the highest value and return it as an informational piece. We'll do that in a few minutes at the end of this section. But first, let's talk about filtering data, which we can do in two different ways – adding another data frame condition similar to how we've done earlier or the subset() function.

Selecting all of the versicolor species out of the iris dataset can be done using this command:

```
iris[iris$Species=="versicolor",]
```

Or if we'd like something a bit more human-readable, we could use the `subset()` function, which I find makes it easier when sharing scripts with someone for them to understand what we're filtering for.

```
subset(iris,Species == "versicolor")
```

With `subset()` we can also add multiple conditions easily:

```
subset(iris,Species == "versicolor" & Sepal.Width == 3.2)
```

This will pull all of the `versicolor` with a Sepal.Width of 3.2. What if we wanted those in `versicolor` or Sepal.Width of 3.2? It would look like this:

```
subset(iris,Species == "versicolor" | Sepal.Width == 3.2)
```

Let's put together a few things we've had earlier into a simple example: imagine that you want to report back to the user the highest Sepal.Length for the `versicolor` species. You don't want to show the user the data, just give them the information on one line in a report. Here's how we could do it:

```
versicolor.only <- subset(iris, Species == "versicolor");
highlen <- max(versicolor.only$Sepal.Length);
paste("The highest Sepal Length for Versicolor is", highlen);
```

Congratulations, you've just written your first report output in R! Now we'll spend some time manipulating our data and learn how to write our own functions!

Data Calculation and Structure

Manipulating data in a spreadsheet can be fairly time-consuming. Thinking about writing a function and then having to do a Fill Down or Fill Right to apply it to all of your data values doesn't seem too daunting, until you've wrestled to find the very bottom row without overshooting, or had to be specific about only applying the formula in certain circumstances. This section will start off with basic calculations and formulas, then revisit wide to long and long to wide conversions, and finally finish by talking about recoding variables.

Conversions and Calculations

Simple calculations in R are, as we've seen, fairly easy. For example, if we wanted to calculate a new variable in the `iris` dataset named Petal.Area, we could do that easily by multiplying Petal.Length by Petal.Width.

```
iris$Petal.Area <- iris$Petal.Length * iris$Petal.Width
```

We can also convert values using R's built-in libraries. One case for this might be calculating time between two dates. Here I've coded two dates as strings, and then I've converted them to `Date` objects in R and then subtracted the difference:

```
x <- "2019/01/01"
y <- "2020/01/01"
x.date <- as.Date(as.character(x), format="%Y/%m/%d");
y.date <- as.Date(as.character(y), format="%Y/%m/%d");
paste("The difference between ",x," and ",y," is ", (y.date-x.date), " Days");
```

You'll notice that the `as.Date()` function takes a `format` argument, which you can use to let R know if your date values are in a different format, such as 01/01/2019 or 23-2-2019, and so on. We also did a fair bit of casting there that we might not have needed – x and y were already cast as characters; however, it doesn't hurt to make sure that they are properly casted in our code.

Lastly, you'll notice that when I recast x and y as dates, I appended `.date` to their variable name. It's a good practice to do this, especially on large datasets with many different variables. By appending the data type to the end of the data, you ensure that you will know later, at a glance, the type of variable you're working with. I generally use `.f` for factors, `.chr` for characters, `.date` as dates, and so on. Pick a system that works for you and go with that!

Finally, let's briefly talk about conditional statements and loops and useful functions for them. R supports a few common structures, which I've demoed as follows.

If-else or ifelse

```
if (iris$Sepal.Length[1] > 5) {paste("Greater than 5") } else {paste("Less
than 5")}
```

This checks the first row. If we wanted to do all rows, we could use `ifelse()`:

```
ifelse(iris$Sepal.Length > 5,"Greater than 5","Less than 5")
```

This code returns the value of either "Greater than 5" or "Less than 5" for each of the rows in the dataset, in essence summarizing them. In general use, I find `ifelse()` is much more commonly used than `if` unless I'm working inside a loop or function.

For

```
for (i in 1:10) {print(i)}
```

This declares a new variable named i and works through it ten times, printing 1–10 as output.

While

```
i <- 1
while (i < 10) {
print(i)
i = i+2
}
```

This code declares a new variable named i, and while i is less than 10, it prints the value and then adds 2 on to it. The output lists odd numbers: 1, 3, 5, 7, and 9. Since the last loop sets i to 11, the loop doesn't work.

Functions to Create Data

Finally, we have functions that create data: `rep()` and `seq()`, `runif()`, and `rnorm()`. See the following example:

```
x <- rep(1:5,5) # Creates a variable with 1-5, repeated 5 times.
y <- seq(1,100,10) # Creates a sequence of 1-100, by 10s
r <- runif(5) #Creates 5 random numbers between 0 - 1.
rn <- rnorm(5) #Creates 5 random numbers that follow the normal
distribution (mean = 0, standard deviation = 1)
```

You could use these functions to select subsets of data, or random sequences, as necessary for your work.

Now that we've seen some of the control functions in R, let's reshape data in more detail!

Reshaping

In the last chapter, we used the `reshape2` package to reshape data. We'll explore that a little more here as we convert the `iris` from wide data to long and back again.

To do this, we first load the `reshape2` package. We then "melt" our data into "identification" variables and "value" variables. In the following code, I've loaded the package and then created a unique ID variable for each entry using the `runif` function from earlier. Finally, I've melted the entire dataset.

```
library("reshape2")
iris$ID <- paste(iris$Species,runif(150))
melted <- melt(iris, id.vars=c("ID","Species"))
```

Looking at the first six lines, we can see how our data has changed (see Figure 5-1).

```
> head(iris)
  Sepal.Length Sepal.Width Petal.Length Petal.Width Species Petal.Area                        ID
1          5.1         3.5          1.4         0.2  setosa       0.28 setosa 0.830270135309547
2          4.9         3.0          1.4         0.2  setosa       0.28 setosa 0.830270135309547
3          4.7         3.2          1.3         0.2  setosa       0.26 setosa 0.830270135309547
4          4.6         3.1          1.5         0.2  setosa       0.30 setosa 0.830270135309547
5          5.0         3.6          1.4         0.2  setosa       0.28 setosa 0.830270135309547
6          5.4         3.9          1.7         0.4  setosa       0.68 setosa 0.830270135309547
> head(melted)
                         ID     variable value
1 setosa 0.830270135309547 Sepal.Length   5.1
2 setosa 0.830270135309547 Sepal.Length   4.9
3 setosa 0.830270135309547 Sepal.Length   4.7
4 setosa 0.830270135309547 Sepal.Length   4.6
5 setosa 0.830270135309547 Sepal.Length     5
6 setosa 0.830270135309547 Sepal.Length   5.4
```

Figure 5-1. *The original* `iris` *dataset and the* `melted` *dataset*

Now that we have the data "melted", we can cast it however we like. I'm going to cast it back to the way that it had been:

```
newiris <- dcast(melted,ID + Species ~ variable))
```

We can see in Figure 5-2 that `iris` and `newiris` have been resorted; however, they still contain the exact same data, as Line 1 in `iris` matches with Line 2 in `newiris`. Line 5 of `iris` also matches up with Line 4 of `newiris`.

```
> newiris <- dcast(melted,ID + Species ~ variable)
> head(iris)
   Sepal.Length Sepal.Width Petal.Length Petal.Width Species Petal.Area                    ID
1          5.1         3.5          1.4         0.2  setosa       0.28  setosa 0.10579918907024
2          4.9         3.0          1.4         0.2  setosa       0.28  setosa 0.225900596007705
3          4.7         3.2          1.3         0.2  setosa       0.26  setosa 0.857473941985518
4          4.6         3.1          1.5         0.2  setosa       0.30  setosa 0.64388625882566
5          5.0         3.6          1.4         0.2  setosa       0.28  setosa 0.137810364598408
6          5.4         3.9          1.7         0.4  setosa       0.68  setosa 0.408119145547971
> head(newiris)
                             ID Species Sepal.Length Sepal.Width Petal.Length Petal.Width Petal.Area
1 setosa 0.0416964574251324  setosa          5.4         3.9          1.3         0.4        0.52
2  setosa 0.10579918907024   setosa          5.1         3.5          1.4         0.2        0.28
3  setosa 0.13674538792111   setosa          4.6         3.4          1.4         0.3        0.42
4 setosa 0.137810364598408   setosa          5.0         3.6          1.4         0.2        0.28
5 setosa 0.138342033838853   setosa          4.8         3.1          1.6         0.2        0.32
6 setosa 0.149875388247892   setosa          5.0         3.4          1.5         0.2        0.30
```

Figure 5-2. *Comparing* `iris` *and* `newiris`

We've now just converted from wide to long then back to wide. In our data, we had the advantage that we didn't have multiple values in long format for any particular entry (e.g., multiple Sepal.Lengths for the same ID). In most long formats, that's not going to be the case. Thankfully, the `dcast()` function can also take an argument of `fun.aggregate` with options such as `mean`, `median`, or `sum`. This tells R what you'd like it to do when it encounters multiple lines in long format – basically how should it summarize those lines?

Once you've started playing around with the `reshape2` package, you can think of ways it might work into your daily life. Here are a few that come to my mind:

- Sales teams send you daily reports that you need to summarize. Each day you add the data to a CSV file, and once a week, you pull that file into R and have it reshape the long data (sales each day) to wide (a sales report for the week).

- Your assistant is collecting ratings on various new products from everyone in the office. She's placed all of the ratings in a spreadsheet, with each product getting its own line and each rater having their own column. You're curious if you have some people who just love everything, or others that love nothing, and particularly if the color of the item matters. So you pull the data into R, set the id.var to be the color of the item, and convert the data to wide format aggregating on color of the item. Suddenly you notice that 2–3 people like all of the products in black more so than anything else.

- You're analyzing the grades of students in your class. They've each done the same assignment five times in five different subjects, and you're curious to see which subjects each person is strongest in. You melt the data down to have the subject and student name and then use the fun.aggregate feature to get the mean for each group of five assignments.

There are many different possibilities for converting data from wide to long, so I'd encourage you to start looking at the data you see around you on a daily basis to consider ways you might want to summarize it! You may also notice that data isn't always coded in the ways you'd like, which is where our next section comes into play: recoding data!

Recoding

Recoding variables can be useful for two primary reasons: first to summarize data by reducing it in scope (e.g., a median split, either "above median" or "below") and second to change the reporting style of the variable (e.g., converting 1–5 to a scale of agreement). We'll look at both in our examples as follows.

The first and perhaps most obvious way that we could recode variables is to use the `ifelse()` function that we saw earlier. This is good for single criteria recoding. Returning to the `iris` dataset, we find that we have three species: setosa, versicolor, and virginca. Imagine wanting to simply have two groups: Setosa and "Other". We could do something like this:

```
iris$Species.new <- ifelse(iris$Species == "setosa","Setosa","Other");
```

We could also accomplish this by using the R control structures:

```
iris$Species.control[iris$Species != "setosa"] <- "Other"
iris$Species.control[iris$Species == "setosa"] <- "Setosa"
```

Both Species.new and Species.control now have the exact same information in them; we just went about coding it in two different ways. The difference is that our second method could be used for more than just an "either-or" decision, since the first line sets all of the Setosa lines to NA until the second line fills them in with Setosa. You could, therefore, have as many lines like this as you have levels of your variable, gradually assigning everything a line at a time, something like this:

```
iris$Sepal[iris$Sepal.Length > 6] <- "Long"
iris$Sepal[iris$Sepal.Length > 5 & iris$Sepal.Length < 6] <- "Medium"
iris$Sepal[iris$Sepal.Length < 5] <- "Short"
```

A third way to recode data comes from the recode() function from the car package. I'm a fan of this method because it gives us the flexibility of the control structures approach while also putting most everything on one human-readable line. Here's an example of it adapted from the documentation for the recode() function:

```
library("car")
x <- rep(1:5,4);
x
recode(x, "1='A'; 2='B'; c(3,4) = 'C'; else='D'")
```

That fourth line makes it pretty easy to see what we're doing – 1 becomes A, 2 becomes B, 3 or 4 becomes C, and everything else becomes D. The only trickiness is getting the syntax right – starting the recode argument with a quotation mark, any character with an apostrophe, and using semicolons between each "clause". Even after using this command for years, I sometimes still find myself with an error the first time using it in a project. Indeed, when I wrote this code earlier, I had accidentally placed a comma after "C", and R was not happy with me!

Finally, it's usually a good idea to recode into a different variable name. While R will let you "overwrite" an existing variable, it can be hard to tell what's going on by doing so. Adding a new variable, by appending something like .recoded onto the end, will help you keep your data straight as you work through your task.

Before we move on to different ways to report data, let's talk about a situation where you may need to recode data quite often and want to centralize your code into your own function. As you'll see, writing a function in R is pretty simple!

Writing Our Own Recode Function

OK, so here's our scenario: you are a teacher, and your students want you to tell them their letter grade. You have a standard letter grade sequence that's pretty straight forward: 90% and above gets an A, 80% to 89% gets a B, 70% to 79% gets a C, 60% to 69% gets a D, and everyone else fails. Using the recode() function, we could write this as

```
library("car")
recode(88,"lo:59 = 'F'; 59.01:69 = 'D'; 69.01:79 = 'C'; 79.01:89 = 'B';
89.01:hi = 'A'")
```

Now every time you want to recode a percentage to a letter grade, you could use that recode line; however, it's going to cause a lot of typing. Instead, let's wrap it in a function called LetterGrade(). Here's the code:

```
LetterGrade <- function(percentage) {
library("car")
return(recode(percentage,"lo:59 = 'F'; 59.01:69 = 'D'; 69.01:79 = 'C';
79.01:89 = 'B'; 89.01:hi = 'A'"))
}
```

Now all we need to do is run LetterGrade(88) to get the letter grade for a score of 88. If we ever make a change to our grade mapping, we only need to change it in one place – the LetterGrade() function.

Using custom functions in R merely requires that they be loaded into your script before they're used. A common way to do this is to have all of your custom functions at the top of your scripts, along with any packages that you need to have loaded. Some choose to place all of these in a separate file and then use the source() function in R to execute that entire file every time they load their project. And if you're using RStudio or saving your image in R, you'll have those functions reloaded every time you open your project, which can save time.

Finally, it's important to note that functions can return any type of data object or type. You can get very complex with your functions – in fact, this is how whole packages are born! If you start using R for a lot of your daily work, you'll likely amass a large collection of your favorite functions to use and reuse, again and again.

Speaking of using R for your daily work, at some point, someone is probably going to want to see that work. And we can produce a very nice product for them using a few different data reporting methods. In the next section, I'll discuss one of the most popular ways to report your data – RMarkdown!

Data Reporting Using RMarkdown!

Creating reports with data can be a daunting task – you generally need to crunch the numbers and then find some way to move them into a word processor or web editor to show them off to others. In RStudio, however, you can make extensive use of RMarkdown to show off your work without having to copy and paste (and introduce the possibility of errors).

To get started, create a new RStudio project and install the rmarkdown package:

```
install.packages("rmarkdown")
```

From there, create a new RMarkdown document (Figure 5-3). For our first example, we'll use HTML (Figure 5-4).

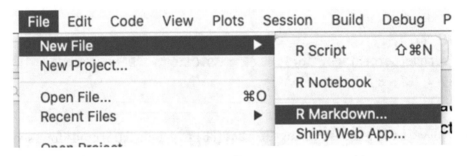

Figure 5-3. *File, New RMarkdown Menu Item in RStudio*

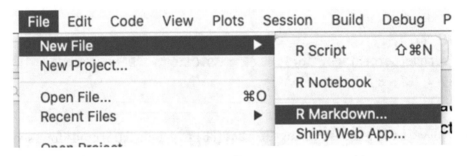

Figure 5-4. *The New RMarkdown Box*

As you can see in Figure 5-5, RStudio opens a new document with some basic markdown examples in it.

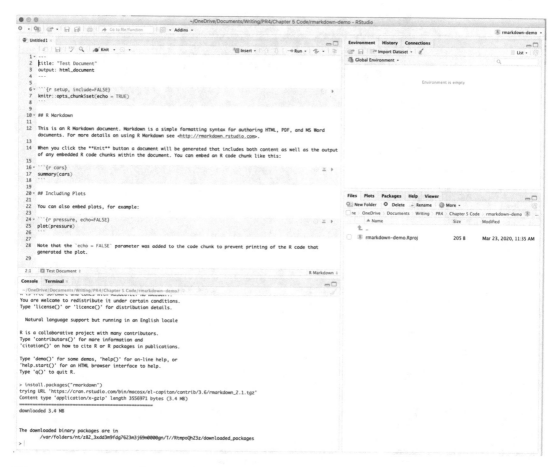

Figure 5-5. *Example RMarkdown File*

From this, we can actually compile the document immediately and see how the output would look. To do this, we'll have RStudio run the RMarkdown through a program called knitr. Knitr takes the RMarkdown file, parses it, executes any R code in it, and weaves it all together into one HTML document. To get it to "knit", click the "Knit" button shown in Figure 5-6. We can see it doing this in Figure 5-7 and see the final output in Figure 5-8.

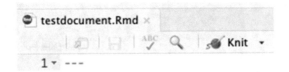

Figure 5-6. *The "Knit" button*

```
processing file: testdocument.Rmd
  |.........                                              |  14%
   ordinary text without R code

  |..................                                     |  29%
label: setup (with options)
List of 1
 $ include: logi FALSE

  |..............................                         |  43%
   ordinary text without R code

  |.........................................              |  57%
label: cars
  |.................................................      |  71%
   ordinary text without R code

  |.........................................................  |  86%
label: pressure (with options)
List of 1
 $ echo: logi FALSE

  |...........................................................| 100%
   ordinary text without R code


/Applications/RStudio.app/Contents/MacOS/pandoc/pandoc +RTS -K512m -RTS testdocument.utf8.md --to html4 --from markdow
n+autolink_bare_uris+tex_math_single_backslash --output testdocument.html --smart --email-obfuscation none --self-cont
ained --standalone --section-divs --template /Library/Frameworks/R.framework/Versions/3.6/Resources/library/rmarkdown/
rmd/h/default.html --no-highlight --variable highlightjs=1 --variable 'theme:bootstrap' --include-in-header /var/folde
rs/nt/z82_3xdd3m9fdg7623m3j69m0000gn/T//RtmpbPxTvr/rmarkdown-str17a0767d596a9.html --mathjax --variable 'mathjax-url:h
ttps://mathjax.rstudio.com/latest/MathJax.js?config=TeX-AMS-MML_HTMLorMML'
output file: testdocument.knit.md


Output created: testdocument.html
```

Figure 5-7. *Knitr "knitting" everything together*

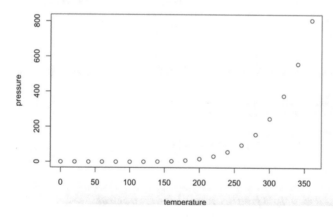

Figure 5-8. *A preview of the finished HTML document*

You probably saw other options for output, including PDF. However, as seen in Figure 5-9, this fails if you do not have MiKTeX (Windows) or TeX Live (Mac) installed.

```
 |.....................                                    |  29%
label: setup (with options)
List of 1
 $ include: logi FALSE

 |.............................                            |  43%
  ordinary text without R code

 |........................................                 |  57%
label: cars
 |..................................................       |  71%
  ordinary text without R code

 |..............................................................  |  86%
label: pressure (with options)
List of 1
 $ echo: logi FALSE

 |................................................................| 100%
  ordinary text without R code


/Applications/RStudio.app/Contents/MacOS/pandoc/pandoc +RTS -K512m -RTS testdocument.utf8.md --to latex --from markdow
n+autolink_bare_uris+tex_math_single_backslash --output testdocument.tex --self-contained --highlight-style tango --la
tex-engine pdflatex --variable graphics --variable 'geometry:margin=1in'
output file: testdocument.knit.md

! sh: pdflatex: command not found

Error: LaTeX failed to compile testdocument.tex. See https://yihui.org/tinytex/r/#debugging for debugging tips. See te
stdocument.log for more info.
In addition: Warning message:
In system2(..., stdout = if (use_file_stdout()) f1 else FALSE, stderr = f2) :
  error in running command
Execution halted

No TeX installation detected (TeX is required to create PDF output). You should install a recommended TeX distribution
for your platform:

  Windows: MiKTeX (Complete) - http://miktex.org/2.9/setup
  (NOTE: Be sure to download the Complete rather than Basic installation)

  Mac OS X: TexLive 2013 (Full) - http://tug.org/mactex/
  (NOTE: Download with Safari rather than Chrome _strongly_ recommended)

  Linux: Use system package manager
```

Figure 5-9. *Error message if the TeX installation is not present*

Installing MacTeX (which provides TeX Live) and having it take up a whopping 10 GB of space between installer and installed files and restarting RStudio, I now have the ability to knit PDF files (Figure 5-10 shows the compile output; Figure 5-11 shows the PDF document).

```
processing file: testdocument.Rmd
  |..........                                              |  14%
     ordinary text without R code

  |...................                                     |  29%
label: setup (with options)
List of 1
 $ include: logi FALSE

  |.............................                           |  43%
     ordinary text without R code

  |......................................                  |  57%
label: cars
  |...............................................         |  71%
     ordinary text without R code

  |........................................................|  86%
label: pressure (with options)
List of 1
 $ echo: logi FALSE

  |........................................................| 100%
     ordinary text without R code
```

```
/Applications/RStudio.app/Contents/MacOS/pandoc/pandoc +RTS -K512m -RTS testdocument.utf8.md --to latex --from markdow
n+autolink_bare_uris+tex_math_single_backslash --output testdocument.tex --self-contained --highlight-style tango --la
tex-engine pdflatex --variable graphics --variable 'geometry:margin=1in'
output file: testdocument.knit.md
```

```
Output created: testdocument.pdf
```

Figure 5-10. *The output of the knitr compiler for PDF*

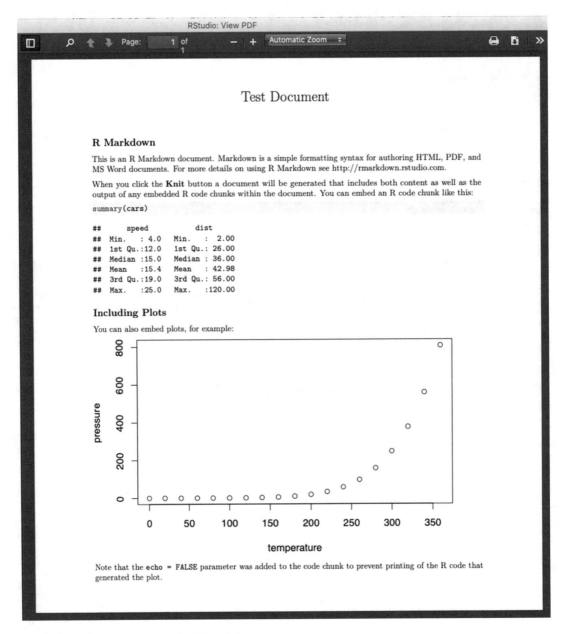

Figure 5-11. *The compiled PDF document*

And finally, since I have Microsoft Office installed on my machine, I can use the Knit to Word option (See Figure 5-12) to create a word document. First Word does ask permission to allow R to write to it (shown in Figure 5-13), and from there, it creates the document automatically (See Figure 5-14).

```
processing file: testdocument.Rmd
  |..........                                                    |  14%
    ordinary text without R code

  |..................                                            |  29%
label: setup (with options)
List of 1
 $ include: logi FALSE

  |............................                                  |  43%
    ordinary text without R code

  |......................................                        |  57%
label: cars
  |.............................................                 |  71%
    ordinary text without R code

  |.......................................................       |  86%
label: pressure (with options)
List of 1
 $ echo: logi FALSE

  |..............................................................| 100%
    ordinary text without R code


/Applications/RStudio.app/Contents/MacOS/pandoc/pandoc +RTS -K512m -RTS testdocument.utf8.md --to docx --from markdown
+autolink_bare_uris+tex_math_single_backslash --output testdocument.docx --smart --highlight-style tango
output file: testdocument.knit.md

Output created: testdocument.docx
```

Figure 5-12. *The output of the knitr compiler for Word*

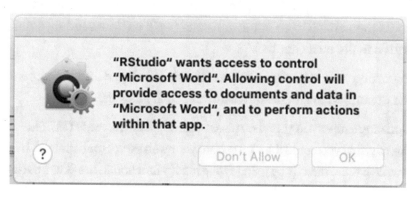

Figure 5-13. *Allowing permission to use Microsoft Word*

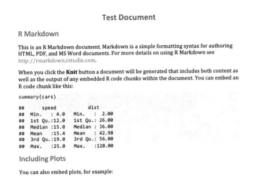

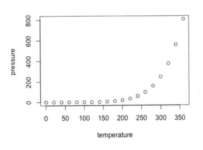

Figure 5-14. *The Word Document*

All four test documents area available in the rmarkdown-demo code for this chapter. I'd encourage you to play around with Markdown in R to create reports that will be useful to you, in the proper format. I'd then encourage you to think about the possibilities such as

- Each week having an R script run to create a PDF report, that you could then attach to an email and send (we'll explore sending emails with R in the next chapter).

- Exporting your statistical analysis straight into Word and then opening the document to add narrative around each analysis.

- Updating a report on your web page by having R create the HTML file directly, that you could then drop onto your web server (or better yet, have R write it there directly by using ftpUpload() function in the RCurl package.

Conclusion

We've covered a lot of basics in this chapter that take R from simply running statistical analysis to creating rich datasets that are formatted exactly as you'd want them and then output into formats that others could easily utilize such as PDF or Word. Along the way, I've shared some of my favorite tips, and we've seen that there is often more than one way to do something in R. Our next two chapters focus on projects that amp up workplace productivity – an R Form Mailer in Chapter 6 and an R Powered Presentation in Chapter 7!

CHAPTER 6

Project 3: The R Form Mailer

Email is something that we simultaneously love and hate. It's great in that it allows us to conduct quite a bit of business and pleasure through its use, but it can also be an overwhelming avalanche of information when we log in for the first time in several days (or hours, if you're unlucky!). In this chapter, we're going to discuss how R can work with email in a few interesting ways. First, we'll talk about the email packages that R supports. We'll then dig into one specific package that hooks R up to one of the most popular email providers on the Web: Gmail. We'll take a side trip down the road of data encryption and security and then return to the big payoff: the R Form Mailer – automated email sending through just a script, making it more flexible than alternatives such as Mail Merge. By the end of this chapter, you'll be able to send out a bulk email that calculates a salesperson's commission, without ever needing to take out your calculator. Let's jump in!

Packages and Packages of Email

Before we actually send some mail, we should talk about the packages that R makes available to send mail, as some are more flexible or specialized than others. Searching the CRAN package list, we find several packages that specify email. Here's a list of them, along with use scenarios:

© Jon Westfall 2020
J. Westfall, *Practical R 4*, https://doi.org/10.1007/978-1-4842-5946-7_6

Package Name	Use Scenario
blastula	A versatile package that can send HTML encoded emails. Flexible, and offers support for a few third-party APIs
blatr	A Windows-only package that sends mail through the command-line program blat
edeR	A bit of the reverse – it doesn't send, but rather reads email. Imagine having data sent to an email box – this package can access that mailbox and download the data directly!
emayili	An email library that supports sending through an SMTP server, with minimum R dependencies
IMailgun	A library to send mail through the Mailgun service (from http://mailgun.com)
mail	One of the oldest mail libraries. Doesn't support some of the newer features you might need, such as SMTP authentication or HTML. Perfect for quick notifications
'mailR'	A wrapper for the Apache Commons Email API
sendmailR	A simple SMTP client that allows R to send email directly to receiving servers, although this may run into issues if your machine is not properly set up as an SMTP server (e.g., your mail may be blacklisted for failing a reverse DNS test)
gmailR	An email library specifically designed to work with Gmails RESTful API. This is the package we'll further explore as follows.
ponyexpress	A community project to bring automated email list distribution to Gmail through R. You can find more about this at https://docs.ropensci.org/ponyexpress/.
RDCOMClient	Another Windows-only package; however, this one utilizes Windows DCOM methods, which allow it to send email as well as send data to other applications.

As you can see, depending on what you want to accomplish, you may be better off with certain clients over others. The simpler clients that directly connect to an SMTP server (or include one themselves) may work just fine on their own if they're within your own small network, where you control spam filtering and access. However, they might not work well with the "wider" world, where email must be somewhat vetted to prevent as much SPAM as possible. At the end of this chapter, I will provide a few links to email providers that I've found especially helpful and useful to me as a small developer and system administrator. In many cases, these services are free to small quantities of mail, which make them ideal for your own personal productivity. Before we get into those, however, let's work with a pretty large player: Gmail.

Sending Gmail

Gmail has come a very long way since its founding on April 1, 2004 (when many thought that its 1 GB of space was an April Fools' Day joke!). Today Gmail serves more than a billion users, making it the most popular email service in the United States and in many other countries. As it has "grown up," Gmail has added a plethora of features from robust search to spam filtering. Given its size and scope, unfortunately, it means that setting it up for automated email sending can be a bit of a hassle. However, in this section, I'll walk you through setting up your Gmail account for API access (by creating your own application), downloading the credentials you need, and ultimately sending a test email. Later we'll use these same credentials and set up for our R Form Mailer!

Setup: Google Developer Console and API Access

The process to set up your authentication credentials in Gmail is a little bit more complex than simply providing a username and password, as you might do with an SMTP server. This is because, as one of the largest email providers, Gmail can be a rather large target for hackers as well as a very rich ecosystem for developers. Google has had to walk a line between protecting users and providing robust tools for a developer to interact with Gmail to build neat things. Over the next steps, we're going to create a developer project in Google Developer Console and download credentials to authenticate with it – the same process we would use if we were going to build an application used by hundreds, thousands, or millions of people. A bit overkill for just one person, but still necessary in the ecosystem. Here are the steps to follow to get set up. Keep in mind that some of the wording may change over time – Google is notorious for changing interfaces fairly often, which in the past has made it hard to keep a consistent set of steps. However, the basic premise is "New Project" and "OAuth Client ID" credential:

1. Visit http://console.developers.google.com/ and log in. If this is the first time you've used the Google Developer Console, you'll have to agree to a terms of use and specify your region, as seen in Figure 6-1.

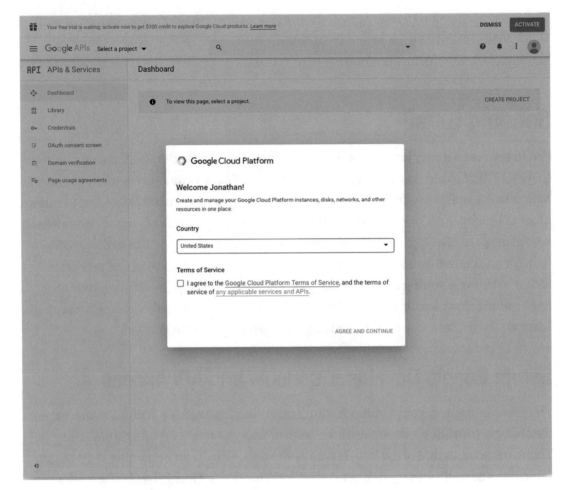

Figure 6-1. *Console Developers Screen*

2.   Once you've gotten into the console, you'll want to find the
     "Create Project" button. Give your project a descriptive name that
     you'll recognize (as you're likely the only one to ever see it!). I've
     called mine "Email from R" as you can see in Figure 6-2.

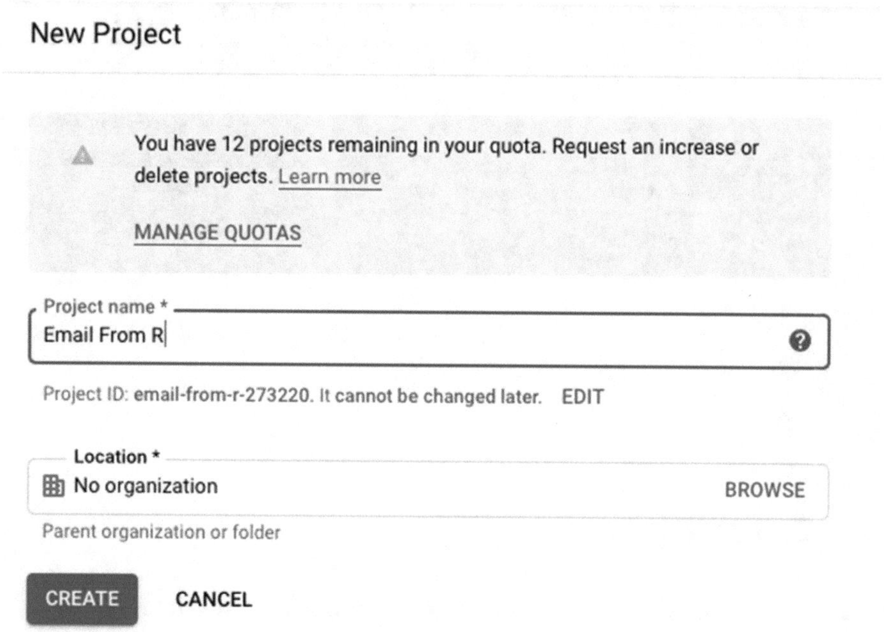

New Project

⚠ You have 12 projects remaining in your quota. Request an increase or delete projects. Learn more

MANAGE QUOTAS

Project name *

Email From R   ❓

Project ID: email-from-r-273220. It cannot be changed later.   EDIT

Location *

🏢 No organization   BROWSE

Parent organization or folder

CREATE   CANCEL

Figure 6-2. *Email From R Project*

Here is a good place to note that you'll see Google make a distinction between External and Internal in a few places. If you're a Google Apps customer, you can create applications that are internal to your specific Google Apps installation. If you have a regular Gmail account, as I'm using here, all of your applications are "external" as they're able to be used by any other Gmail account. However, external apps that are not validated by Gmail have certain limits – they are only open to 100 users at the most, and they also have lower rate limits. For a single person, this is not a problem. However, if you build an R script that sends email, you'll want to remind your users to create their own application and not use yours. In fact, in the code that I'll be distributing with this book, I'll be removing my application information (and in places where it's visible in screenshots, I'll be deleting the project, so those values won't authenticate further).

After creating the project, you should get a confirmation that it was successfully added. Figure 6-3 shows this message.

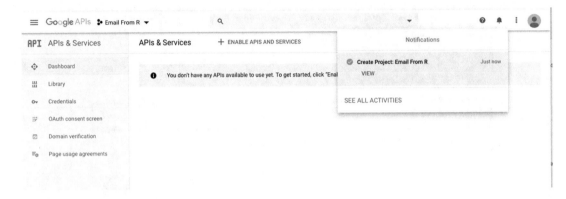

Figure 6-3. *Project Added*

3. Next, from the dashboard, you're going to want to find the APIs & Services area. You'll see a link at the top of Figure 6-3 that says "ENABLE APIS AND SERVICES". Figure 6-4 shows the API and Services page that we're looking for. Alternatively, you can search "Gmail API" in the search box above. Regardless of how you get there, you want to get to the Gmail API screen, either by jumping through Figure 6-4 or going there directly. Figure 6-5 shows the screen we're after.

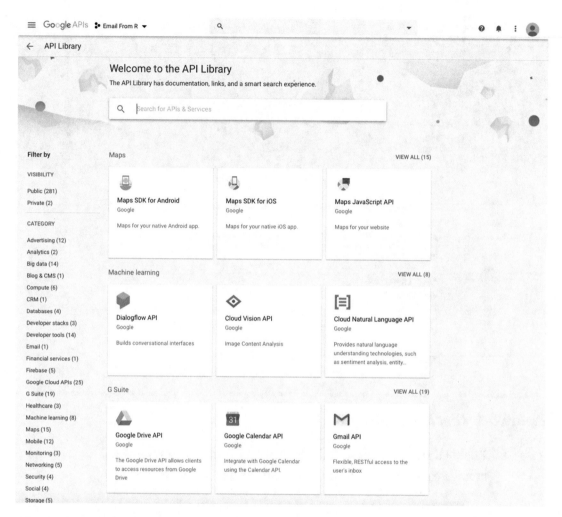

Figure 6-4. *Enable APIs and Services Screen*

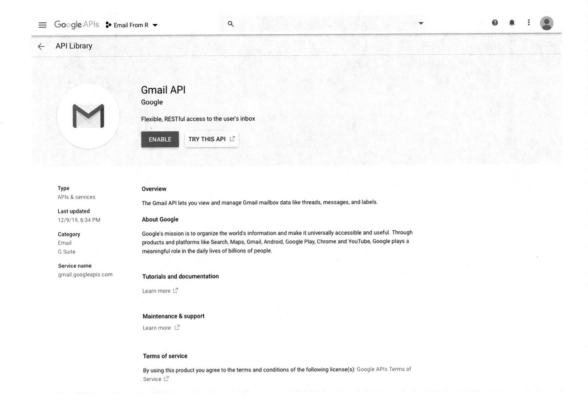

Figure 6-5. *Gmail API*

4. Enable the API by clicking the ENABLE button. The screen will change to show the API status for your project (see Figure 6-6).

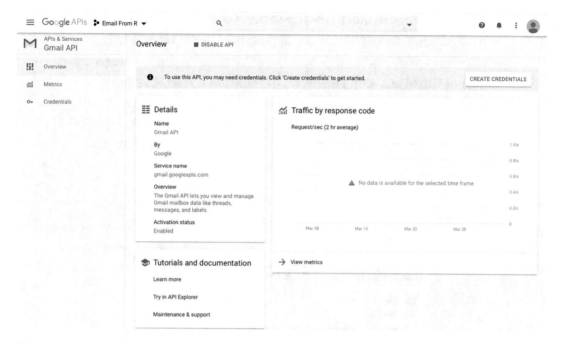

Figure 6-6. *Gmail API enabled*

5. Now that we have the Gmail API enabled, we need to create a
    credential to authenticate our R script with Gmail. To do this, click
    "Credentials" on the left-hand side menu to get a screen similar to
    Figure 6-7.

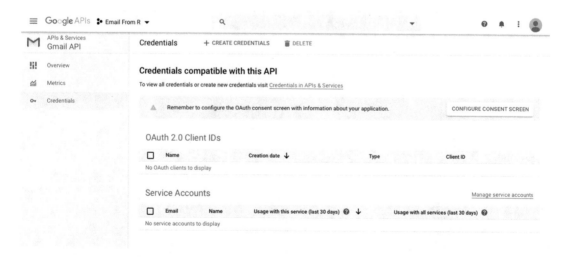

Figure 6-7. *Google Developer Console Credentials Area*

6. We need to make a quick side trip to the "OAuth consent screen"
    configuration, mostly to add our app name. Click "CONFIGURE
    CONSENT SCREEN" and then choose "External" if you're using a
    regular Gmail account. Finally, on the consent screen, give your
    application a name you'll recognize, and leave the rest blank.
    Unless you're building an app that you want to release publicly,
    your consent screen will only ever be seen by you. Figures 6-8, 6-9,
    and 6-10 show the screens in the order you'll see them.

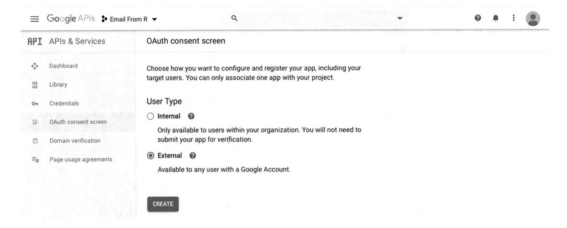

Figure 6-8. *Internal or External Choice*

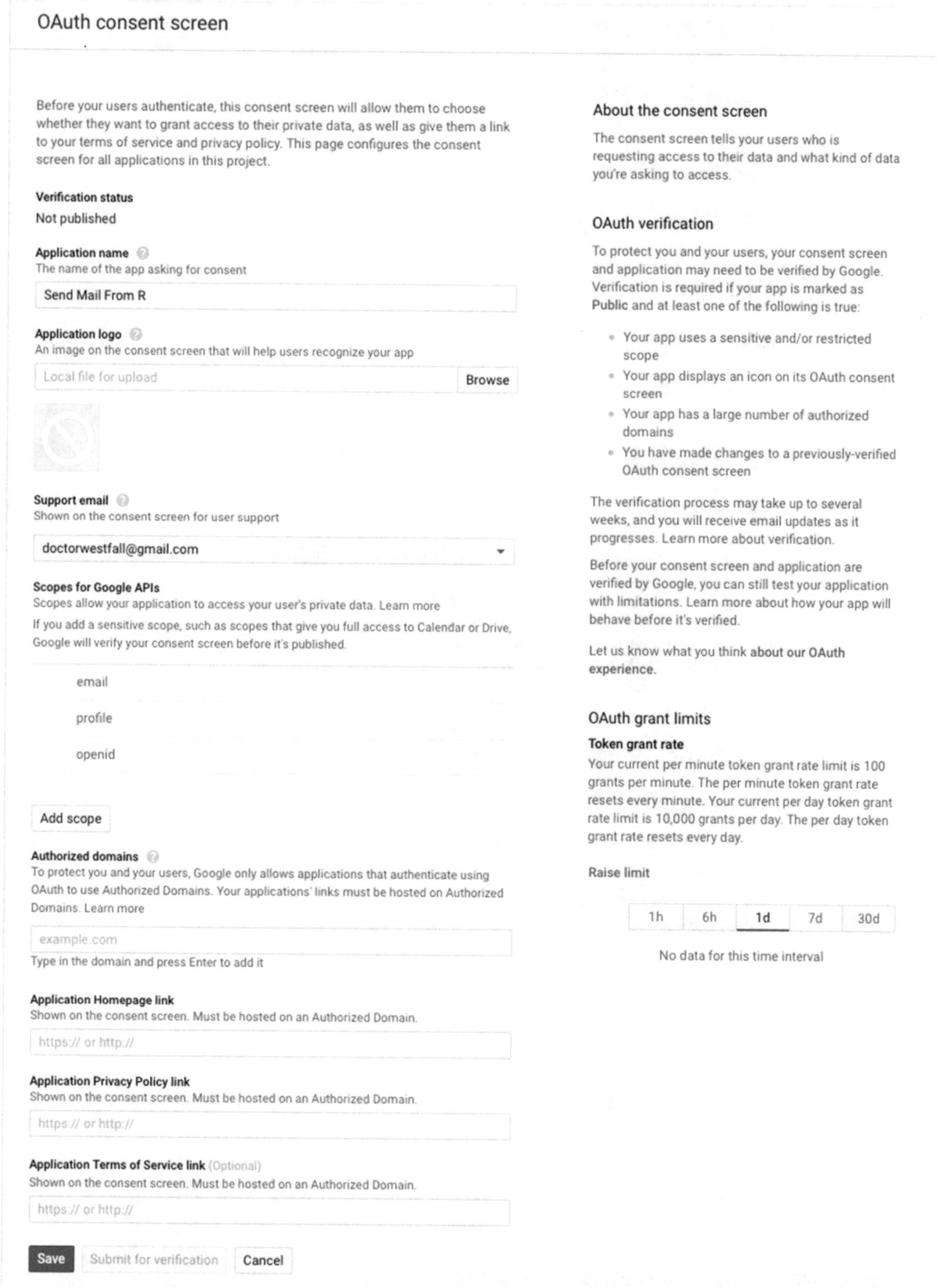

OAuth consent screen

Before your users authenticate, this consent screen will allow them to choose whether they want to grant access to their private data, as well as give them a link to your terms of service and privacy policy. This page configures the consent screen for all applications in this project.

Verification status
Not published

Application name ⓘ
The name of the app asking for consent

> Send Mail From R

Application logo ⓘ
An image on the consent screen that will help users recognize your app

Local file for upload	Browse

Support email ⓘ
Shown on the consent screen for user support

doctorwestfall@gmail.com	▾

Scopes for Google APIs
Scopes allow your application to access your user's private data. Learn more

If you add a sensitive scope, such as scopes that give you full access to Calendar or Drive, Google will verify your consent screen before it's published.

email

profile

openid

> Add scope

Authorized domains ⓘ
To protect you and your users, Google only allows applications that authenticate using OAuth to use Authorized Domains. Your applications' links must be hosted on Authorized Domains. Learn more

example.com

Type in the domain and press Enter to add it

Application Homepage link
Shown on the consent screen. Must be hosted on an Authorized Domain.

https:// or http://

Application Privacy Policy link
Shown on the consent screen. Must be hosted on an Authorized Domain.

https:// or http://

Application Terms of Service link (Optional)
Shown on the consent screen. Must be hosted on an Authorized Domain.

https:// or http://

> Save   Submit for verification   Cancel

About the consent screen

The consent screen tells your users who is requesting access to their data and what kind of data you're asking to access.

OAuth verification

To protect you and your users, your consent screen and application may need to be verified by Google. Verification is required if your app is marked as Public and at least one of the following is true:

* Your app uses a sensitive and/or restricted scope
* Your app displays an icon on its OAuth consent screen
* Your app has a large number of authorized domains
* You have made changes to a previously-verified OAuth consent screen

The verification process may take up to several weeks, and you will receive email updates as it progresses. Learn more about verification.

Before your consent screen and application are verified by Google, you can still test your application with limitations. Learn more about how your app will behave before it's verified.

Let us know what you think about our OAuth experience.

OAuth grant limits

Token grant rate
Your current per minute token grant rate limit is 100 grants per minute. The per minute token grant rate resets every minute. Your current per day token grant rate limit is 10,000 grants per day. The per day token grant rate resets every day.

Raise limit

1h	6h	**1d**	7d	30d

No data for this time interval

Figure 6-9. *OAuth Consent Screen Configuration*

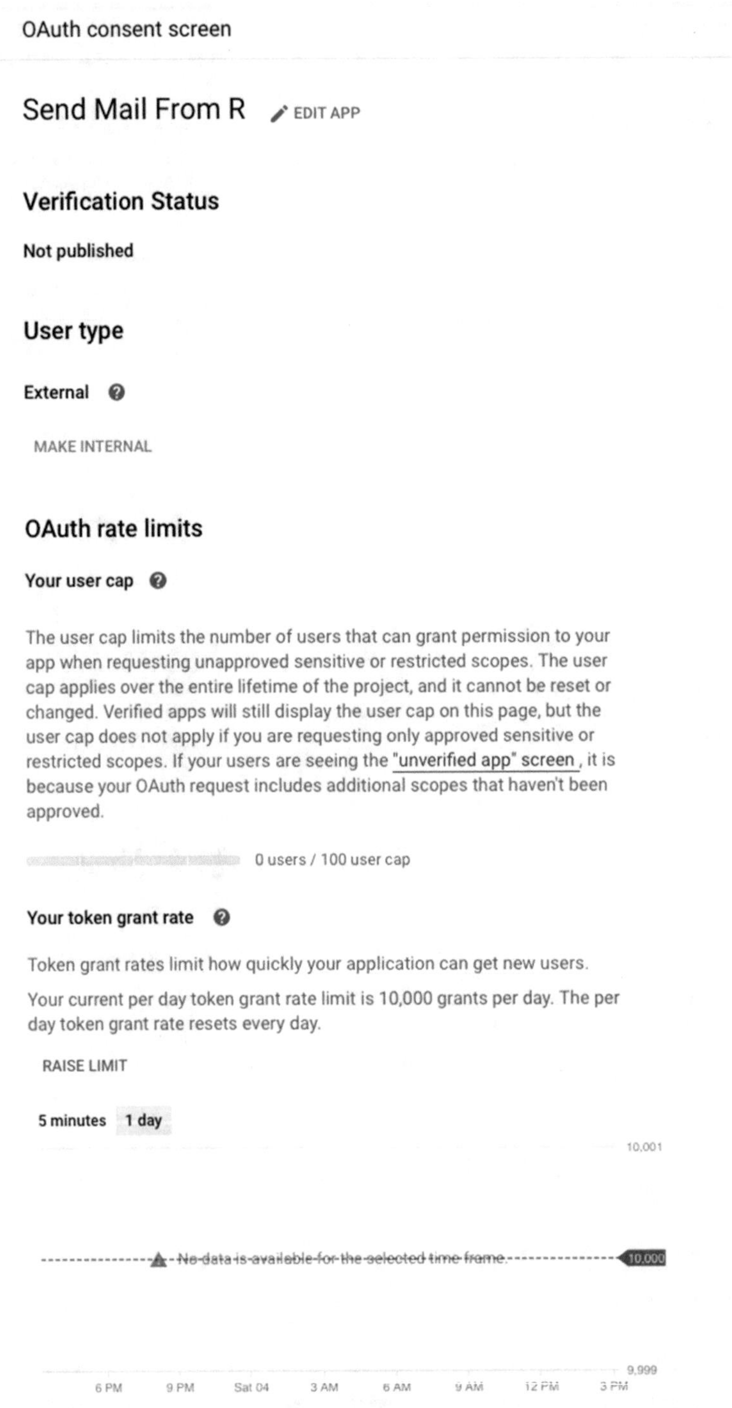

OAuth consent screen

Send Mail From R ✏ EDIT APP

Verification Status

Not published

User type

External ❷

MAKE INTERNAL

OAuth rate limits

Your user cap ❷

The user cap limits the number of users that can grant permission to your app when requesting unapproved sensitive or restricted scopes. The user cap applies over the entire lifetime of the project, and it cannot be reset or changed. Verified apps will still display the user cap on this page, but the user cap does not apply if you are requesting only approved sensitive or restricted scopes. If your users are seeing the "unverified app" screen , it is because your OAuth request includes additional scopes that haven't been approved.

0 users / 100 user cap

Your token grant rate ❷

Token grant rates limit how quickly your application can get new users.

Your current per day token grant rate limit is 10,000 grants per day. The per day token grant rate resets every day.

RAISE LIMIT

5 minutes   1 day

10,001

⚠ No data is available for the selected time frame 10,000

9,999

6 PM   9 PM   Sat 04   3 AM   6 AM   9 AM   12 PM   3 PM

Figure 6-10. *OAuth Consent Screen Saved*

7. OK, we're almost there. Now that we have the consent screen done, we can return to the "Credentials" option in the left-hand menu bar. Click the "CREATE CREDENTIALS" option and choose "OAuth client ID", as seen in Figure 6-11.

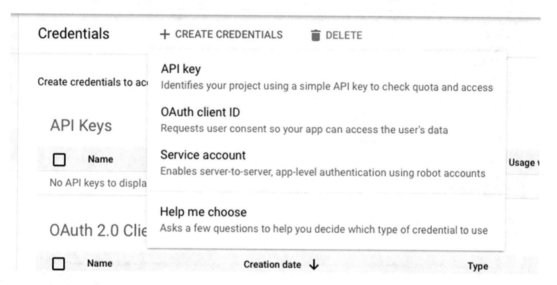

Figure 6-11. *Create Credentials Options*

8. Choose "Other" as your Application type (and give it a name; I chose "R"), and click Create (See Figure 6-12). A box similar to Figure 6-13 will appear with your credential information. You can click "OK" – in the next step, we will download these credentials in a way that R can easily open them.

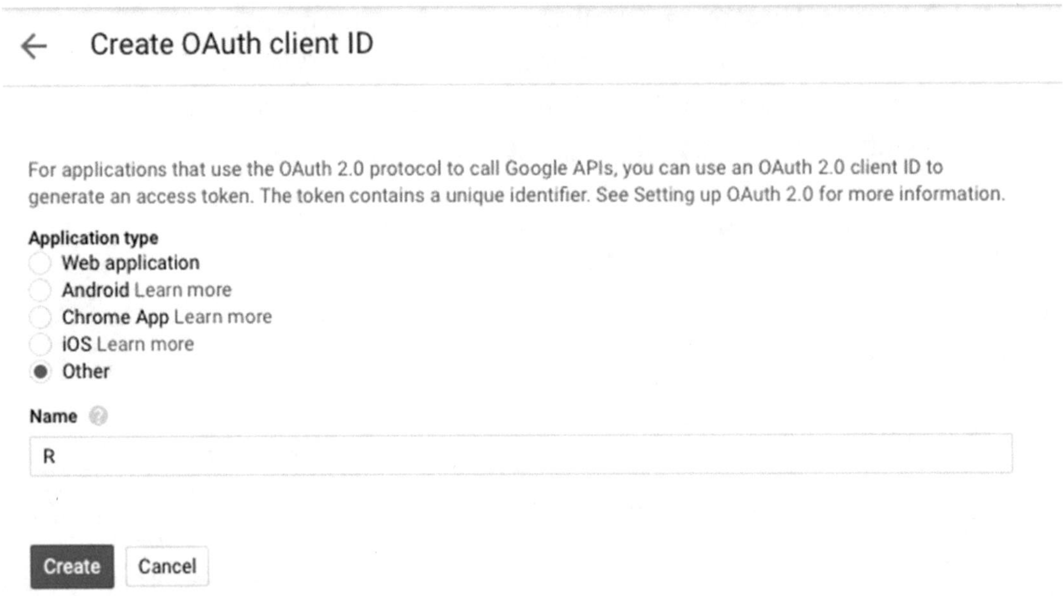

←   Create OAuth client ID

For applications that use the OAuth 2.0 protocol to call Google APIs, you can use an OAuth 2.0 client ID to generate an access token. The token contains a unique identifier. See Setting up OAuth 2.0 for more information.

Application type
- ○ **Web application**
- ○ **Android** Learn more
- ○ **Chrome App** Learn more
- ○ **iOS** Learn more
- ● **Other**

Name ⓘ

R

[Create]   Cancel

Figure 6-12. *Device Name*

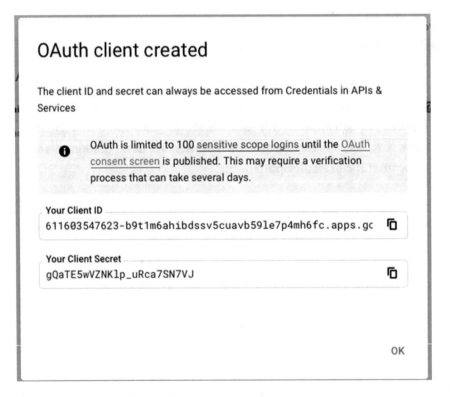

OAuth client created

The client ID and secret can always be accessed from Credentials in APIs & Services

ⓘ   OAuth is limited to 100 sensitive scope logins until the OAuth consent screen is published. This may require a verification process that can take several days.

Your Client ID

611603547623-b9t1m6ahibdssv5cuavb59le7p4mh6fc.apps.gc   🗐

Your Client Secret

gQaTE5wVZNKlp_uRca7SN7VJ   🗐

OK

Figure 6-13. *Credentials Created*

9. Finally, once you're back at the main Credentials screen, you'll see your new OAuth 2.0 Client ID. There is a download arrow at the far right of Figure 6-14 (to the right of the trashcan). Click it to download your file as a JSON data file. This is the file that R will open and read your credentials from. You don't want to give out this file as anyone who has it can use your application to send email from their Gmail account.

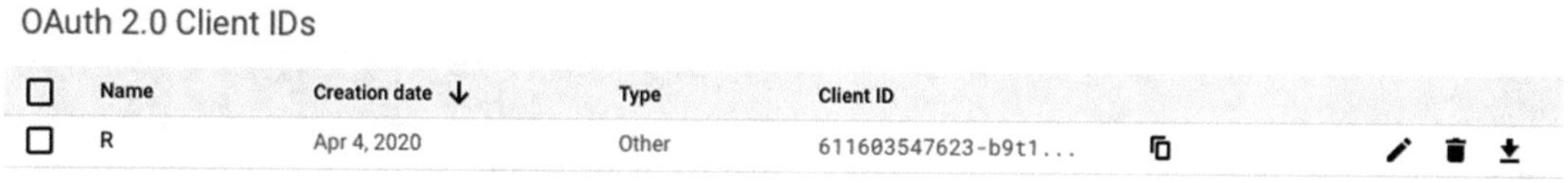

OAuth 2.0 Client IDs

	Name	Creation date ↓	Type	Client ID				
☐	R	Apr 4, 2020	Other	611603547623-b9t1...	🗐			

Figure 6-14. *OAuth Client IDs*

That was a laborious process, but it only has to be done one time – you now have your application set up to interface between Gmail and R, and you have the client credential you need for it. In the next section, we're going to set up an RStudio project named "Mailer" that is going to house the code for all three of our examples in this chapter – sending an individual email, securing data through encryption, and, finally, sending out bulk mail through R!

RStudio Project: Mailer

We're finally ready to send some email! To do so, I've created a new RStudio project named "Mailer". The first thing we want to do is move our client_secret JSON file that we downloaded in step 9 into our project directory. I've renamed mine to simply client_secret.json as the default name is quite long and annoying to keep track of. You could name yours whatever you like, as long as you adjust the code to account for it. As you can see in Figure 6-15, my project directory is pretty barren aside from the client_secret file and my first-mail.R script.

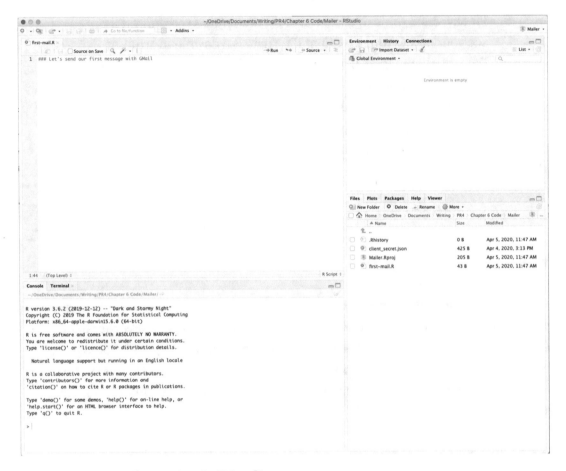

Figure 6-15. *Mailer project in RStudio*

Sending Your First Email Message

To get started, we'll need to install the `gmailr` package and then load it into R. The following lines will take care of that:

```
install.packages("gmailr")
library("gmailr")
```

Next, we need to specify the Gmail credentials. If you've changed the name of your OAuth JSON credentials, here's the line to modify. Since mine are named "client_secret.json", my code is simply

```
gm_auth_configure(path="client_secret.json")
```

This tells the `gmailr` package what authentication credentials to use. Next, I'm going to set up my email – the subject, the from header, the to header, and the body:

```
msg_subject <- "This is the second email I've sent.";
msg_from <- "Jon Westfall <doctorwestfall@gmail.com>";
msg_to <- "Another Jon Westfall <jon@jonwestfall.com>";
msg_body <- "<html>There is no attachment in this email. You already got
the file in the last one!</html>";
```

Since Gmail works with MIME message objects, I can then use the following code to create a MIME mail object named `email_msg`:

```
email_msg <- gm_mime() %>%
  gm_to(msg_to) %>%
  gm_from(msg_from) %>%
  gm_subject(msg_subject) %>%
  gm_html_body(msg_body)
```

It's worth noting that this is the first time we're seeing the %>% notation in R. This is a forward pipe infix operator – it forwards information to the next function or expression. It provides a mechanism to create a bit more readable code, although it can look a little strange at first. You can learn more about it by looking at the `magrittr` package that initially created it.

At this point, we're ready to send the email. However, the first time we do so, we need to authenticate with Gmail and grant it permissions to send from our Gmail account. As you can see in Figure 6-16, I've done nearly everything, and I'm on the last line.

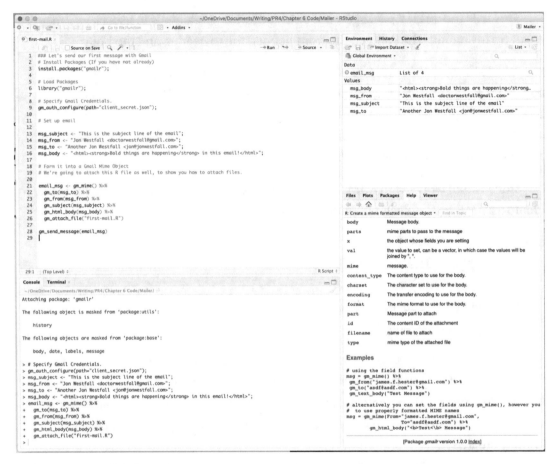

Figure 6-16. *Ready to send mail, all but the last line has been executed*

Now I execute the line gm_send_message(email_msg) and get the message "httpuv not installed, defaulting to out-of-band authentication", with a line asking me for an authorization code. At the same time, a browser window opens in my default browser to the Google Sign in page (Figures 6-17 and 6-18).

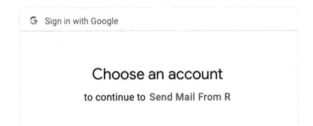

Figure 6-17. *Choosing an account to authenticate with*

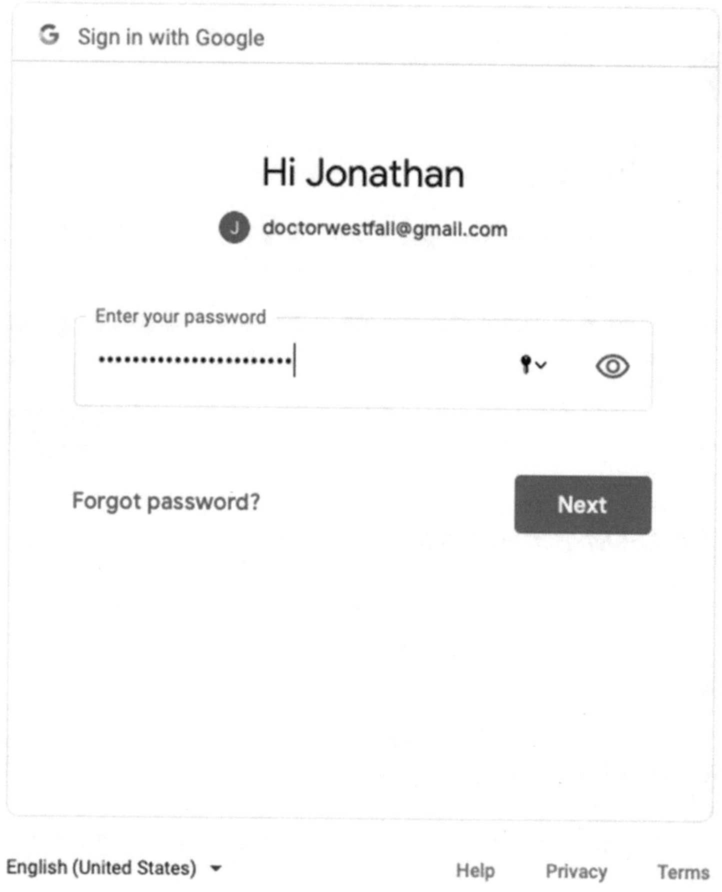

Figure 6-18. *Logging into Gmail*

Once I've logged in, I'm taking to a warning screen that I'm trying to authenticate to an unverified application. This is the application I created earlier, so while, yes, it is unverified, I'm reasonably sure it's safe since I'm the only one who has been using it and the only one who has authentication credentials for it! So it is safe for me, in Figure 6-19, to click "Advanced" and then "Go to Send Mail From R (unsafe)" in Figure 6-20.

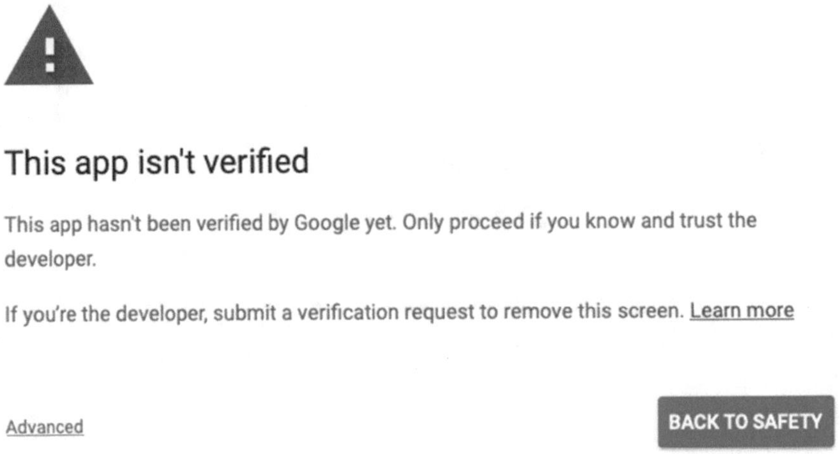

This app isn't verified

This app hasn't been verified by Google yet. Only proceed if you know and trust the developer.

If you're the developer, submit a verification request to remove this screen. Learn more

Advanced   BACK TO SAFETY

Figure 6-19. *The Unverified Application Screen*

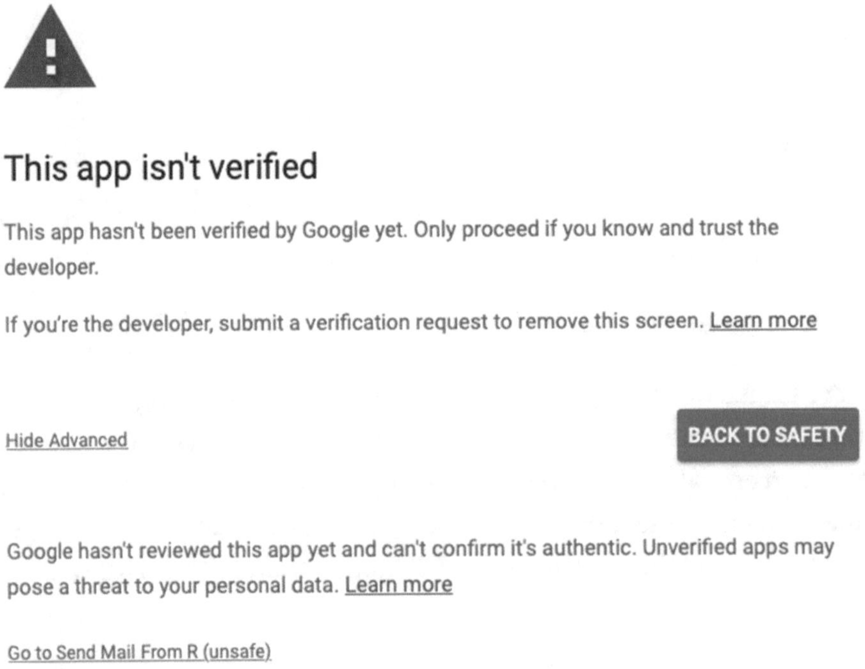

This app isn't verified

This app hasn't been verified by Google yet. Only proceed if you know and trust the developer.

If you're the developer, submit a verification request to remove this screen. Learn more

Hide Advanced   BACK TO SAFETY

Google hasn't reviewed this app yet and can't confirm it's authentic. Unverified apps may pose a threat to your personal data. Learn more

Go to Send Mail From R (unsafe)

Figure 6-20. *Clicking "Advanced"*

With that warning aside, I now have to grant permission to my Gmail account to use the Gmail API (See Figures 6-21 and 6-22), and eventually, I'm given an authorization code, in Figure 6-23.

194

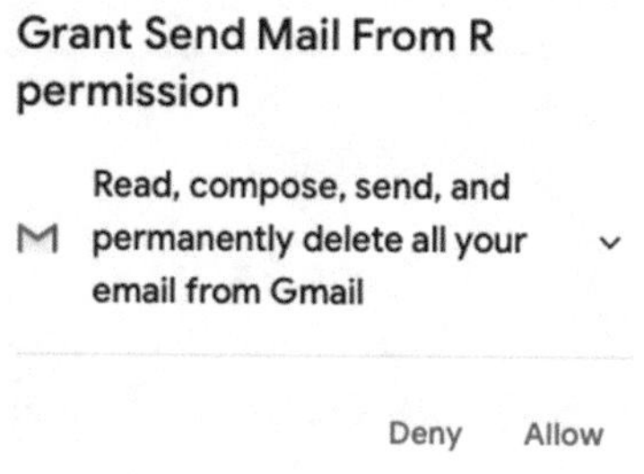

Grant Send Mail From R
permission

M Read, compose, send, and
permanently delete all your   ⌄
email from Gmail

Deny   Allow

Figure 6-21. *Granting Permission*

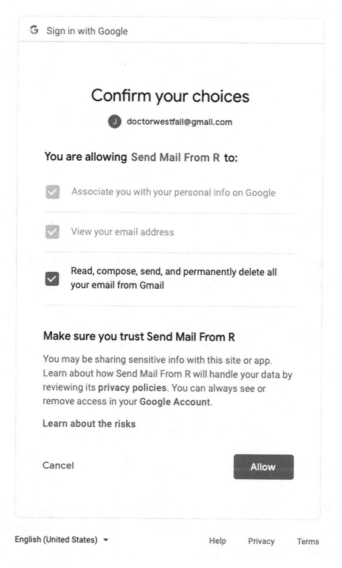

Figure 6-22. *Confirming Selections*

Google
Sign in
Please copy this code, switch to your application and paste it there:
4/yQFnrt43hnRB-
QGSQQ1mwuxEYcwn5OpbYEcosxc4OBZZf8KiIRSVFSg

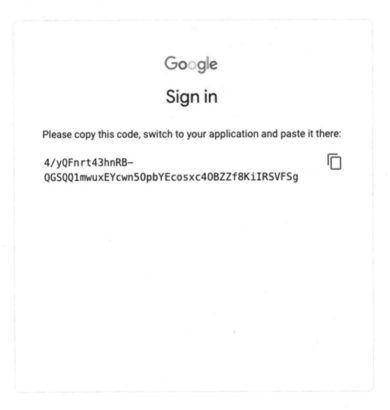

Figure 6-23. *The Authorization Code*

Returning to RStudio, I paste that authorization code into the prompt and press Enter. The email is then sent, and I receive a confirmation ID (Figures 6-24 and 6-25).

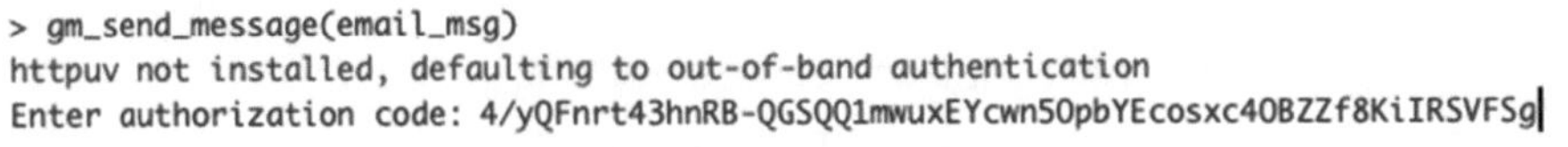
> gm_send_message(email_msg)
httpuv not installed, defaulting to out-of-band authentication
Enter authorization code: 4/yQFnrt43hnRB-QGSQQ1mwuxEYcwn5OpbYEcosxc4OBZZf8KiIRSVFSg

Figure 6-24. *Entering the code in R*

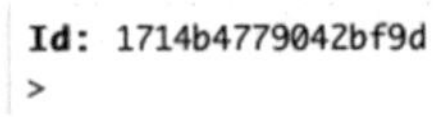
Id: 1714b4779042bf9d
>

Figure 6-25. *Receiving a confirmation ID in R*

And that's it! My message has been sent. On the receiving end, I can see it in Microsoft Outlook (Figure 6-26), and if I log into the sending Gmail account, I can see the message in my sent list (Figure 6-27).

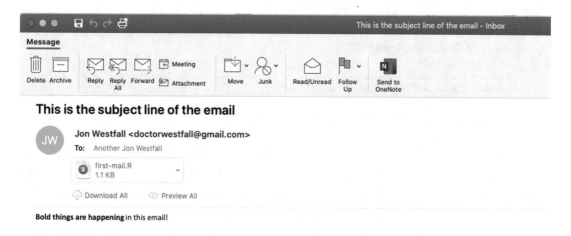

Figure 6-26. *The email, as it appears in Microsoft Outlook*

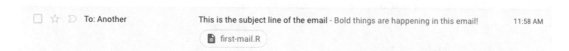

Figure 6-27. *The sent mail in the senders Gmail account*

Now that I've authenticated one time, the `gmailr` package can cache my authorization, if I let it. So the next time that I send email, in Figure 6-28, it goes through without any prompting (See Figure 6-29).

```
> msg_subject <- "This is the second email I've sent.";
> msg_from <- "Jon Westfall <doctorwestfall@gmail.com>";
> msg_to <- "Another Jon Westfall <jon@jonwestfall.com>";
> msg_body <- "<html>There is no attachment in this email. You already got the file in the last one!</html>";
>
> # Form it into a Gmail Mime Object
> # We're going to attach this R file as well, to show you how to attach files.
>
> email_msg <- gm_mime() %>%
+   gm_to(msg_to) %>%
+   gm_from(msg_from) %>%
+   gm_subject(msg_subject) %>%
+   gm_html_body(msg_body)
>
> gm_send_message(email_msg)
Id: 1714b49775f14a9c
```

Figure 6-28. *Sending a second email, the credentials are cached*

This is the second email I've sent.

 Jon Westfall <doctorwestfall@gmail.com>   Today at 12:00 PM
To: Another Jon Westfall

There is no attachment in this email. You already got the file in the last one!

Figure 6-29. *The second email in Microsoft Outlook*

Finally, you'll notice that if you log back into the Google Developer Console, you now have one user who has used your application (see Figure 6-30), viewing the OAuth User Count. Unverified apps can have up to 100 users to test them out as they're being built, so in practice, you're well under the limit and can continue using your application in Gmail for likely as long as you want. If you do ever want to build out a public application, however, you'll need to have your application verified and potentially pay Google to conduct a security audit on it. Speaking of security, how about we think about how we want to secure our information that we send out from R?

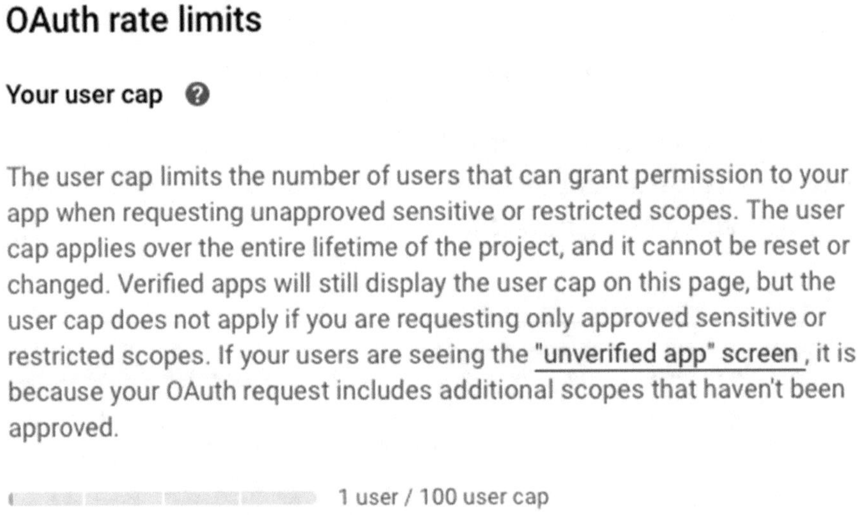

OAuth rate limits

Your user cap   ❓

The user cap limits the number of users that can grant permission to your app when requesting unapproved sensitive or restricted scopes. The user cap applies over the entire lifetime of the project, and it cannot be reset or changed. Verified apps will still display the user cap on this page, but the user cap does not apply if you are requesting only approved sensitive or restricted scopes. If your users are seeing the "unverified app" screen, it is because your OAuth request includes additional scopes that haven't been approved.

▬▬▬▬▬▬▬▬▬▬▬▬   1 user / 100 user cap

Figure 6-30. *The OAuth User Count*

Securing Communications

Email is a protocol that harkens back to a simpler time on the Internet, where things were not as secure as they are today. In its basic implementation, it's 100% plain text. Today we typically want a bit more security around our communications, and we get that through SSL encryption in many places we go on the Web. However, sometimes you want to have a bit more security – something that you control yourself. In this section, I'll talk about two packages that can help you with that in R. Once your data is secured, you can then send it directly from R using the preceding example. Our first package is a simple form of encryption that is useful within R only. Our second is an industry standard that takes a bit more to set up, but can be used in a wide variety of use scenarios.

The sodium Package

Cryptography can be a difficult subject to master, and as we'll see in our next section, it can get quite complex. However, for something simple, perhaps wanting to send data output from R to a friend who is also using R, a simpler way can be very appreciated. This is the point of the sodium package by Jeroen Ooms. The package offers a few different ways to encrypt data, and in the following example, we're using one of the simplest: secret key encryption, or commonly thought of – a password!

Here's how this might work: I'm working with a friend on a project, and we want to share data back and forth via email. However, we need our data to be secure, so that someone can't easily intercept it. We agree on a passphrase, something like **you can grow ideas in the garden of your mind** (a quote from Fred Rogers). Imagine that I want to encrypt a dataset in R (we'll use ChickWeight that we talked about in Chapter 2) using that passphrase. I can do this by installing the sodium package and using the following code:

```
install.packages("sodium")
library("sodium")
passphrase <- "you can grow ideas in the garden of your mind"
key <- hash(charToRaw(passphrase))
secret_message <- serialize(ChickWeight, NULL)
noise <- random(24)
encrypted_text <- data_encrypt(secret_message, key, noise)
```

I now have an encrypted text variable that isn't very useful to anyone. You can see a snippet of it in Figure 6-31.

```
> encrypted_text
  [1] 45 8f 66 7e 2c 11 28 4a 74 29 ca 9b bb 29 dd 15 7e 24 29 be 1a 3b a9 c7 19 f5 26 73 39 8d 17 6c f1 0f d6
 [36] dd c7 83 d4 1d 47 6a 31 aa f2 5e 54 e0 bc fc 96 1b d9 3c 86 d7 d6 4d 24 88 95 4f ee 36 46 98 b4 15 09 be
 [71] 41 38 75 15 2d ef 66 13 80 21 74 1f 7f e3 fd ee 3f 6d ba 1f 4f c7 ac b5 05 92 3a eb 9c d0 c2 41 0b 6b 8f
[106] a4 6e 22 65 5b d6 79 50 5a a3 96 74 62 4a cd bf 8d 64 ff f5 04 02 e2 d6 f5 a3 e8 e4 ce 3f a5 3c 01 ab 06
[141] 98 45 c1 42 a9 9d 30 8b cc ea 25 93 c3 53 ea 3f 55 e8 d7 5b 6d a3 61 8a 2b 11 8f d3 c5 66 4a 5e 84 96 32
[176] 2c 36 30 32 a3 7d aa 40 50 4c a4 7f 35 3b 37 56 0b 05 a3 4d 6c 4c a8 2d 92 0e 97 1e 8e fb df 79 ec 6d 05
[211] d8 60 e6 c4 bd 6b c0 18 ac ec fe 40 dc 8d b9 b6 d7 ad bf af c9 b7 2f 5e 35 ba 4e 3e 71 de e5 a4 ff 38 db
[246] 7f 92 42 da 16 d2 3a c8 5c 16 bb a6 05 42 76 2d c6 50 b3 65 88 b9 ce 29 ad 39 bc cf 1f 4c 52 ce 7b b3 80
[281] 44 df d8 8f 69 3a b9 45 88 a7 52 f6 8a da 08 83 7e b6 87 c6 37 bb 4f 1e d5 a6 16 35 59 68 bf fa 69 2b 29
[316] e7 1e 3f 90 5d 3c 2a 0c 28 b9 6c d9 4b 27 78 66 12 49 2a 4f 80 d0 00 37 38 1d 3c 2b 32 80 1a 8e ae 81 3f
[351] 70 f5 fb 88 3f 0a 85 66 f3 f7 43 ee b8 d1 a6 c8 25 e5 ba 34 f6 6e b4 3e 18 24 2d 23 6f c8 a4 f1 b1 a9 a8
[386] e7 d0 b7 8d 40 aa d1 33 be c0 67 d1 2d 7b 71 dd ba 2c 04 68 a5 3a 86 f6 52 8b cf 3c f6 9d c0 72 91 c5 49
[421] 93 1c 9d 24 0b 1a 29 6d 4b b1 11 b5 c7 19 7e bb ef 5f 71 e0 65 14 7c 6b 70 b6 62 87 a3 79 87 86 5b fc 70
[456] 0e d0 37 eb 38 d4 f9 3d 58 7b 99 36 e9 b5 df 9b fa 70 7f 53 88 a9 36 d8 7f 3f 67 3f 93 42 f6 5a 3c f8 f5
[491] 13 47 27 91 b1 1d a9 8e 26 6b b2 57 cf 8e b0 28 be 17 47 05 0c b3 4c a7 1b cd 9c c9 ba 82 25 e8 3b 0c 8f
[526] 8d db 90 d6 87 bc 27 b0 1e fb d3 06 17 82 f5 ac cd 37 56 98 32 d2 b3 c7 f5 18 e7 2c f3 72 5b d9 4e 15 c7
[561] cb 98 d9 3b 38 ac e7 cb 8d 15 9d f3 af eb 02 89 2c 25 e6 69 2a f5 9d 61 79 6e 69 69 e3 3b a5 7a 1f 2d 7e
[596] 78 19 34 d4 44 50 ef 68 c2 67 27 ad 4e 17 d9 db 49 37 dc e7 54 c9 5e 47 37 f6 15 e5 db f2 c6 ca 91 0e 85
```

Figure 6-31. *Encrypted Message*

Now all I have to do is send my friend the random noise I used to encrypt with (the noise variable) and the text (encrypted_text). Something like this will work:

```
saveRDS(noise, file="noise.rds");
saveRDS(encrypted_text, file="text.rds");
library("gmailr");
gm_auth_configure(path="client_secret.json");
msg_subject <- "Encrypted Data";
msg_from <- "Jon Westfall <doctorwestfall@gmail.com>";
msg_to <- "Another Jon Westfall <jon@jonwestfall.com>";
msg_body <- paste("See the data attached");
email_msg <- gm_mime() %>%
  gm_to(msg_to) %>%
  gm_from(msg_from) %>%
  gm_subject(msg_subject) %>%
  gm_html_body(msg_body) %>%
  gm_attach_file("noise.rds") %>%
  gm_attach_file("text.rds")
gm_send_message(email_msg)
```

This first saves our random noise variable and our encrypted text to an R Data object and attaches it to an email. When our receiver gets the message (Figure 6-32), they can load and restore the data using the secret key that you've agreed upon, using code like this:

```
library("sodium")
noise <- readRDS(file="noise.rds")
encrypted_text <- readRDS(file="text.rds")
passphrase <- "you can grow ideas in the garden of your mind"
key <- hash(charToRaw(passphrase))
data <- unserialize(data_decrypt(encrypted_text,key,noise))
```

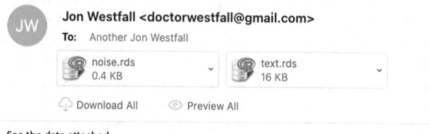

Figure 6-32. Encrypted email attachments

And just like that you've got your data securely transported. Our limitation, though, is that we have to use both R to encrypt and decrypt our data. Our next encryption method is a bit more complex, but it overcomes this problem by using an industry standard: GPG, the free replacement for Symantec's PGP cryptography.

The gpg Package

One of the most established cryptographic technologies on the Web today is GNU Privacy Guard (GPG or GnuPG). It works off of a principle called Public-Private Key cryptography. In a very simple sense, imagine that you have a lock with two keys: Key A and Key B. Key A can lock the lock in a way that only Key B can unlock it. Key B can lock the lock in a way that only Key A can unlock it.

Now imagine that you gave all of your friends Key B, and you kept Key A somewhere secret. When they wanted to secure something, they'd put the lock on it and lock it with Key B. The other friends with Key B can't use Key B to unlock it – only Key A can unlock it. You'd use your Key A to open the message, assured only you could.

And when you wanted to send something to a friend, you'd use Key A to lock it, and using Key B, they could ensure that you were the one who actually sent it. Now call Key A your "Private Key" and Key B your "Public Key" and you have the concept of Public-Private Key cryptography. It's a way for me to ensure that only the recipient of the message can read it, and it's also a way for me to "sign" my own documents so that people know it's really me.

Back when PGP/GPG was first started, individuals would go to "key signing" parties to build up a "web of trust." Imagine a bunch of people in a room meeting each other, showing each other documents that proved their identity (e.g., driver's licenses, passports), and the other person saying "Yep, that's you, I'll sign your key". Eventually you'd have a key that was well trusted. Today that same principle is used in a few different areas, including a popular platform named Keybase (`https://keybase.io`).

Figure 6-33 shows my Keybase profile. Through Keybase, one can know that all of the web profiles that I've associated with it are truly me. Keybase also allows people to securely talk with me through the Chat feature. What's very interesting, though, is the line of seemingly random numbers at the top that starts with 1396. Clicking that, we see my PGP/GPG public key fingerprint and full public key (see Figure 6-34).

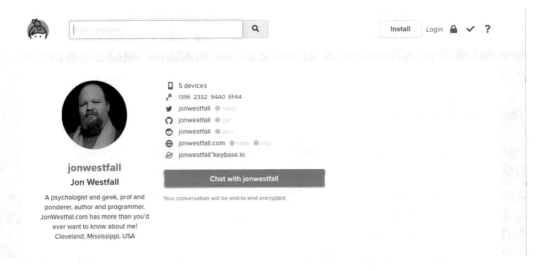

Figure 6-33. *My Keybase Profile at* `http://keybase.io/jonwestfall`

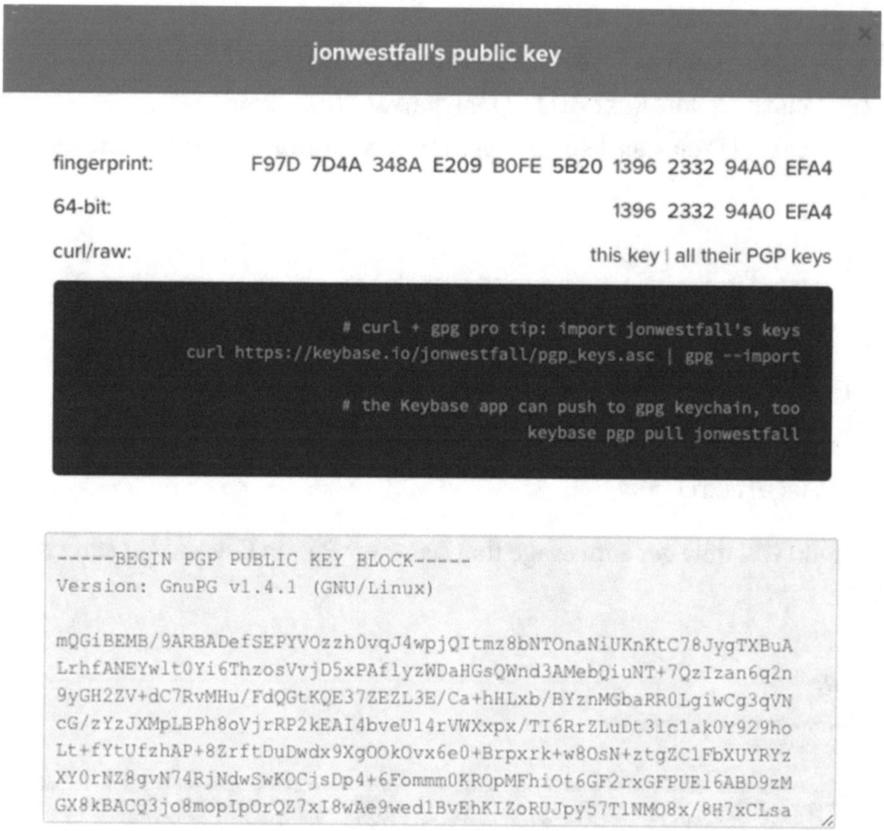

jonwestfall's public key

fingerprint:	F97D 7D4A 348A E209 B0FE 5B20 1396 2332 94A0 EFA4
64-bit:	1396 2332 94A0 EFA4
curl/raw:	this key	all their PGP keys

```
# curl + gpg pro tip: import jonwestfall's keys
curl https://keybase.io/jonwestfall/pgp_keys.asc | gpg --import

# the Keybase app can push to gpg keychain, too
keybase pgp pull jonwestfall
```

```
-----BEGIN PGP PUBLIC KEY BLOCK-----
Version: GnuPG v1.4.1 (GNU/Linux)

mQGiBEMB/9ARBADefSEPYVOzzh0vqJ4wpjQItmz8bNTOnaNiUKnKtC78JygTXBuA
LrhfANEYwlt0Yi6ThzosVvjD5xPAflyzWDaHGsQWnd3AMebQiuNT+7QzIzan6q2n
9yGH2ZV+dC7RvMHu/FdQGtKQE37ZEZL3E/Ca+hHLxb/BYznMGbaRR0LgiwCg3qVN
cG/zYzJXMpLBPh8oVjrRP2kEAI4bveU14rVWXxpx/TI6RrZLuDt3lc1ak0Y929ho
Lt+fYtUfzhAP+8ZrftDuDwdx9XgOOkOvx6e0+Brpxrk+w8OsN+ztgZC1FbXUYRYz
XY0rNZ8gvN74RjNdwSwKOCjsDp4+6Fommm0KROpMFhiOt6GF2rxGFPUE16ABD9zM
GX8kBACQ3jo8mopIpOrQZ7xI8wAe9wed1BvEhKIZoRUJpy57TlNMO8x/8H7xCLsa
```

Figure 6-34. *My Public Key*

We'll use this data in a moment in an example of how one can send an encrypted message using the gpg package in R. But first, before you can send me a message, you must have your own public and private keys. Thankfully, they're pretty easy to create using the gpg package. This code will create a public/private key pair and then email the public key to a friend:

```
install.packages("gpg")
library("gpg")
my_key <- gpg_keygen(name = "Testy McTestperson", email="doctorwestfall
@gmail.com")
public_key <- gpg_export(id = my_key)
library("gmailr");
gm_auth_configure(path="client_secret.json");
```

```
msg_subject <- "My Public Key";
msg_from <- "Jon Westfall <doctorwestfall@gmail.com>";
msg_to <- "Another Jon Westfall <jon@jonwestfall.com>";
msg_body <- paste("You can use the public key below to communicate with me: ",
public_key);

email_msg <- gm_mime() %>%
  gm_to(msg_to) %>%
  gm_from(msg_from) %>%
  gm_subject(msg_subject) %>%
  gm_html_body(msg_body)

gm_send_message(email_msg)
```

Your friend will now get a message that has your Public Key, as you can see in Figure 6-35.

My Public Key

 Jon Westfall <doctorwestfall@gmail.com>   Today at 1:55 PM
To: Another Jon Westfall

You can use the public key below to communicate with me: -----BEGIN PGP PUBLIC KEY BLOCK----- mQENBF6KKWYBCAC3sEjkLkZPbq3lGhwQ/PzHV5blgpRQaCMb8CvDKmNsqhZDabg1
yRLdJaOef1GEuOmGZjuZoZiB1sF3JE1bjappuQT8IO1AsKijpZg6qrBW1dwhK4oK QCSMDbSOy1j37gs4st7Bc+vXy5Am/YnkNahKloCD7ammDKqBSZYPX86Fv5909xln
u9VHCATQZZOBOY/rAcdDbwpf4UbPmTGl13a7hlX8L40MGpULqCioaYbel1COPrxX lpMpZM9PBJ+A3Gd2MP/dRjJqmNBK3i/8d5SocxQjUV2TBJGnhF4cta3P6sRSyOM9
Q6ce93wyZv3DJIrxeM/NB/VfuuXol7weHxRjABEBAAG0LVRlc3R5Rl5lE1jVGVzdHBl cnNvbiA8ZG9jdG9yd2VzdGZhbGxAZ21haWwuY29tPokBVAQTAQgAPhYhBDinNJxa
npi+7GpTLQCG/HTn2sERBQleiilmAhsPBQkDwmcABQsJCAcCBhUKCQgLAgQWAgMB Ah4BAheAAAoJEACG/HTn2sERULwIAJnZzs5OohUlXf9iagxod3tq8JlFcyfyolgZ
8KI9WDZXIswPts/si2hfM3lOv8jUL2uM1uHDoBTyFba7wQTiPA2+zlndVzqI6GRl NacxcF1gxB+lcxZWZjB2UlgMNoq8EM2TJaNu4Cnkeogvqzv4DTrldPPJOMSkf8Vs
lpYJM59fZG6XfKjjQzLwAF7ZHiZOQOlmprF3zChw3RnWYCY/anCey2Avk8+TuqUJ 1YWCNR1StuxlT2V4l9yPzvNMdqAmFdyzMSYrU7bdB5/gdvAe+Z1DN3qMPso22+we
pcev61gWLnwWa6M7A8DSrPW2XYNuWs7q/N3qSxlNRNkytSfGA9s= =B9C1 -----END PGP PUBLIC KEY BLOCK-----

Figure 6-35. *The PGP Public Key*

This allows my friend to send messages to me by encrypting them using the public key that I just sent them. I can decrypt it using the private key.

Once you have created your public/private key, GPG will store them on your GPG keyring. However, it's a good idea to back them up by using the following commands:

```
gpg_export(id = my_key) #exports public key
gpg_export(id= my_key, secret = TRUE) #exports private key - do NOT give
this to anyone!
```

Another way to get someone's PGP/GPG key, other than having them email it to you, is through that fingerprint we saw in Figure 6-34. The following code will download my public key to my GPG keyring directly. The second half of the code then encrypts the contents of the secure-communications.r file using the public key I downloaded.

```
library("gpg")
jon <- "F97D7D4A348AE209B0FE5B201396233294A0EFA4"
gpg_recv(jon)
library("gmailr");
gm_auth_configure(path="client_secret.json");
msg_subject <- "Encrypted Message";
msg_from <- "Jon Westfall <doctorwestfall@gmail.com>";
msg_to <- "Another Jon Westfall <jon@jonwestfall.com>";
msg_body <- gpg_encrypt("secure-communications.R",receiver=jon)
email_msg <- gm_mime() %>%
  gm_to(msg_to) %>%
  gm_from(msg_from) %>%
  gm_subject(msg_subject) %>%
  gm_html_body(msg_body)
gm_send_message(email_msg)
```

On the receiving end of the message (Figure 6-36), the message appears to be gibberish. However, since it's been encrypted with my public key, I can use my private key to decrypt it.

Encrypted Message

 Jon Westfall <doctorwestfall@gmail.com>   Today at 2:02 PM

To: Another Jon Westfall

-----BEGIN PGP MESSAGE----- hQIOA39xvs9UDTTsEAf+LG/6yl24k2oyXuSWaCjEdH0vdBWh1Bni+aOdawOo2luf X/ffeHCPmxxycijL/P8Sc6XkLFTE4m2ZmcQKpPEWaD4AWiQTkalB74KC5Bqam39d
lfGj6d0wecSHP0jYYjuIgN5yWYclzbzxY+eJ0Iv6XKQW2LyyCgyW/8xZ7bxDMveC dn0IW+3dnUwixWcopD8dbB61Nw8fQNYyeDIAAHYoMv/1qto4TsZlXK/xncBW/hjr
wnsqA1H98wAAFpxmm/cNiikZd6hGfo1qkHiGel/LKybShNJGL9n2T37rug6BKWBR DixwC3/tFblYLiju9ZjmNFYYQNF5SChUFyL8uqEcLgf7BUhFil/Mtna7rqxOZkg7
o20WT7E6uyJgs15UqD9VZpCIyYxlmjlc+S99RDCW2/Y9coXAilgvdkucRAMn4Wz+ 65XOZ4b7AWHBTa3t/H3zvubpRfwpddD7nbfLojAe6R6ik6DYWhlB3eUYhE2A0KjR
n5A9EaPloAuVqNJBVPkpcTSB9MPYtNVSCQct2UK1VvLMn35r/FD9bOghGOCIsIU 0di21D6ULDgvFR9PsF3qhxOe924SnPnEcDXbNF9BXdeSrOYJT57wSZVteUk4Yb3d
f9dL9ckiwS/Vnk6YZsI1lTzKKXdXOlZRIdSCbU3flePo2X2wmtwHhCP55FQ7Ls50 B9LpAST2day1M1OnS/6Iy47SK2mDePfNI7pbOR0RhPxZSpv61gdO9arufkKtqwd/
8NTd22i0yi82r/pHJhWEzFh/1+Hpu7FUZOLRUD4dLUkh+IsGLMjpLiu2jIm6YMoN WpqvVgVHZ410MEiJNIlbg0xZYEaxcqjMXwjDyn6fWXTxoAhyGYN4ld9Q7Qzrc934
Fe8W2Ribn541dNZy+wHGOu0DXQ6egO2afHUByOqhKZR4z5eNBpQR5iTDsY90eSzb 0AYGyakb50cpaKfQ/W8/8miQqHMhBZ7lz7rqOqdeLFEGdXv/sv7sXj99Pm+L7qsE
U6k2L0AAUIq+cASwwNm1ue07T2GXz8X6VtTpUO6ObLFtQEgKoknOLklwQqhzlqGO +oe7DeMhwuzdUCNGOZa2+b5e5exARqV0dmMcOV125gbZuLpfM/bC2M63BVH79q2G
7nK4hrj9Cs6Su3PK/nYRDjMpWSyNY3Mv5Dse0REQtZnUNJrkzQw2lXIKO9g2RwYZ 8vf6mPOrkbJjoppSxFWtRxDFyWqfYDiwA6NzjZgKAqINfVINHetMfWOuz3HA2OVd
fp0fA8G09CMnGNQ6XNFqkHHJDKGLji1dSkWYorXrLsNJWznUMG/+C1ribFn4bz+Q ikpw562HfP30+7YOWB1wmtOiy3K7XEK5gtlarqiys+VPL5x6Fdfe+rY8H4GKMNsP
8StwhS83ih4NH1bkkpnb+vTq9TafUsdfXard6ob4j0RUZ0IVF78IOHZOtpfsMucv BzVFWtHgID8A8Xei3+8yYQHKRqFPI8YhxOHiKLX6FvbAgKDkywlTJ7iuDMLLQ/Eo DyM83ZF2raRDl2g1IJk= =MSb8 -----END PGP MESSAGE-----

Figure 6-36. *Encrypted result*

GPG/PGP is an excellent cross-platform cross-application method to secure your data and send it back and forth to others. It can be encrypted in R and then opened in any other tool that supports it. By backing up and keeping your public and private keys safe, you can begin to build up a reputation of trust around them, so that your friends know that what you sent them is truly from you and not someone who has just changed the "From" header of their email to be your name. As you can see, R is pretty flexible in using GPG or other encryption methods to secure your data.

Now that we've talked about security, we can talk about automation – taking a fairly complex task of sending multiple emails and breaking it down into an easily modified script we can use again and again!

The R Form Mailer

Long the domain (in the world of business) of "Mail Merge" in Microsoft Office, or dedicated software, sending out mass emails can be a challenge to an intrepid office worker. While Mail Merge does a good job and is very customizable, it also takes time to set up and can be difficult to modify in a hurry. It's also nearly impossible to script.

R, however, does not have those limitations. Imagine a scenario where we need to email out sales commissions for the week. We've got a spreadsheet with each salesperson's name (in this case, my alternative identities), their gross sales, and their commission rate. We could have a very simple CSV (comma-separated values) file that looks like this:

```
lastname,firstname,commission-rate,gross-sales,email_address
West, Jon, 1.5, 1500, jon@jonwestfall.com
Westfall, Prof Jon, 3.25, 1000, jwestfall@deltastate.edu
```

Jon West, who likes to shorten his last name so it's easier to reserve tables at restaurants, sold $1500 in product last week and has a 1.5x commission rate (because my business is about to go out of business, I pay people more than they bring in each week. My bad business practices should not be copied by you!). My professor identity gets even more money. It's a good thing I'm using an open source product, because I won't have much money left after I pay out more than I'm taking in. (Or do I just have a whole salesforce that I pay much lower commission rates? Probably!)

Taking a look at the following code, we can see that it borrows from our generic mailing earlier to create a series of emails and then send them out:

```
library("gmailr");
library("dplyr");
library("purrr");

gm_auth_configure(path="client_secret.json");
form_data <- read.csv("form-mail.csv");
```

```
## Calculate commissions
form_data$commission <- form_data$commission.rate * form_data$gross.sales;

##
msg_from <- "Jon Westfall <doctorwestfall@gmail.com>"
body <- "Hi, %s. Your commission for this week is %s."

# Uses the mutate() function from dplyr to insert the correct variables.
sending_data <- form_data %>%
  mutate(
    To = sprintf('%s <%s>', paste(firstname, lastname), email_address),
    From = msg_from,
    Subject = sprintf('Sales Commission for %s', firstname),
    body = sprintf(body, firstname, commission)) %>%
    select(To, From, Subject, body)

# Use the pmap() function and safely function from "purrr" package.
emails <- sending_data %>%
  pmap(mime)

send_message_safe <- safely(send_message)
sent_mail <- emails %>%
  map(send_message_safe)
```

Reading from top down, we first see that we are loading three libraries, gmailr, dplyr, and purrr. Their use will be discussed as follows.

Next, we load in our Gmail credentials and the CSV file that has our form mails. Then I calculate my commissions by multiplying my very generous rates by my grow sales.

Moving along, we get to the portion of the email that has our From header as well as our body. Since we're inserting information into the body based on each line, we need a function to help accomplish that. We'll use the mutate() function from dplyr as well as the base sprintf() function.

Finally, we use two functions from the purrr() package to format the email into MIME and then to send it out. The safely() function provides a bit of redundancy in case one email in the middle of a large job has an error. The results can be seen in the Outlook emails in Figures 6-37 and 6-38.

Sales Commission for Jon

Jon Westfall <doctorwestfall@gmail.com>   Today at 2:54 PM

To: Jon West

Hi, Jon. Your commission for this week is 2250.

Figure 6-37. *Sales Commissions 1*

[EXT]: Sales Commission for Prof Jon

● Jon Westfall <doctorwestfall@gmail.com>   Today at 2:54 PM

To: Jon Westfall

External Email

Hi, Prof Jon. Your commission for this week is 3250.

Figure 6-38. *Sales Commissions 2*

In researching for this chapter, it should be noted the excellent blog post by Artur Hebda at the Mailtrap.io blog (`https://blog.mailtrap.io/r-send-email/`). It provides a few nice tweaks to my simplified examples earlier, including tracking success and failures of the sent email and exporting the finished emails to a CSV file before they are sent as a record of exactly what was sent to each person. The blog post also covers some of the other R email packages and gives example code. Their service, Mailtrap, is also very interesting – I'll discuss it more here in the final section of this chapter.

Once you have your basic form mail setup going, you can think about ways to extend it. In our preceding example, we calculated a simple commission value. Here are some more complicated things that are possible:

- Collecting the times everyone is available to meet via a Google Form, downloading the data from Google Sheets via a CSV link (as outlined in Chapter 2), and looking for the most commonly available time – then emailing out everyone with the results.

- Opening a report that is generated nightly and stored on your server and emailing encrypted copies of it to partners outside your company that don't have access to the server directly.

- Drawing a winning raffle ticket number and then emailing all of the raffle winners and losers with the results.

- Downloading quiz responses from Google Forms, grading them, and then emailing students with their grades. A lot is possible, and much of it can be done without a lot of modification. I'd encourage you to think about how you might be able to use R anytime you're sending more than three emails out that are very similar. Could you script them?

Useful Email Services

As mentioned earlier, researching for this chapter uncovered a lot of interesting packages and use scenarios for R when it comes to email. I also was able to find a few services that would be especially useful to you when testing out these scripts as well as when sending mail in general. They include

- SMTP2GO (`https://smtp2go.com`) is an SMTP delivery service. It allows you to send your email through their well-established and reliable servers to users across the Internet. I've used their free plan for several years on my virtual private servers, which allow applications on my servers to email anyone on the net without fear of being a false positive in a spam filter. Prior to using their service, I'd have to configure the SMTP server on my servers to send directly, which usually meant that once or twice a year (or more), I'd be tweaking settings because my email was either bouncing back or it was getting silently dropped – a very annoying situation to be in for a mail administrator, but even worse for a programmer without mail administration background!

- Mailtrap (`https://mailtrap.io`) is an email playground, for lack of a better term. Imagine having a self-contained email system that you could use when testing out your application or script, without worrying that you would accidentally send an email to a real person and confuse or scare them. It collects all of the email that you're sending, puts them in special inboxes that you specify, and lets you see how the email looks as if you were the user that received it – very useful when testing out email scripts to make sure they aren't sending misformed or horrendously laid out emails!

- Mailgun (`https://mailgun.com`) offers a lot of services that interface with email, including regular delivery and tracking. What makes it useful and gives it the "gun" in its name is the Burst Sending feature, which can send over 1.2 million emails in a minute. If you're building a system that alerts users and time is of the essence, Mailgun might be an option that will help you get the word out – quickly!

- Mailchimp (`https://mailchimp.com`) is one of the leading email newsletter providers, which also offers a free tier to lower volume users. While you cannot send mail through Mailchimp in R, there are a series of tools on GitHub (`https://github.com/sckott/chimpr`) that allow you to query Mailchimp in R to get information on your subscribers, campaigns, and more.

Email is an essential service for many, and it makes sense that you might find it useful to integrate into R. However, it's not the only way to communicate information into the world. In the next chapter, we'll discuss how to use R when building a presentation to seamlessly incorporate information in. And later in the book, in Chapter 9, we'll talk about push notifications through a product named Pushover, which can be faster than email and more robust. Email is just the beginning of where you can use R to increase your productivity!

## CHAPTER 7

Project 4: The R Powered Presentation

Years ago, I was asked by a colleague to give a presentation to a group of my peers on statistical reliability and validity. It was at the end of a "retreat" day that was also a Friday – at 3:00 PM. Nobody wants to give or be in a presentation at 3:00 PM on a Friday for any reason. Yet it was the situation I was in.

In an attempt to make the presentation more interesting and engaging, I decided to put in two "live data" demonstrations. In one, participants would be assessing face validity of items presented, and in another, they would be counting the number of times that a friend's six-year-old daughter made pronunciation errors in a pre-recorded video. For the pronunciation example, I wanted to calculate a measure of interrater reliability based on a published paper. Interrater reliability refers to how often experts agree with one another when rating something subjectively. The higher the value, the easier to show that experts agree not only on what they're viewing but also the criteria by which to rate it.

This posed a bit of a problem, in that the calculation on the live data was something a little more complex than could be done on a hand calculator in front of the group. So I turned to R. In this chapter, I'll walk you through creating and giving a live data presentation, in which your participants are able to give a rating while sitting in their seats, and you are able, as the presenter, to show their results nearly instantly. I can't say for sure that this woke up my 3:00 PM Friday crowd years ago, but I can say that it was well received by those who asked me to give the talk!

© Jon Westfall 2020
J. Westfall, *Practical R 4*, https://doi.org/10.1007/978-1-4842-5946-7_7

The Setup

Before we can address the task at hand, we'll need to do a little bit of thinking and preparing. The first task is, simply, deciding what you'd want to incorporate into your presentation. A few thoughts come to mind:

- Like my example, having individuals give rating data or opinion data and calculating or tabulating results to share with the group. Simple polling all the way up to complex multi-part assessments could be done this way.

- Quizzing and testing could be done this way as well – think about offering a test preparation course that requires you to assess where your students are struggling each day. The students could take an end-of-day quiz, and the teachers could meet 10 minutes later to review them as a group.

- Analyzing live analytics data could be done by connecting R straight to the analytics source. Imagine launching a product and having daily meetings with the same metrics each day. R could create a new PowerPoint each day with the new data and email it out (see Chapter 6) automatically.

- On a lighter note, R includes packages for some pretty interesting diversions, including the `casino` package that allows you to play poker, blackjack, or a slot machine. One could track their gameplay and produce a presentation to share with co-workers on the perils of gambling.

Thinking about your own task is the first step, and after that, one needs to consider how to get the data and where to analyze it.

Methods of Getting Data

There are a few ways one might want to get the data into R to analyze in real time. Here are a few suggestions:

- Real-time data entry: Simply going around a room and asking each person for their result and typing it into a spreadsheet or even directly into the R script using the Input method mentioned in Chapter 2. This really is only useful if you are collecting a small amount of data and you don't mind people broadcasting it out to others.

- Data entry through a survey service that can export to CSV: This is the method I chose for the following example. I set up a very quick Google Forms spreadsheet that I connected to a Google Sheet and then got the Google Sheet CSV file results (as mentioned in Chapter 2). More robust survey systems could also be employed such as LimeSurvey (see Chapter 3) or a commercial alternative. If it can export to a "live" link or you can download a file from it, it could conceivably be your source. I might stay away from some purpose-driven options though, such as tools that integrate into PowerPoint to run polls. They often don't support downloading of data in an automated way (or sometimes in any way!).

- Data retrieval from a database: As discussed in Chapter 2, this might be your best bet if your data is constantly changing and you want to take a quick "snapshot" of it every day. At my workplace, we have a report that is generated each day for the first 15 days of the academic semester and then emailed to a set of individuals. That could be automated completely in R.

One caveat to live data, however, is that it must be "cleaned" in some way. For example, years ago I asked students to enter their pulse, in beats per minute, into a Google Form. I found that even with very explicit instructions, I would still get more information than just a two- or three-digit number. Think "89 bpm", "89 beats per minute", "89bpm", "89beats", and so on instead of simply "89". R can clean up some of this data *if* you can predict what problems you'll have. However, it's always possible that someone in your audience will come up with a new way to misform their data before it gets to your spreadsheet.

Now that we've talked about sources of your data, let's talk about the computer needs you might have in analyzing it.

Computing Needs

Depending on your technology setup, you may need to do a lot or a little planning before you run your presentation. I'll outline the easiest to the most difficult in the following table:

Scenario	Presentation Runs Off...	Setup Needed
Best case	Your sufficiently powerful laptop	Basic connectivity to projector and audio. R running on your laptop with the script and packages ready to go. Tool to open PowerPoint presentation and project
Second best	A powerful dedicated presentation computer that you can install software on	You can access the computer early and install R and script/packages that you'll need. Testing will need to be done to make sure the script runs.
Mediocre	Your underpowered laptop	If your laptop cannot crunch the numbers fast enough, you may want to investigate using RStudio Server, which I'll discuss in Chapter 8, to run the analysis somewhere else. You can then download the file it creates to project on your slower computer.
Somewhat painful	A underpowered or locked down dedicated presentation computer	In this scenario, you'll probably want to bring your own laptop or remotely connect to your computer to run the analysis and create the file. Dropping the file into cloud storage would then allow you to open it on the dinosaur computer you're stuck with.
Excruciating	An underpowered/locked down dedicated presentation computer without network access in a room without Wi-Fi or cell signal	In this case, you're probably not going to be able to create a live data presentation. If your participants can connect, you might be able to run the analysis through your smartphone or laptop and then report it verbally to the group.

Different businesses and locations have different ways of connecting; however, as you can see from the table, there are ways you can off-load some of the processing power needed to other systems. The processing power most likely won't be very extreme; however, I've worked on a few shared presentation computers that struggle to open PowerPoint!

Now that you've got the setup ready, let's walk through getting and analyzing the data!

Getting and Analyzing the Data

As I mentioned earlier, my presentation revolved around calculating a measure of interrater reliability called the Single Score Intraclass Correlation. To get my data, I first showed the slide in Figure 7-1 to let them know what to count.

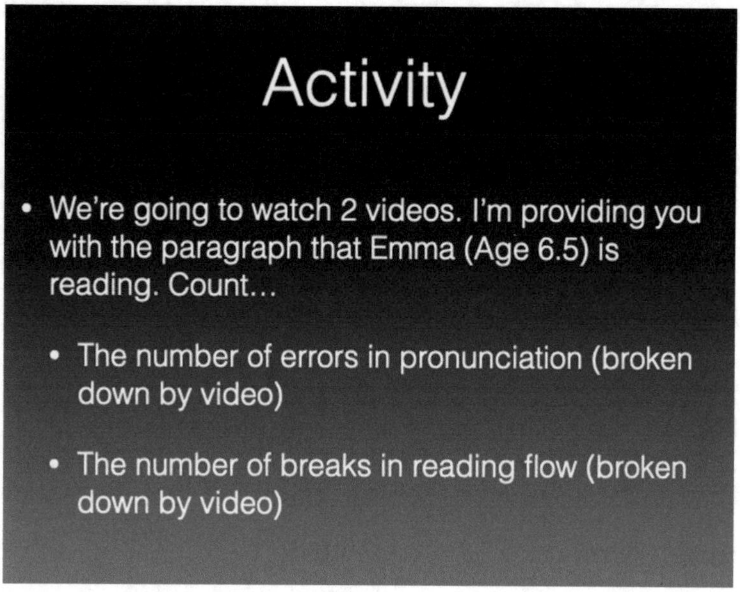

Figure 7-1. *Presentation Slide of Instructions*

We then watched both videos. After the videos, I provided a link to the group that took them to the Google Form in Figure 7-2, which my participants then took on their phones or tablets.

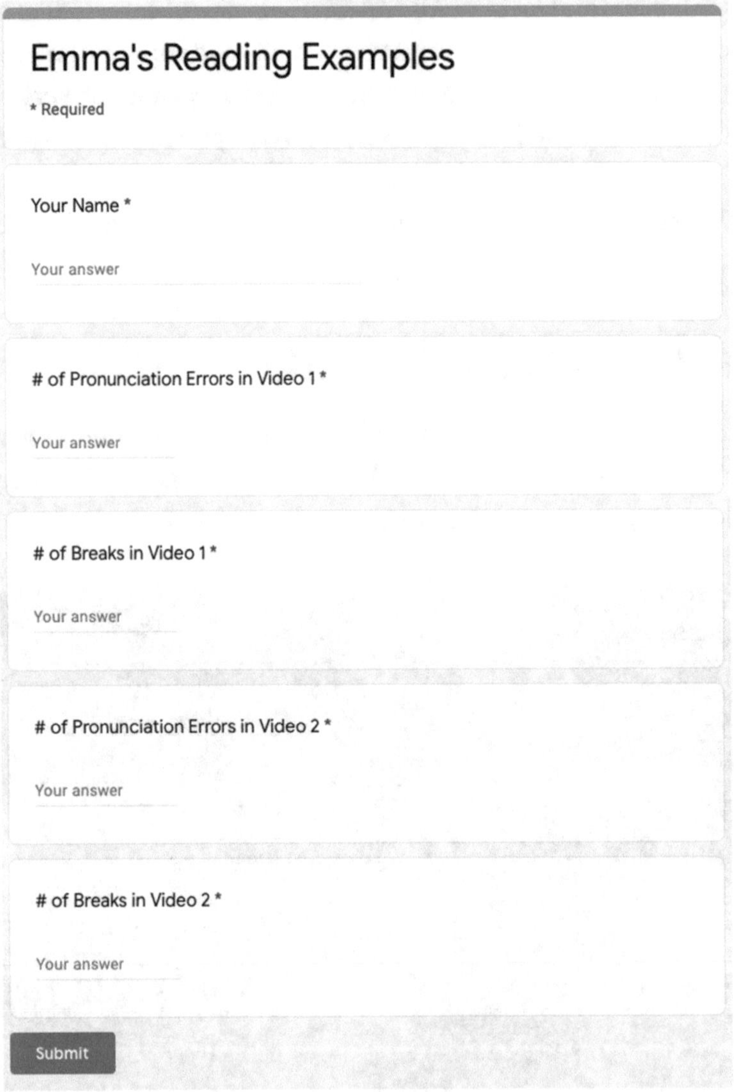
Emma's Reading Examples

* Required

Your Name *

Your answer

# of Pronunciation Errors in Video 1 *

Your answer

# of Breaks in Video 1 *

Your answer

# of Pronunciation Errors in Video 2 *

Your answer

# of Breaks in Video 2 *

Your answer

Submit

Figure 7-2. *Google Form*

Because my participants had two videos to watch, one in which Emma read a simple paragraph and one in which she read a more difficult paragraph. I not only wanted the overall Single Score Intraclass Correlation but also wanted to break it down by video. I also wanted to print out the raw values from each person who rated the videos, so that I could use those as I discussed the results.

The following code is what I used to take the data from Google Forms and analyze it. Your code will almost certainly look different; however, I'm providing this code as it reshapes the Google Forms data into a long format from its original wide shape (see Chapter 5).

```
## Interrater Statistics
## Original Article in http://www.ncbi.nlm.nih.gov/pmc/articles/PMC3402032/
##
## Enter Data
data <- read.csv("PATH_TO_CSV_FILE");
## Take out Test Data
data <- data[-c(1:5),]
data <- data[,c(3:7)]
names(data) <- c("Rater","Pronunciation1","Breaks1","Pronunciation2","Breaks2");
library(reshape)
library(irr)
mdata <- melt(data,id.vars="Rater");
mdata$video <- NA;
mdata$video <- ifelse(mdata$variable == "Pronunciation1","EasyEmma",mdata$video);
mdata$video <- ifelse(mdata$variable == "Breaks1","EasyEmma",mdata$video);
mdata$video <- ifelse(is.na(mdata$video),"HardEmma",mdata$video);
mdata$score <- NA;
mdata$score <- ifelse(mdata$variable == "Pronunciation1","Pronunciation",
mdata$score);
mdata$score <- ifelse(mdata$variable == "Pronunciation2","Pronunciation",
mdata$score);
mdata$score <- ifelse(is.na(mdata$score),"Breaks",mdata$score);
mdata <- mdata[,-2]
## Pronunciation Data Only
pro <- subset(mdata,score == "Pronunciation");
br <- subset(mdata,score=="Breaks");
easyemma <- subset(mdata,video == "EasyEmma");
hardemma <- subset(mdata,video == "HardEmma");
pro <- pro[,-4];
```

```
br <- br[,-4];
easyemma <- easyemma[,-3];
hardemma <- hardemma[,-3];
pro <- cast(pro,video~Rater);
br <- cast(br,video~Rater);
easyemma <- cast(easyemma,score~Rater);
hardemma <- cast(hardemma,score~Rater);
# Looking at task, pronunciation or breaks. Higher correlation = easier to rate
print(head(pro));
print(icc(pro,model="oneway",type="consistency",unit="single"));
print(head(br));
print(icc(br,model="oneway",type="consistency",unit="single"));
print(head(easyemma));
print(icc(easyemma,model="oneway",type="consistency",unit="single"));
print(head(hardemma));
print(icc(hardemma,model="oneway",type="consistency",unit="single"));
```

My output looked like this:

```
> print(head(pro));
      video rtr1 rtr2 rtr3 rtr4 rtr5 rtr6 rtr7 rtr8 rtr9
1 EasyEmma    3    2         3    0    0    0    0    4    3
2 HardEmma    5    9         7    4   10    5    5    7   14
> print(icc(pro,model="oneway",type="consistency",unit="single"));
 Single Score Intraclass Correlation

   Model: oneway
   Type : consistency

   Subjects = 2
     Raters = 9
     ICC(1) = 0.702

  F-Test, H0: r0 = 0 ; H1: r0 > 0
     F(1,16) = 22.2 , p = 0.000234

  95%-Confidence Interval for ICC Population Values:
   0.226 < ICC < 1
```

```
> print(head(br));
     video rtr1 rtr2 rtr3 rtr4 rtr5 rtr6 rtr7 rtr8 rtr9
1 EasyEmma   7     5          9     6  5  9    23  10   0
2 HardEmma   7     9          8     9 20 11    44  28  10
> print(icc(br,model="oneway",type="consistency",unit="single"));
 Single Score Intraclass Correlation

   Model: oneway
   Type : consistency

   Subjects = 2
     Raters = 9
     ICC(1) = 0.178

 F-Test, H0: r0 = 0 ; H1: r0 > 0
    F(1,16) = 2.94 , p = 0.105

 95%-Confidence Interval for ICC Population Values:
  -0.061 < ICC < 0.997
> print(head(easyemma));
          score rtr1 rtr2 rtr3 rtr4 rtr5 rtr6 rtr7 rtr8 rtr9
1        Breaks   7    5         9    6  5  9    23  10   0
2 Pronunciation   3    2         3    0  0  0     0   4   3
> print(icc(easyemma,model="oneway",type="consistency",unit="single"));
 Single Score Intraclass Correlation

   Model: oneway
   Type : consistency

   Subjects = 2
     Raters = 9
     ICC(1) = 0.474

 F-Test, H0: r0 = 0 ; H1: r0 > 0
    F(1,16) = 9.11 , p = 0.00815

 95%-Confidence Interval for ICC Population Values:
  0.052 < ICC < 0.999
> print(head(hardemma));
```

```
           score rtr1 rtr2 rtr3 rtr4 rtr5 rtr6 rtr7 rtr8 rtr9
1        Breaks   7    9         8    9  20  11   44  28   10
2 Pronunciation   5    9         7    4  10   5    5   7   14
> print(icc(hardemma,model="oneway",type="consistency",unit="single"));
 Single Score Intraclass Correlation

   Model: oneway
   Type : consistency

   Subjects = 2
     Raters = 9
     ICC(1) = 0.267

 F-Test, H0: r0 = 0 ; H1: r0 > 0
    F(1,16) = 4.28 , p = 0.0552

 95%-Confidence Interval for ICC Population Values:
  -0.035 < ICC < 0.998
```

Because I was going to be discussing this data with my colleagues, I did not put them directly into the PowerPoint presentation. However, in the next section, I will do exactly that by using a rather robust and useful package in R named officer.

Creating the PowerPoint Presentation

Now we're going to take the data that we've calculated and generate a PowerPoint presentation from it. I've gone step by step in the following, and the full code may be found in the code download for this book.

First, we might want something attractive. Recently, Microsoft has introduced a "Design Ideas" area into PowerPoint – powered by AI that attempts to provide a dynamic template that suits your presentation. As you can see in Figure 7-3, opening PowerPoint shows these design ideas before anything is even entered.

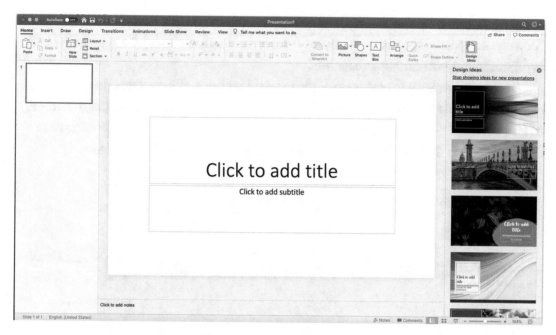

Figure 7-3. *Microsoft PowerPoint with Design Ideas*

I like those ideas, but nothing really screams "Data Analysis" to me. So I'll just enter the name of the presentation ("Data Presentation") and what do you know – the ideas changed to those in Figure 7-4. I like the second one, so I'll choose that.

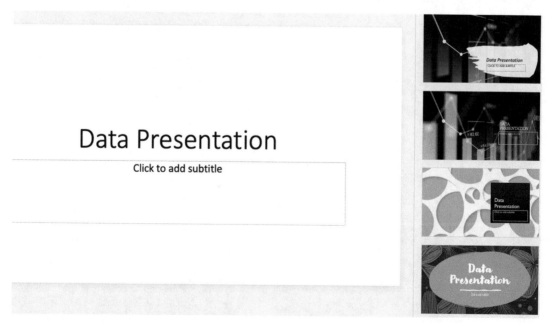

Figure 7-4. *Design Ideas for "Data Presentation"*

Now that we have the presentation template, I'll save the file and name it "powerpoint.pptx" (because sometimes I run out of fun filenames). I've placed it inside my RStudio project named "PresenteR".

Of course, because "pptx" is not a file format that normally contains data, R doesn't exactly know how to handle it at first. Thankfully, there is an excellent package named `officer` (Figure 7-5) that can work with office documents within R. As you can see in Figure 7-6, it has a number of commands for working with PowerPoint files.

Figure 7-5. *The homepage of the officer package*

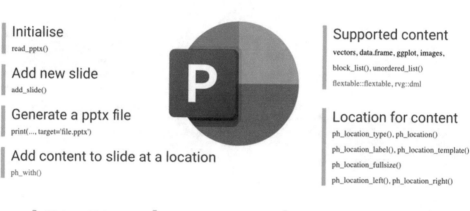

Figure 7-6. *The commands available for Powerpoint*

In Figure 7-7, you can see what happens when we install the package and load up the PowerPoint file that we just created. The `officer` package reads the presentation and tells us the layouts available to us and the template that they are using.

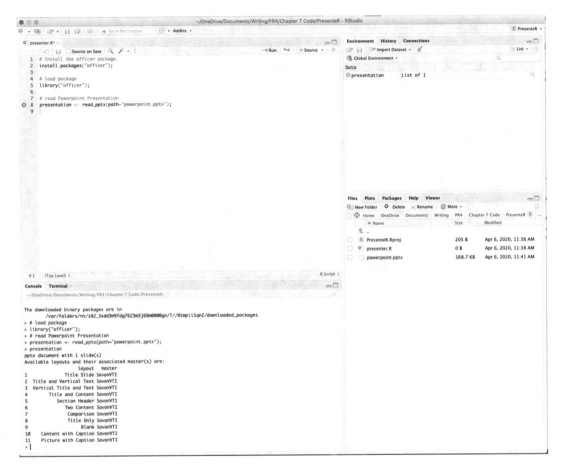

Figure 7-7. *Reading a PowerPoint File in R*

From here, we simply need to add a few features. First, I'm going to recreate my slide from Figure 7-1, giving the instructions to my audience. I'll do this by adding a slide and putting the text on to it using this code:

```
# Add new slide
presentation <- add_slide(presentation, layout="Title and Content",
master="SavonVTI");
# Modify new slide to have a title.
presentation <- on_slide(presentation, index=2)
presentation <- ph_with(presentation, value = "Activity", location =
ph_location_type(type = "title"))
presentation <- ph_with(presentation, value = c(We're going to watch 2
videos. I'm providing you with the paragraph that Emma (Age 6.5) is reading.
```

Count...", "The number of errors in pronunciation (broken down by video)","The number of breaks in reading flow (broken down by video)"), location = ph_location_type(type = "body"))

You can see the output of this slide in Figure 7-8.

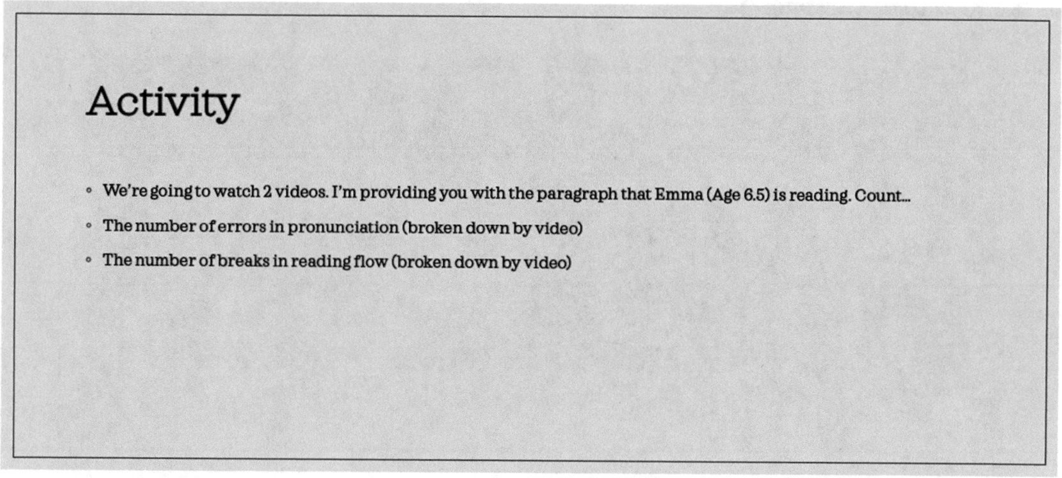

Figure 7-8. *Output of Introduction Slide*

Next, I'd like to add in the overall data tables for each dependent variable – pronunciation and number of breaks. I can do that with this next snippet of code:

```
presentation <- add_slide(presentation, layout="Title and Content",
master="SavonVTI");
presentation <- on_slide(presentation, index=3)
presentation <- ph_with(presentation, value = "Overall Ratings of
Pronunciation", location = ph_location_type(type = "title"))
presentation <- ph_with(presentation, value = pro, location = ph_location_
label(ph_label = "Content Placeholder 2") )

presentation <- add_slide(presentation, layout="Title and Content",
master="SavonVTI");
presentation <- on_slide(presentation, index=4)
presentation <- ph_with(presentation, value = "Overall Ratings of Breaks",
location = ph_location_type(type = "title"))
presentation <- ph_with(presentation, value = br, location = ph_location_
label(ph_label = "Content Placeholder 2") )
```

The output of these slides can be found in Figure 7-9. You'll notice the table overshot the slide a bit in Figure 7-9. I simply grabbed the lower edge and resized to fit the slide in Figure 7-10 – a simple 1-second fix, which is a bit annoying but not difficult. The `officer` package unfortunately has some issues properly sizing data tables. There are options you might want to explore that can reformat the tables before placing them into a slide, such as the `flexible` package.

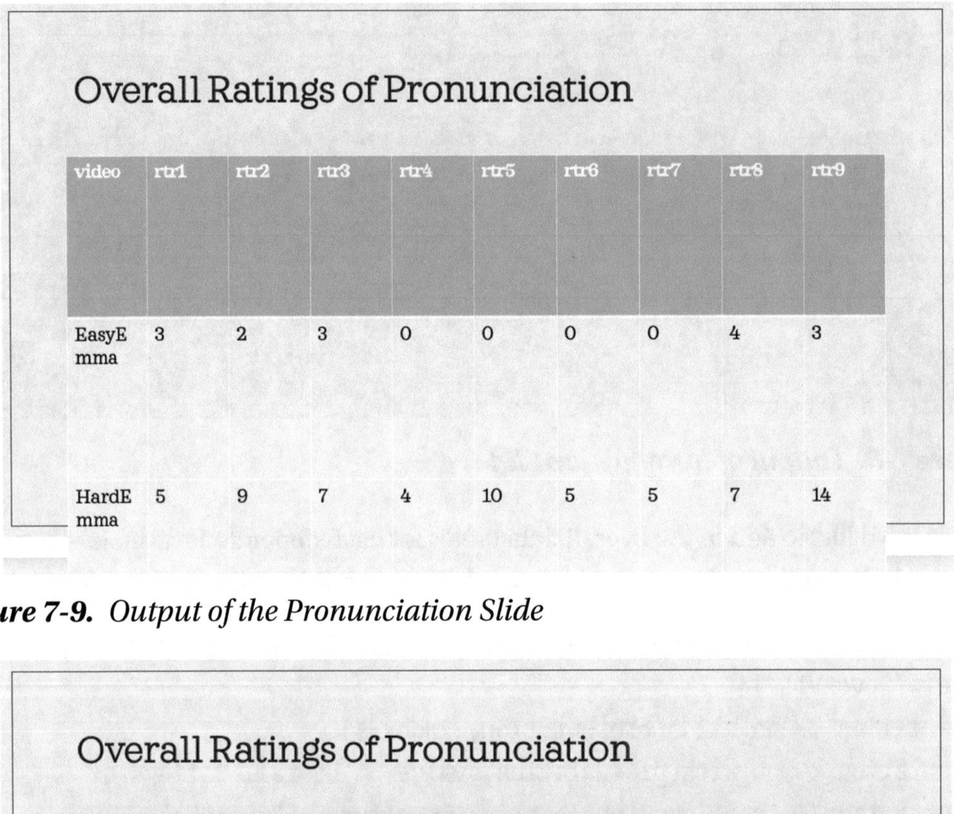

Figure 7-9. *Output of the Pronunciation Slide*

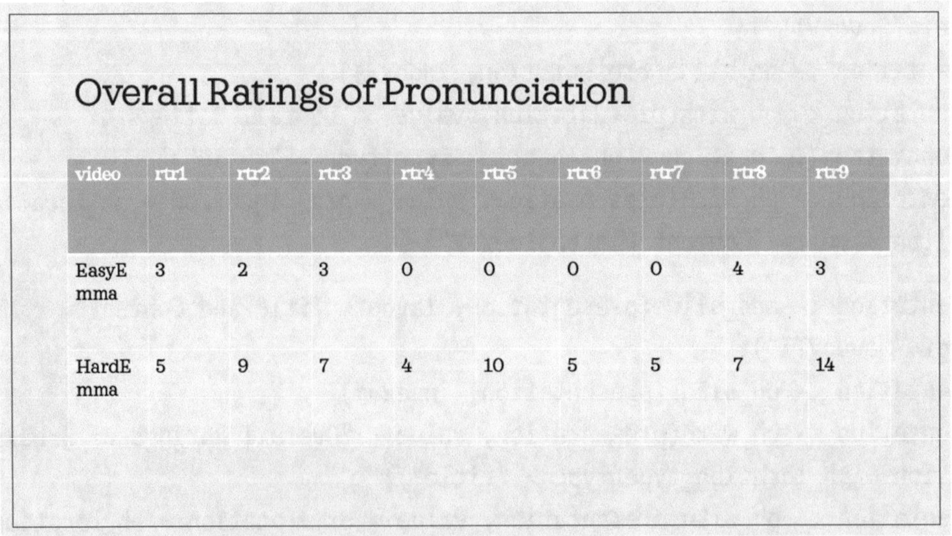

Figure 7-10. *Output of the Pronunciation Slide, Fixed*

Now we're rolling. Next, we'll tackle adding in the results of the Single Score Intraclass Correlation. I could do this by simply outputting the results, but I'll format it to be a little more English-readable by accessing the elements of the output of the icc() function.

```
proicc <- icc(pro,model="oneway",type="consistency",unit="single");
bricc <- icc(br,model="oneway",type="consistency",unit="single");
presentation <- add_slide(presentation, layout="Title and Content",
master="SavonVTI");
presentation <- on_slide(presentation, index=5)
presentation <- ph_with(presentation, value = "Results of the ICC
Calculations", location = ph_location_type(type = "title"))
presentation <- ph_with(presentation, value = c(sprintf("The Pronunciation
ICC is %s, with an ANOVA results of F(%s,%s)=%s, p = %s", round(proicc$value,
digits=2), round(proicc$df1, digits=2), round(proicc$df2, digits=2),
round(proicc$Fvalue, digits=2), round(proicc$p.value, digits=2)),sprintf("The
Breaks ICC is %s, with an ANOVA results of F(%s,%s)=%s, p = %s",
round(bricc$value, digits=2), round(bricc$df1, digits=2), round(bricc$df2,
digits=2), round(bricc$Fvalue, digits=2), round(bricc$p.value, digits=2))),
location = ph_location_type(type = "body"))
```

The output to this slide can be seen in Figure 7-11, in human-readable form!

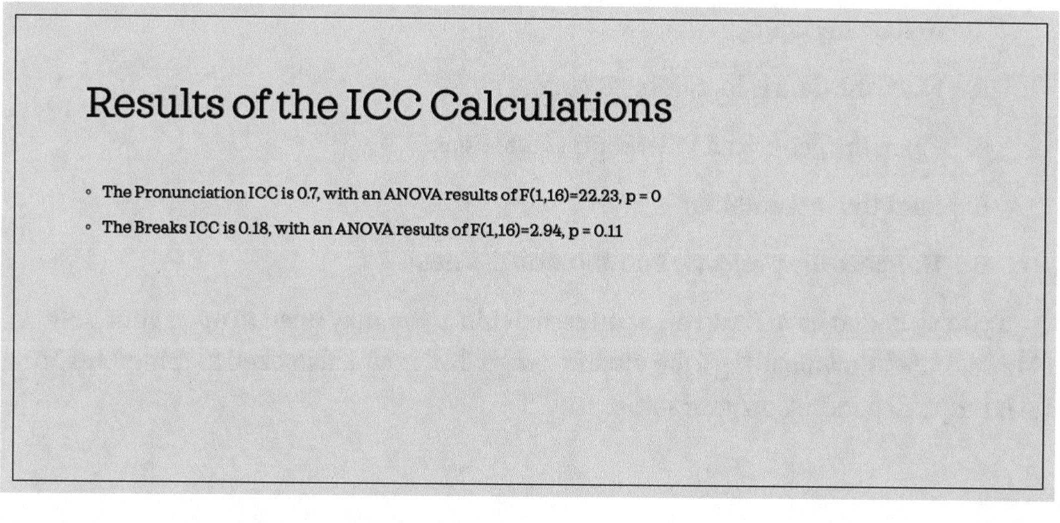

Results of the ICC Calculations

- The Pronunciation ICC is 0.7, with an ANOVA results of F(1,16)=22.23, p = 0
- The Breaks ICC is 0.18, with an ANOVA results of F(1,16)=2.94, p = 0.11

Figure 7-11. *Output of ICC Slide*

Finally, once I'm done making my slides, I can compile them into a PowerPoint show with the following line of code:

```
print(presentation, target="completed-powerpoint.pptx");
```

At this point, one could simply continue adding as much or as little information as they like. The example pages for the `officer` package show how to add graphics, images, and more depending on what you'd like to show off. Another added benefit of creating your PowerPoint presentation like this is that you can easily create batches of slides with minimal code changes. Perfect for long reports that contain a lot of repetition! You can also combine what we've done here with what we've seen in earlier chapters, such as email the presentation directly to someone.

Now that you've got your code all set, let's talk about presentation flow!

The Flow of the Presentation

Now that everything is set, the basic flow of your presentation is as follows:

1. Build a normal slide deck of slides to start your presentation. Once you get to the point that you want your audience to participate, tell them how to do so (e.g., Google Forms link? Read off their answers, etc.).

2. Generally, I freeze the display on the instructions and switch over to R on my laptop.

3. Once the data is in, run the R code.

4. Open the generated PowerPoint slide deck.

5. Start the presentation.

6. Unfreeze the projector and show off the data.

If you've had to have R run on another machine, you may need to open your new slide deck after downloading from cloud storage. You might also need to remotely run the R script, depending on your setup.

And that's it – we've successfully embedded nearly live data into our R-generated PowerPoint presentation. If you don't use PowerPoint, preferring other formats, then earlier examples of using RMarkdown might be better for you to create a PDF or Word version to share. However you do it, it is tremendously powerful to show an audience their own data, whatever point you're trying to make.

This brings us to the last section of our book. In the next chapter, we'll talk about R running without some of the limitations we've discussed so far (e.g., running on your laptop, not accessible on iOS or a Chromebook, hard to collaborate with others, etc.). We'll be running R on a server, away from your computer, in a space that you and others can easily access from nearly anywhere. We'll also talk about other ways to show off data, using a product called Shiny. We're taking R anywhere we need to be!

CHAPTER 8

R Anywhere

As we've seen in the first two parts of this book, R can really help you in very noticeable ways: formatting and manipulating data, analyzing complex problems and relationships, and even automating some of your daily tasks. One problem, though, is that we have to actually have a computer running R in order to do these things. As I mentioned very far back in Chapter 1, R runs on a lot of systems – Macs, Windows PCs, Linux desktops and servers, some android devices, and even devices like a Raspberry Pi. But it doesn't run everywhere. It can be frustrating in a time when many people are turning to Chromebooks, and Apple iOS devices, to not have R. And even if R runs on your device, you need to be physically at your device to run something, and a longer job may mean that your computer is tied up for hours chugging away at something. In this chapter, we'll discuss a way around this limitation – putting R "in the cloud" or (in other terms), somewhere else and remotely accessing it. We'll see that there are some really useful tools that help us achieve that, and all we need is a spare computer at home, a virtual private server on the Internet, or even a cloud computing service account like Amazon Web Services!

The Basics: What We're Doing, and Where We're Doing It

In this first portion of the chapter, we need to talk about our overall goal and how we can accomplish that with appropriate software and hardware or cloud resources. Let's start with the software products in question and then move on to where we might run them and access them.

© Jon Westfall 2020
J. Westfall, *Practical R 4*, https://doi.org/10.1007/978-1-4842-5946-7_8

Software

Here's the software you'll need in order to achieve your R Anywhere dream. Along the way, I've given my tips and tricks for getting it installed.

R

Well, this one was kind of obvious. Using the instructions that I gave in Chapter 1, you should start by installing R on your target machine or cloud. R, by default, not only installs its graphical environment that we've used for several projects but also its command-line interface and its script interface, `rscript`. While it is not very pretty, it is functional to use R in a command-line environment, as I will discuss in a few moments in the following.

A bit of a caveat though to installing R on a machine that isn't sitting right in front of you, with your user account logged in, relates to packages. If you're installing R on a Unix-style machine, such as a Linux server, you'll need to think about the user account that is running R in the following examples. It may be sufficient for your user account to run R in all examples; thus, if you install packages that are in your local account, you won't have any issues. However, if you decide to use some of the more advanced R Anywhere tips as follows, such as running a Shiny Server, you may need to install packages as the `root` user so that they are available to all user accounts. Often tutorials on the Web will subtly indicate this by the command they tell you to run to install packages. As an example, the command provided to install the `shiny` package (discussed later) begins `sudo su` which executes the code as the `root` user on your machine.

If you don't realize that packages must be installed by `root` and available to all, you might find yourself in a maddening situation of knowing you installed a package using the `install.packages()` function in R, but having error logs that tell you the package cannot be loaded. Executing the code in your local user account will likely work fine, assuring your frustration as things look OK to you!

RStudio – Server

For a good portion of our book, we've used RStudio, an open source IDE for R. RStudio PBC, the company behind RStudio, also makes a version of RStudio named RStudio Server. A server in the sense that it typically runs on a computer that you designate as a server, I actually think of it more as RStudio Web. While the professional version offers a ton of resources around project sharing, multiple R versions and sessions, administrative and security tools, and auditing, the open source edition is perfect for an individual user or a small group. Here I've opened our PresenteR example from Chapter 7 in RStudio (Figure 8-1). Copying the R project files over to my RStudio Server, I log in (Figure 8-2) with my username and password and open the same project (Figure 8-3). As you can see, aside from the RData file not being read properly to restore the workspace, and a message that certain packages that I have required are not installed, things look pretty similar. The difference is, though, that I now have these files and interface running in a web server. Figure 8-4 is the same screen loaded up on my iPad – bringing R to a device that I formerly wouldn't have been able to use it on!

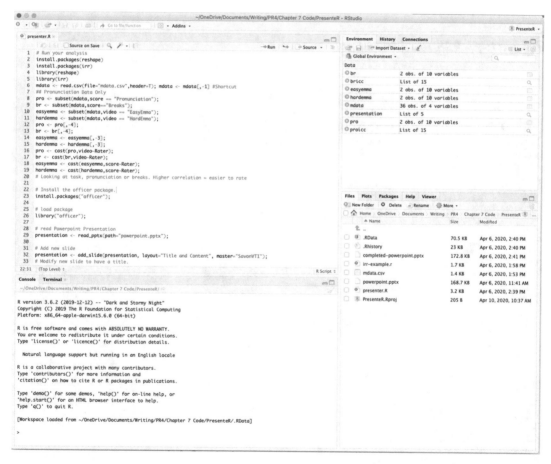

Figure 8-1. *PresenteR in RStudio Desktop*

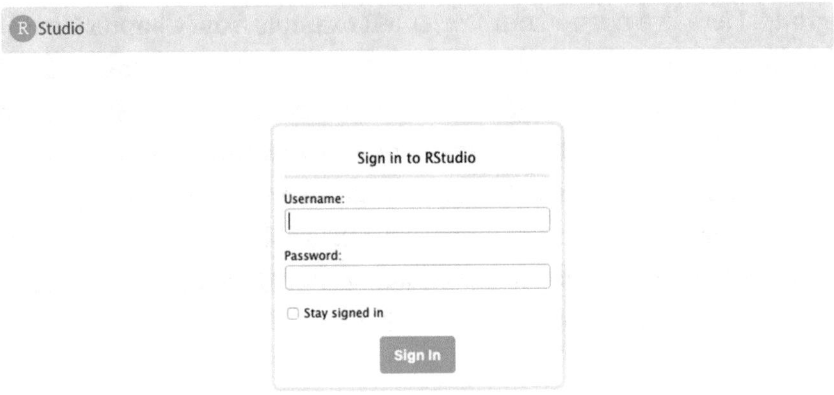

Figure 8-2. *RStudio Server Login*

Figure 8-3. *PresenteR in RStudio Server on a Desktop Computer*

Figure 8-4. *PresenteR in RStudio Server on an iPad*

One thing to note with RStudio Server is that it is limited to one browser connected to a session at a time. When I loaded up the server on my iPad, I found the error in Figure 8-5 on my desktop. Hitting reconnect got me back to my working session.

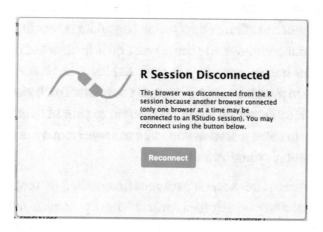

Figure 8-5. *Reconnect Error*

To install RStudio Server, you'll need to visit `https://rstudio.com/products/` `rstudio/download-server/` and choose your platform, the majority of which are Linux based. Theoretically, it is possible to install RStudio Server from source on a Windows or Mac, but it's probably easier to use RStudio Desktop on those machines and then use some sort of remote access tool (e.g., VNC, TeamViewer, RemotePC, etc.) to log into the desktop and run your R analyses. This also can be accomplished via those "hard to reach from" devices, such as an iPad or iPhone, although it will likely be difficult to access everything on, say, a 27″ monitor, on a 6″ iPhone screen!

Shiny Server

Shiny Server is another excellent tool from RStudio PBC. Imagine wanting to share data with the world, perhaps even allowing them to work with the data to visualize or analyze it however they choose. While you could create an RStudio Server interface that everyone logged into, that would likely be overkill. Shiny Server serves small R scripts called Shiny apps. These are interactive applications that display, manipulate, or analyze data so that the information the data pertains to is easier to understand to a person viewing a web page. In other words, it lets you grab the graph and change it to suit how you would best understand or explore the data.

Like RStudio Server, Shiny Server comes in two flavors – an open source edition and a professional version named RStudio Connect. One downloads Shiny Server by going to `https://rstudio.com/products/shiny/download-server/` and choosing your platform. There are a few issues that you will want to consider before you install and during your installation:

- The open source version of Shiny Server does not support any sort of native authentication or encryption (e.g., data is sent in cleartext between your computer and the server and is in cleartext on the server). This means that you can easily deploy it, but it also can be vulnerable to people snooping around your data. You'll want to either run your Shiny Server on an internal server to your network or find a secure way to serve just what you need to serve from it out onto the Internet through your firewall.

- Shiny Server requires several packages be installed by `root` in order to function properly (see earlier). These packages include `shiny` (obviously!), `rmarkdown`, and others. When I first installed

Shiny Server, the applets (i.e., small windows containing example programs) on the test page (shown in Figure 8-6) did not load at all. Tracking down the logs, which on a Debian or Ubuntu machine are housed in /var/log/shiny-server, revealed the missing packages to me. I then logged into R as root using the command sudo R and installed them. After that, the server was up and running.

- Shiny Server will, by default, serve files under a document root, such as /srv/shiny-server. These files are owned by root which can make it hard for regular user accounts to write and read them. You'll want to think about where you want to store your files so that you can easily update them as needed. You can modify the document root and the log document in /etc/shiny-server/shiny-server.conf, as seen in Figure 8-7. The Shiny Server documentation also addresses the issues of multiple users and how to allow everyone to have their own "publishing" space (e.g., off of their home directory or another central location on the server).

Welcome to Shiny Server!

If you're seeing this page, that means Shiny Server is installed and running. **Congratulations!**

What's Next?

Now you're ready to setup Shiny — if you haven't already — and start deploying your Shiny applications.

If you see a Shiny application running on the right side of this page, then Shiny is configured properly on your server and already running an example. Bravo! You can see this application on your server at /sample-apps/hello/.

If you see a gray box or an error message, then there's a bit more work to do to get Shiny running fully. You can continue with the installation instructions or use the Admin Guide for more information. If you're seeing an error message in the panel to the right, you can use it to help diagnose what may be wrong. If you think Shiny is installed and setup properly and things still aren't working, you can look in the Shiny Server log which may have more information about what's wrong. By default, the log is stored in `/var/log/shiny-server.log`.

If you're really stuck *and you've read the relevant sections in the Admin Guide* then please ask for help on our RStudio Community forum.

rmarkdown

Once you have Shiny working properly (the top application on the right sidebar), you can optionally proceed to setup rmarkdown to enable your server to host Shiny docs using the `rmarkdown` package.

Once you have `rmarkdown` installed, the lower example to the right should also be available. Once both examples are running, you're all set to host both Shiny applications and Shiny docs!

All Done?

Once you can see the Shiny application on the right, you're off to the races! You can look at shiny.rstudio.com to take a deeper dive into Shiny or take a look at some of the Shiny Server Quick Start Guides to learn about some of the different things Shiny Server can do.

When you're all setup, you can delete this page and/or the sample applications we installed for you if you don't want them anymore. You can delete this page by running `sudo rm /srv/shiny-server/index.html` or delete the sample applications by running `sudo rm -rf /srv/shiny-server/sample-apps`.

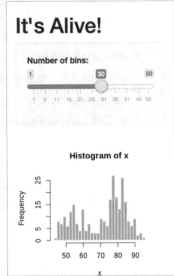

It's Alive!

Number of bins:

Histogram of x

When Shiny is properly configured on your server, you'll see a Shiny app above.

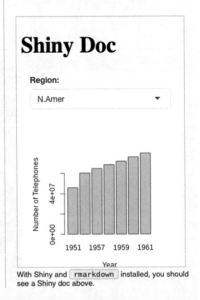

Shiny Doc

Region:

N.Amer

With Shiny and `rmarkdown` installed, you should see a Shiny doc above.

Figure 8-6. *Shiny Server Default Page*

```
jon@WestNix:/srv$ cat /etc/shiny-server/shiny-server.conf
# Instruct Shiny Server to run applications as the user "shiny"
run_as shiny;

# Define a server that listens on port 3838
server {
  listen 3838;

  # Define a location at the base URL
  location / {

    # Host the directory of Shiny Apps stored in this directory
    site_dir /srv/shiny-server;

    # Log all Shiny output to files in this directory
    log_dir /var/log/shiny-server;

    # When a user visits the base URL rather than a particular application,
    # an index of the applications available in this directory will be shown.
    directory_index on;
  }
}
```

Figure 8-7. *Shiny Server Configuration File*

As mentioned earlier, once Shiny Server is installed, you can visit its interface at, by default, port 3838 on your machine. If it's configured properly, the two example scripts at the right will load up their data as seen in more detail in Figures 8-8 and 8-9. Each of them can be adjusted by the user to show data differently. The example in Figure 8-8, a sample app named "hello", allows the user to adjust a slider to display data in different sized bins (as I've done in Figure 8-10). The example in Figure 8-9, a sample app named "rmd", demonstrates the use of RMarkdown to display the requested data. Changing the region in the drop-down box (Figure 8-11) changes the data as seen in Figure 8-12.

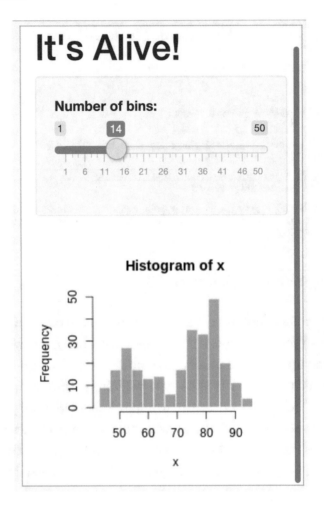

Figure 8-8. *hello app*

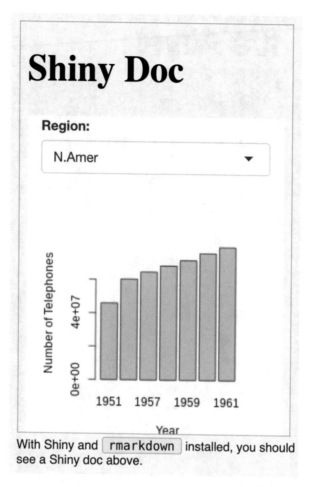

Figure 8-9. rmd App

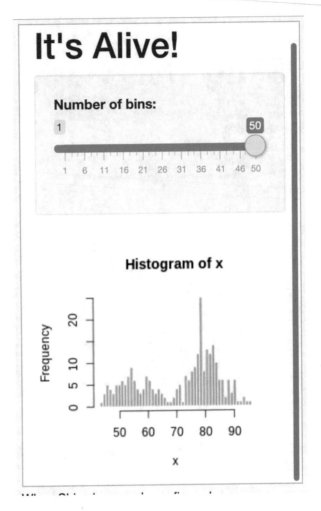

Figure 8-10. *Adjusting the bin size*

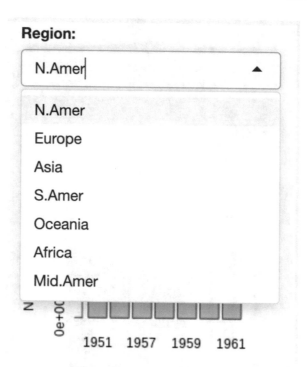

Figure 8-11. *Region Dropdown box Region Dropdown box*

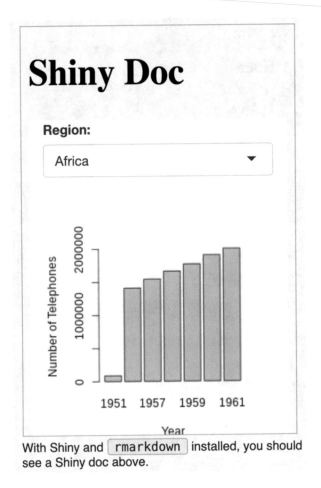

Figure 8-12. *New output for a new region*

If you think this looks like it would take a lot of work to create, it actually isn't as complex as it looks. Shiny apps consist of, at bare minimum, a function to tell Shiny Server what to do and an interface that tells Shiny Server how to display the data. We'll build a few simple Shiny apps in the following, and you can also jump in by viewing the tutorial video at https://shiny.rstudio.com/tutorial/.

R Packages

Finally, the last piece of software we're going to need are the R Packages that we use to create our applications or projects. Later on in this chapter, I'm going to highlight some of those packages in a section of ideas that you may want to investigate for your "always-on" R server.

Speaking of which, let's talk about where that R instance lives.

Hardware or Cloud

R Anywhere is only possible if R is *somewhere*. That somewhere might be a few different places, depending on your needs. Here are a few options, along with the pros and cons of each:

Option/ Location	Description	Pros	Cons
A computer you own/use	If you have an old computer lying around at home or work, you could install R, RStudio, and Shiny on it.	• Ability to access the hardware directly in case of issue • Physical security, you know exactly where your data is. • Easy to upgrade • Low cost	• May not have the fastest upload connection to the Internet, slowing down remote access • May not have full control over security, especially if the computer is at work – might not be able to access over the Internet or may need to set up and use a virtual private network (VPN; an encrypted connection between your location and your home or work network) • If the hardware is older, it may be more prone to fail or may take an exceedingly long time to perform simple tasks. • If you break it, you need to fix it – no one is available to call.

(continued)

Option/ Location	Description	Pros	Cons
A virtual private server (VPS)	Many Internet service providers and hosting providers offer virtual private servers or dedicated servers that you can customize as you like.	• You administer the server, but it's someone else's headache if the hardware fails. • Typically provides good connectivity to the Internet for both upload and download • May allow dynamic allocation of resources depending on the provider, so you can increase resources as you need them	• Requires knowledge of server administration and security • Seldom offers built-in backup functionality, requiring you to safeguard your own data and copies of it • Can be very pricey if you go with a well-established and reliable company (e.g., \$50/month) • Can be very inexpensive (e.g., \$12/year) if you go with a "low end" provider. This is a great option if you're comfortable with it, but a terrible option for a beginner who isn't aware of the risks.
A cloud service	Several cloud services, such as Amazon Web Services (AWS), Google Cloud Compute, and Microsoft's Azure support running R either natively or in a container (i.e., small self-contained set of files that can be easily moved) you'd create.	• Allows for rapid creation and deployment of R, RStudio, or Shiny • Provides a high level of reliability and functionality such as snapshot backups and dynamic resource allocation • Allows for easy sharing/copying of R projects	• Pricey if you take advantage of all of the services, although low cost options on par with a virtual private server are also available • Again, relies on you to do most of the administration. You have support options; however, they might not be as supportive as you need depending on your ability level.

(*continued*)

Option/ Location	Description	Pros	Cons
A portable device (e.g., a Raspberry Pi)	It is possible to run R on a device you take with you, such as an older laptop or an ultra-small form factor computing device like the Raspberry Pi.	• You literally are taking it with you anywhere you need to go, so Internet access is not required. • It could be powered in your bag to allow analyses to continue while you're on the move, using a portable battery. • Data is very safeguarded in that it's not connected to the Internet or only connected when you're using it. • Not going to lie – it's pretty cool to show off to friends!	• The computing requirements may be more than the device can handle. • You will need some way to interface with the device while on the go. An ad hoc wireless network or cabled interface. • It's another thing to carry, in a world where we increasingly want to be more portable!
RStudio Cloud	Recently RStudio PBC has started offering RStudio Cloud free of charge (Figure 8-13).	• Allows you to easily get started with RStudio and Shiny in the cloud • Allows for collaboration and easy sharing/ modifying of existing R projects	• In beta test now, and may not be free forever • Data uploaded is in the care of RStudio PBC, which means you may not be comfortable uploading sensitive data.

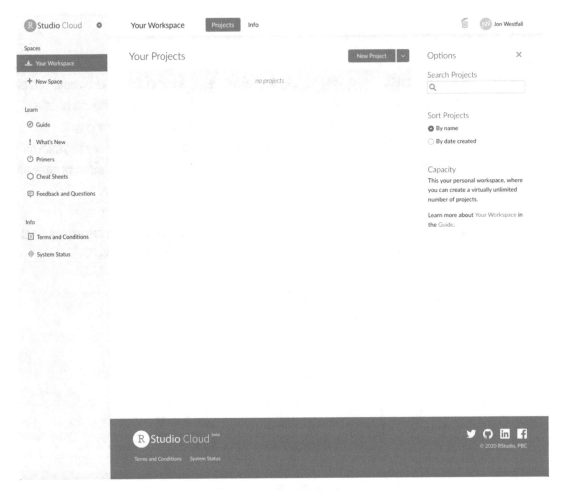

Figure 8-13. *RStudio Cloud Interface*

As you can see, there are a lot of options of where to put your RStudio or Shiny Server project. Not all options will be appropriate for everyone, and in some cases, you may have a bit of a hybrid. I could imagine hosting a simple project on RStudio Cloud that doesn't contain private data, hosting a multi-user collaborative project on a VPS or cloud service, and hosting my own "automation server" at home off of an old laptop. Since the software we're using is free from licensing costs, you might be able to run all three of those examples without spending little more than your time.

Use Scenarios

Now that we've covered what you can do and where you can do it, let's walk through a few examples. We'll cover the following three scenarios in a broad sense in this section. In the next section, Scripts to Tinker With, I'll provide three short projects that you could take and modify for your own use. Let's start with perhaps the simplest interface – the command line.

Command Line via SSH

Opening a command line either locally on your computer with R installed or remotely on another computer through a protocol like Secure Shell (SSH), you can run the easy-to-remember R command to start R (see Figure 8-14). While not pretty, it is very functional. Any device that supports an SSH client could therefore connect. Figure 8-15 shows the same interface through my SSH client, Prompt, on my iPhone. It's a bit small and cramped, for sure, but functional.

```
jon@WestNix:~$ R

R version 3.4.4 (2018-03-15) -- "Someone to Lean On"
Copyright (C) 2018 The R Foundation for Statistical Computing
Platform: x86_64-pc-linux-gnu (64-bit)

R is free software and comes with ABSOLUTELY NO WARRANTY.
You are welcome to redistribute it under certain conditions.
Type 'license()' or 'licence()' for distribution details.

  Natural language support but running in an English locale

R is a collaborative project with many contributors.
Type 'contributors()' for more information and
'citation()' on how to cite R or R packages in publications.

Type 'demo()' for some demos, 'help()' for on-line help, or
'help.start()' for an HTML browser interface to help.
Type 'q()' to quit R.

> █
```

Figure 8-14. *R in Command-Line*

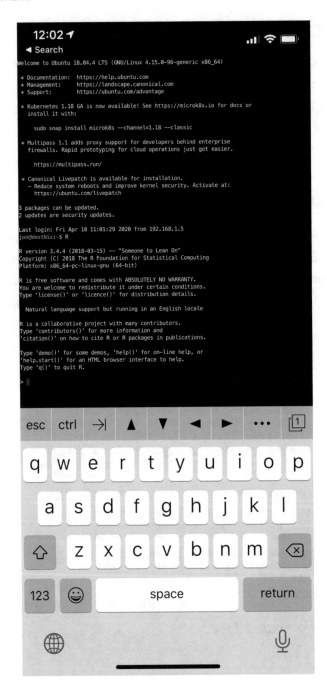

Figure 8-15. *R on the Prompt SSH client on an iPhone X*

Using this interface, I can execute basic R functions by typing them in. If I want to plan ahead, however, I can also write an R script that I can execute using the `rscript` command. The following script, named `test.R`, outputs Figure 8-16 when I run `rscript test.R`:

```
print("Hello World with Line Numbers")
cat("Hello World with a line break \n")
cat("Hello World without a line break")

cat("User Info \n")
cat("Your login name is ")
cat(Sys.getenv("LOGNAME"))
cat("\n")
```

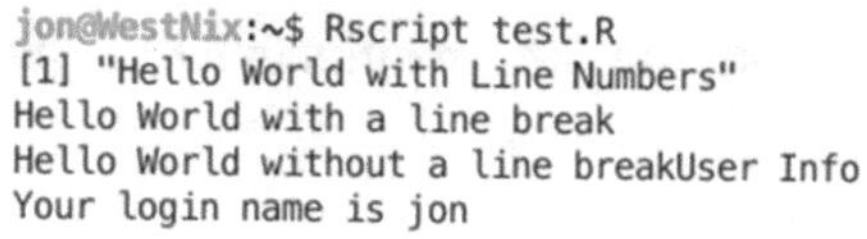

```
jon@WestNix:~$ Rscript test.R
[1] "Hello World with Line Numbers"
Hello World with a line break
Hello World without a line breakUser Info
Your login name is jon
```

Figure 8-16. *Output of test.R*

This script shows the basics of getting output from a script that's running in "headless" mode – meaning without interactivity by the user. Using the `print()` command outputs the text with a line number, which is what we're generally used to in R. However, if I wanted to print something without line numbers, I can use the `cat()` function. Adding \n inside my output creates a line break, which helps clean up the output a little bit.

We can get a little more fancy by modifying one of our earlier examples. In Chapter 2, we used the following example:

```
OurData = ("
Student Pretest Posttest
A 25 27
B 23 23
C 21 22
D 23 29
E 23 24
F 21 19
")
```

```
Data = read.table(textConnection(OurData),header=T)
t.test(Data$Pretest,Data$Posttest,paired=T)
```

Saving that and running it in R script, we get the output in Figure 8-17.

```
jon@WestNix:~/Ch8Code$ Rscript test2.R

        Paired t-test

data:  Data$Pretest and Data$Posttest
t = -1.2286, df = 5, p-value = 0.2739
alternative hypothesis: true difference in means is not equal to 0
95 percent confidence interval:
 -4.123069  1.456403
sample estimates:
mean of the differences
          -1.333333
```

Figure 8-17. *Output of the Paired T-Test*

Imagine that I'd like to output the t-test results in APA style vs. the full output. I could change the script to this:

```
OurData = ("
Student Pretest Posttest
A 25 27
B 23 23
C 21 22
D 23 29
E 23 24
F 21 19
")
Data = read.table(textConnection(OurData),header=T)
res <- t.test(Data$Pretest,Data$Posttest,paired=T)
cat(paste('The output is t(',res$parameter,')=',round(res$statistic,
digits=2),', p = ',round(res$p.value,digits=3),'\n',sep=""))
```

And the output can be seen in Figure 8-18.

```
jon@WestNix:~/Ch8Code$ Rscript test2.R
The output is t(5)=-1.23, p = 0.274
```

Figure 8-18. *Output of the Revised Script*

We can also pipe in arguments to the script from the command line. Here's our final iteration of the script:

```
args = commandArgs(trailingOnly=TRUE)
OurData = ("
Student Pretest Posttest
A 25 27
B 23 23
C 21 22
D 23 29
E 23 24
F 21 19
")
Data = read.table(textConnection(OurData),header=T)
res <- t.test(Data$Pretest,Data$Posttest,paired=T)
cat(paste('The output, ',args[1],', is t(',res$parameter,')=',round
(res$statistic, digits=2),', p = ',round(res$p.value,digits=3),'\n',sep=""))
```

Running `Rscript test2.R "Dear Reader"` provides the output in Figure 8-19.

```
jon@WestNix:~/Ch8Code$ Rscript test2.R "Dear Reader"
The output, Dear Reader, is t(5)=-1.23, p = 0.274
```

Figure 8-19. *Output with Piped Argument*

One can imagine how this might be useful when combining with the concepts we talked about in Chapters 6 and 7. Imagine having a series of pre-built presentations that require the use of live data. The data changes every day. A colleague, Bob, asks you to send him the most up-to-date version you have. You pull out your phone, log into your R server, and type a command similar to `Rscript presentation-email.R "bob@test.com"`. Within a few moments, a freshly written PowerPoint file (see Chapter 7) is sent to Bob (see Chapter 6) with the most up-to-date data pulled from a database server or public website (see Chapter 2). You may even through in some fancy analyses similar to what we did in Chapters 3 and 4 and include another attachment that is the formatted data (Chapter 5). Bob will likely be overwhelmed!

Command line, while powerful, is not everyone's cup of coffee or tea. Let's explore RStudio Server a bit more and see some interesting uses there.

Web Browser via RStudio Server

As mentioned earlier, RStudio Server can open RStudio Desktop projects and vice versa. Creating a new project in RStudio Server looks the same as when you do so in the desktop counterpart. Let's imagine a scenario where we want to get the top thread in the Reddit "Today I Learned" subreddit, and we'd like it every 15 minutes. Our code is pretty simple:

```
install.packages("later")
install.packages("jsonlite")
install.packages("curl")
library("later")
library("jsonlite")

gettoptil <- function() {
toptil <- "https://reddit.com/r/todayilearned/top/.json?count=20"
top.df <- fromJSON(toptil);
later(gettoptil,900) #Have this function call itself every 900 seconds (15 min).
return(cat("\n at ",format(Sys.time(),"%a %b %d %X %Y"), "the top TIL was:
",top.df$data$children$data$title[1]))
}

gettoptil() #Start the loop.
```

This code will download the top Today I Learned every 15 minutes and output it into the R console. It will keep doing that until we restart the R session (using the Session ➤ Restart R command seen in Figure 8-20). As this is running on our server, we can safely close the web browser, and when we return a few hours later, we can see out output (see Figure 8-21 and Figure 8-22). You could imagine using this to track any historical data you'd like – download and scrape data off of a web page every few minutes or hour. Track daily temperatures or stock quotes. Whatever you want to track, your RStudio Server will just keep on ticking, as long as you tell it to.

Figure 8-20. *The Restart R Session Command*

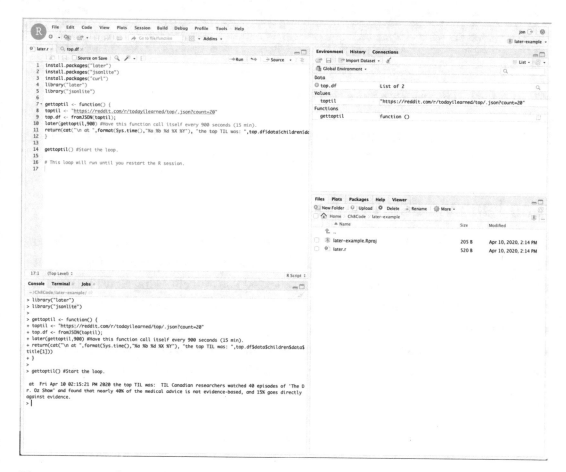

Figure 8-21. *The results of the code running*

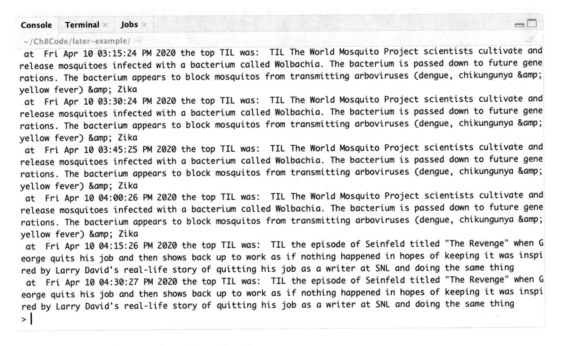

Figure 8-22. *The results after a few hours*

Now that we've played around with RStudio, let's build a simple Shiny app – I think you'll find that you already have most of the skills necessary!

Web Page via Shiny Server

Everything you need to build and test Shiny applications is actually already included in RStudio, so we'll be spending most of our time at the start of this example there. To get started, we create a new Shiny Web App by clicking File and choosing New File ➤ Shiny Web App (Figure 8-23). Next, we give it a name and tell R where it will live. It's important to note that this web app will become a part of your existing project in R; it will not create a completely new project. I've decided to build a simple Latin Square generator by modifying the Shiny Web App template that RStudio creates by default (Figure 8-24).

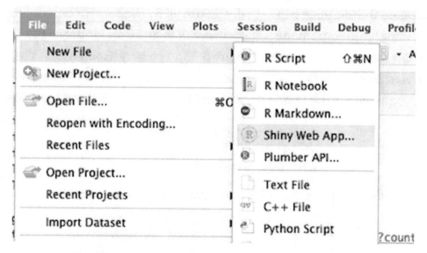

Figure 8-23. *The File, New Shiny Web App option*

Figure 8-24. *The default "Hello" application*

At this point, the template can actually be run all by itself – it's a functioning single file app! Clicking "Run App" in the upper corner of Figure 8-24 launches the Shiny app in a local shiny server web server (see Figure 8-25). You may experience a slight hiccup if you have your browser set to block popups (in the form of the box in Figure 8-26), but eventually, you'll see the the Hello application in its own browser window (Figure 8-27).

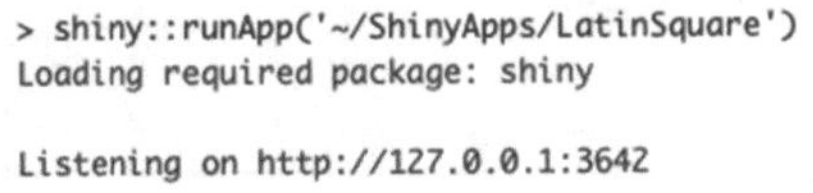

```
> shiny::runApp('~/ShinyApps/LatinSquare')
Loading required package: shiny

Listening on http://127.0.0.1:3642
```

Figure 8-25. *RStudio launching it's own temporary Shiny server*

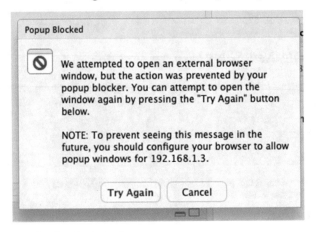

Figure 8-26. *Popup Blocked Warning*

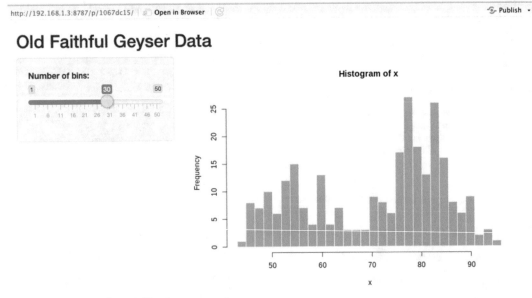

Figure 8-27. *The Hello App running*

Now that we're up and running, we can start modifying the default code to do what we need it to. My first example is pretty simple – I still want the slider from the Hello example, but I want to pipe that value into the rlatin() function from the magic package, which will generate a Latin Square. The following code is broken into two sections – the ui section which tells Shiny what objects I'd like on the web page, where they should go, how they should look, and what they should be called and the second section, server, which tells Shiny what to do when an interactive element, such as the slider, is used. The following code transforms the Hello example into my Latin Square example:

```
library(shiny)
library(magic)

ui <- fluidPage(
    titlePanel("Latin Square Generator"),
    sidebarLayout(
        sidebarPanel(
            sliderInput("steps",
                        "Number of steps:",
                        min = 1,
                        max = 10,
                        value = 3)
        ),
        mainPanel(
            tableOutput("latin")
        )
    )
)
server <- function(input, output) {
    output$latin <- renderTable({
        rlatin(input$steps)
        })
}
# Run the application
shinyApp(ui = ui, server = server)
```

Running this app, I can see the output alongside the code in Figure 8-28. Adjusting the slider value automatically calls the server portion and the output is re-calculated, as you can see in Figure 8-29.

Figure 8-28. *The Latin Square Generator*

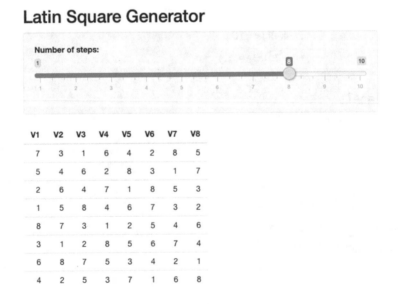

Figure 8-29. *The recalculated Latin Square*

Assuming I'm happy with my code, I can deploy it to my Shiny Server in a few ways. First, there is a Publish option in RStudio that can push the code to your server. In my case, my Shiny Server is running on the same machine as my RStudio Server. So all I had to do was copy the files using a command like this:

```
sudo cp -r /home/jon/Ch8Code/Latin-Square /srv/shiny-server/
```

And when I ran it, I got an error (as seen in Figure 8-30)!

An error has occurred

The application failed to start.

The application exited during initialization.

Figure 8-30. *Unhelpful Error Message!*

My troubleshooting led me to the log file under /var/log/shiny-server where I found this message:

```
Error in library(magic) : there is no package called 'magic'
Calls: runApp ... sourceUTF8 -> eval -> eval -> ..stacktraceon.. -> library
Execution halted
```

I see what the problem is – the magic library isn't installed for the root user, only my account (as I mentioned earlier). Logging in as root, starting R, and using install.pack ages(c("magic","abind"),lib="/usr/local/lib/R/site-library") to install the two packages that I need (magic and a package it relies on, abind) to the site-library, my app loads up fine (see Figure 8-31).

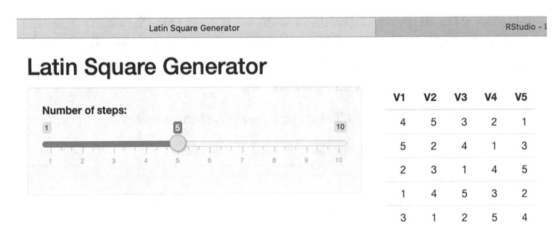

Figure 8-31. *App Running on Shiny Server*

From here, it's really up to you to think about what you want to build. Shiny allows a number of different inputs and outputs. One that I found particularly useful in teaching statistics was the `fileInput()` – it accepts any file and then pipes it through to the server function. I would have my students collect data, enter it into a CSV file template that I provided, and then upload the completed CSV file to my Shiny Server. Students could then get their data analysis and interpret it!

At this point, your brain is probably spinning with a few possibilities of your own for RStudio Server and Shiny Server, and so the last section of this chapter is devoted to some ideas that I had, which you may want to consider for your own scripts. I've included links to a few packages that will, no doubt, also help get your ideas flowing!

R Anywhere Ideas

In this last section, I'm going to highlight a few automation scenarios that you might want to investigate. I'm also going to point out some packages that you'll probably find helpful!

Project Name	Description	Packages to Look Into
The Regularly Tweeted Report	Today a decent amount of news gets consumed through social media. Sharing statistics about something you are passionate in can be a way to help educate others. Perhaps you want to regularly tweet out CO_2 emissions, or sports performances, or the number of people who have signed an online petition. How could you automate that?	A few packages would likely help – twitteR allows you to post tweets to your timeline, and we've seen an example above of the later package allowing you to have something happen every so many seconds. Or you may choose write up a script and use a task scheduler, like Cron to regularly call Rscript. You can even use a package like cronR to modify and manage this job directly from within RStudio Server!
The On Demand Resume Email	Job hunting is hard. Tailoring your resume to a particular job can be even harder. If you've got a wide set of skills, you may want to have different versions of your resume to send based upon the job you want to apply for.	The resumer package in R can generate an attractive resume using RMarkdown. Imagine having a master file of resume material and then writing a function to generate a resume using portions of the master script. You could then couple it with the packages we mentioned in Chapter 6 to write an email cover letter, and attach the appropriate file, to send to a recruiter or hiring manager. If the job is centered on workplace automation and productivity, you may want to even mention how the resume email they received was generated!

(continued)

Project Name	Description	Packages to Look Into
The APA Table Uploaded to a Website	In many industries, regular reports must be made available to the general public. Those reports might need to be standardized and regularly updated, all of which can be done with R.	First, we need to make our data look professional – one very nice package for that is `apaTables` which will take your output from R and form it into an APA Style table, which it can then save directly to Microsoft Word format. Revisiting our friend the `officer` package, we could create the rest of the report. An open source tool named Pandoc (`http://pandoc.org`) could be used to create PDF documents from the Word documents, which you could then use the `pdftools` package to combine into one PDF, and then upload using the `ssh` package to your web server! A little exhausting to set up – but imagine how this could save an hour or two a month if you had to prepare this report regularly by hand!
Building a Process Monitoring Dashboard	Perhaps you work in a manufacturing environment where processes need to be monitored on a high level to ensure productivity? Likely you have a lot of equipment that can either send data to a database or has the ability to have data pulled from a script. R is a great place to centralize and monitor.	bupaR is a suite of R packages (`www.bupar.net`) that allow you to pull in process data, analyze it, and display it. In particular, using the `processmonitR` package would allow you to produce easy-to-read performance dashboards that could be published to a Shiny Server. Since we've already seen notification methods such as email (in Chapter 6) and will see another notification method in Chapter 9 (the `pushover` package), your dashboard could also be a proactive early alert warning system!

Perhaps something from the table struck you as related to your job, but if not, the next two chapters might help you in our longer examples. In the next chapter, the Change Notifier, we're going to return to a concept we introduced in Chapter 2 – web scraping. But we're going to take it up a notch by notifying you anytime something we're "watching" changes. And if it's an emergency, we'll make sure you don't miss the notification by using a versatile service named Pushover. And in our final chapter, we'll build out an R personal assistant. He or she can put together a daily briefing for you, and even read it to you, with the help of other smart assistants you may already have!

CHAPTER 9

Project 5: The Change Alert!

In late January 2020, I sat at my desk thinking about the projects for this book. I had come up with all of the projects except one, the one that we're to talk about in this chapter. Looking for inspiration, I went down the hallway to my colleagues and asked them what "pain points" they dealt with on a daily basis. One of them lamented to me that she wished another office would let her know when they added information to a report. Because they didn't, she had to pull the report every day, just to see if anything had been added. It got me thinking about how many times I do a similar thing – check information just to see if it has changed – thus, the inspiration for this chapter!

We live in a world filled with notifications. We get so many that our smartphones include entire configuration settings around managing the notifications we get so we don't get overwhelmed. But amid all of these notifications, we still don't always know about things when we need to. Forget to check a report for a week and you may find yourself very behind if it's been a busy week. Other weeks, nothing may be added to the report at all, and you've wasted your time pulling it daily. In this chapter, we'll talk about the types of data you might want to monitor, how you could monitor it using R on an RStudio Server, and how to get around some of the limitations that you may have when it comes to interruptions (e.g., your computer loses power) or timely notification (e.g., email might not be fast enough!). Hopefully by the time we reach the ChangeAlert script, at the end of this chapter, you'll be ready to hit the ground running and roll your own business notification system!

© Jon Westfall 2020
J. Westfall, *Practical R 4*, https://doi.org/10.1007/978-1-4842-5946-7_9

Detecting Change – Sources, Situations, and Solutions

Change is the only constant in the universe, yet finding changes can be uniquely frustrating. In a perfect world, anytime someone (or something) made a change, they (or it) would proactively tell us that things were different. Yet the whole point of this chapter is solving the problem that lack of this notification causes. Depending on what you're trying to track, your methods may differ. In this section, I'll talk about three different sources or situations that you might find data in and some solutions for tracking them. I'll also provide example code that you can adapt for your situation.

Typical R Data Formats: Tracking a Data Frame

Perhaps nothing is more frustrating than receiving a dataset from a colleague and having them say "I don't think this is the most up-to-date... I seem to remember another file that had more data" or having them say "Yesterday I could have sworn that there were more people in that other group". In a dataset of a thousand or so observations, no one has time to go through and compare them line by line to see what's changed. That's why we have computers and, in this case, why we have the arsenal package and its function comparedf().

First, it should be noted that there are a lot of packages that will do file difference or data frame differencing. The reason I prefer arsenal is the summary report it can provide and the options that you can use to get exactly the report you need. To show you what I mean, I've taken the survey data we collected in Chapter 3 and provided two versions in the code for this chapter. The file survey_file_1.csv is the same as the complete data from Chapter 3. In survey_file_2.csv I took out ten lines and changed two random demographic variables. Opening the files side by side and we can easily see the ten lines missing (Figure 9-1). However, it can be a bit difficult to see the differences in the demographics.

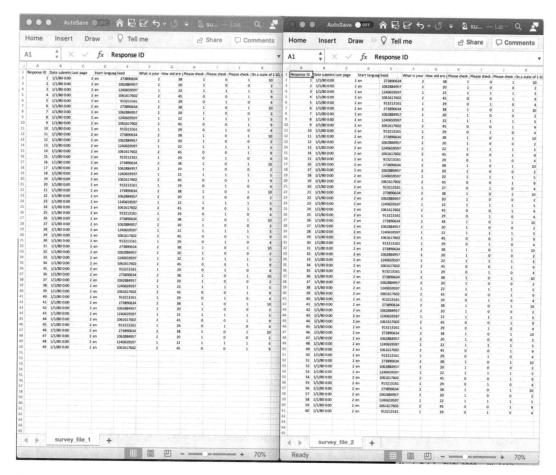

Figure 9-1. *The Two Files Side by Side*

However, the following code will find these two needles in the haystack pretty quickly:

```
install.packages("arsenal")
library(arsenal)
df1 <- read.csv(file="survey_file_1.csv")
df2 <- read.csv(file="survey_file_2.csv") # 10 new rows of data, and 2
demographics changes made
comparedf(df1,df2)
summary(comparedf(df1,df2, by="Response.ID"))
```

Running that code, we get a very comprehensive report that includes the following two snippets:

```
Table: Summary of overall comparison
```

statistic	value
Number of by-variables 1	
Number of non-by variables in common	10
Number of variables compared	10
Number of variables in x but not y	0
Number of variables in y but not x	0
Number of variables compared with some values unequal	2
Number of variables compared with all values equal	8
Number of observations in common	49
Number of observations in x but not y	0
Number of observations in y but not x	11
Number of observations with some compared variables unequal	2
Number of observations with all compared variables equal	47
Number of values unequal	2

Right away we can see that there are 11 observations in y (our second data frame) that aren't in x (our first data frame). Farther down in the list, we actually get a table that lists the Response.IDs of each observation that isn't shared.

And what about those two demographic pieces that I changed? We can find them easily too:

```
Table: Differences detected
```

var.x	var.y	Response.ID	values.x	values.y	row.x	row.y
What.is.your.gender.	What.is.your.gender.	29	2	1	29	29
How.old.are.you.	How.old.are.you.	20	29	27	20	20

These might have been changed for legitimate reasons (e.g., the person entering the data made a typo that they fixed later in the day, after the first report had gone out), or they might have been changed for less than legitimate reasons. Security professionals will tell you that individuals who break into computers can modify log files to cover their tracks. Imagine having a central monitoring script that recorded user activity and periodically auditing the logs to see if the user count was retroactively changed. You might find something before it's too late.

And as I mentioned earlier, `comparedf()` has some features that other packages lack. What if your column names are slightly different ("Response.ID" vs. "response. id")? It can handle that using the `tol.vars` option. What about having a level of acceptable difference? Pass `tol.num.val` with an absolute difference and you'll only trigger differences if the threshold is met. `comparedf()` can also support user-defined tolerance functions, which means you can customize your criteria even more. Example 1 in the comparedf vignette shows how to allow items with a newer date to be ignored, suggesting that those differences are intentional updates.

If only all data could be that nice. And it's possible it might be. It is possible to coerce a lot of data into a data frame in some way. However, in doing so, you may lose some of the things that make that data special – like the actual content! What might we do if the content is what we want to monitor, through either downloading it via an API or directly from the rendered web page or document? Enter the next two scenarios!

Tracking API Data

Data comes in many ways, with a good chunk coming through API calls. One of the more common formats that you can receive data in is JSON (JavaScript Object Notation). R can deal with this data through several packages, one of which is `jsonlite` (if your API of choice uses XML, then you can check out the easily remembered `xml` package).

What makes JSON particularly nice is that in many cases you can download it directly, without having to save it to a file. The data tends to be rather small, and tons of websites support it. In the following example, I'm going to download the current "hot" list of topics from Reddit and display the top item:

```
install.packages("jsonlite")
library("jsonlite")
hot <- "https://www.reddit.com/hot/.json"
hot.df <- fromJSON(hot);
hot.df$data$children$data$title[1]
```

```
> install.packages("jsonlite")
trying URL 'https://cran.rstudio.com/bin/macosx/el-capitan/contrib/3.6/jsonlite_1.6.1.tgz'
Content type 'application/x-gzip' length 1120424 bytes (1.1 MB)
==================================================
downloaded 1.1 MB


The downloaded binary packages are in
        /var/folders/nt/z82_3xdd3m9fdg7623m3j69m0000gn/T//RtmpJeLxmR/downloaded_packages
> library("jsonlite")
> hot <- "https://www.reddit.com/hot/.json"
> hot.df <- fromJSON(hot);
> hot.df$data$children$data$title[1]
[1] "My Great-Grandfather's social security card was made out of metal, not paper"
```

Figure 9-2. *Output from the jsonlite Code*

As we'll see later, once I have the item, there are ways in which I can store it and then compare it later. In the following example, we'll actually check it once an hour to see if it changes, although you can check it as often as you like. Well, almost...

Here's a caveat about API data – not all of it is free. Many websites understand that if you're using an API to access their content, that's fewer eyes that will be on their actual web page. And while it's nice of you to lighten their server load, you're also lightening their pockets by reducing their ad revenue. So for many, they require that you provide an API key in order to access their API. You purchase that key and a certain number of data calls with it. Reddit themselves allow up to 60 requests per minute and require that you authenticate if you're building a client application. So don't look to bog down a server with a ton of calls, because even if you are able to do a few, you might find yourself blocked if you're grabbing the same data 10–20 times per minute.

In situations where the data is expensive or an API isn't available, what option do we have? The majority of the time our best option then is to use some form of web scraping, like I discussed in Chapter 2.

Tracking Web Page

The Web has a ton of data, but it isn't always in a format friendly to us. That's why we have tools like R. In Chapter 2, I gave you a very basic version of scraping data from a web page with the rvest package. When it comes to web scraping, there are likely two different goals you might have in mind: comparing two versions of a page (highlighting the differences) or mining data out of the page to use in your script.

The first is actually easiest thanks to the diffr package. The following code grabs a copy of the homepage of Delta State University from the Internet Wayback Machine at archive.org at two separate points. It then analyzes the differences and produces a difference report of the raw HTML that highlights the differences in file2.html vs. file1.html. As we can see from the report, quite a bit of code changed – mostly due to a difference in file paths.

```
install.packages("diffr")
library(diffr)
install.packages("shiny");
library("shiny");
addr <- "https://web.archive.org/web/20200102195729/http://www.deltastate.edu/"
addr2 <- "https://web.archive.org/web/20191202220905/http://www.deltastate.edu/"
download.file(addr,"file1.html");
download.file(addr2,"file2.html");
diffr("file1.html","file2.html", contextSize=0);
```

```
1  <!doctype html>


4  <html lang="en-US" prefix="og: http://ogp.me/ns#">
5  <head><script src="//archive.org/includes/analytics.js?v=cf34f82" type="text/javascript"></script>
6  <script type="text/javascript">window.addEventListener('DOMContentLoaded',function(){var v=archive_analytics.values;v.service='wb';v.serve
   type="text/javascript" src="/_static/js/ait-client-rewrite.js" charset="utf-8"></script>
7  <script type="text/javascript">
8  WB_wombat_Init("https://web.archive.org/web/", "20200102195729", "www.deltastate.edu");

27     <link rel="shortcut icon" href="https://web.archive.org/web/20200102195729im_/http://www.deltastate.edu/wp-content/uploads/2017/04/fav
28

29
30 <title> Home - Delta State University </title>
31

32
33 <!-- This site is optimized with the Yoast SEO plugin v9.1 - https://yoast.com/wordpress/plugins/seo/ -->
34 <link rel="canonical" href="https://web.archive.org/web/20200102195729/http://www.deltastate.edu/"/>
35 <meta property="og:locale" content="en_US"/>
36 <meta property="og:type" content="website"/>
37 <meta property="og:title" content="Home - Delta State University"/>
38 <meta property="og:url" content="https://web.archive.org/web/20200102195729/http://www.deltastate.edu/"/>
39 <meta property="og:site_name" content="Delta State University"/>
40 <meta name="twitter:card" content="summary"/>
41 <meta name="twitter:title" content="Home - Delta State University"/>
42 <script type="application/ld+json">{"@context":"https:\/\/web.archive.org\/web\/20200102195729\/https:\/\/schema.org","@type":"WebSite","@
   University","potentialAction":{"@type":"SearchAction","target":"https:\/\/web.archive.org\/web\/20200102195729\/http:\/\/www.deltastate.ed
43 <!-- / Yoast SEO plugin. -->
44
45 <link rel="dns-prefetch" href="//web.archive.org/web/20200102195729/http://platform.twitter.com/"/>
46 <link rel="dns-prefetch" href="//web.archive.org/web/20200102195729/http://fonts.googleapis.com/"/>
47 <link rel="dns-prefetch" href="//web.archive.org/web/20200102195729/http://s.w.org/"/>
48 <link rel="alternate" type="application/rss+xml" title="Delta State University » Feed" href="https://web.archive.org/web/20200102195729/ht
49 <link rel="alternate" type="text/calendar" title="Delta State University » iCal Feed" href="https://web.archive.org/web/20200102195729/htt
50     <script type="text/javascript">
51         window._wpemojiSettings =
   {"baseUrl":"https:\/\/web.archive.org\/web\/20200102195729\/https:\/\/s.w.org\/images\/core\/emoji\/2.3\/72x72\/","ext":".png","svgUrl":"h
   {"concatemoji":"https:\/\/web.archive.org\/web\/20200102195729\/http:\/\/www.deltastate.edu\/wp-includes\/js\/wp-emoji-release.min.js?ver=

68 <link rel="stylesheet" id="widget-calendar-pro-style-css" href="https://web.archive.org/web/20200102195729cs_/http://www.deltastate.edu/wp
69 <link rel="stylesheet" id="tribe_events-widget-calendar-pro-style-css" href="https://web.archive.org/web/20200102195729cs_/http://www.delt
   media="all"/>
70 <link rel="stylesheet" id="layerslider-css" href="https://web.archive.org/web/20200102195729cs_/http://www.deltastate.edu/wp-content/plugi
71 <link rel="stylesheet" id="ls-google-fonts-css" href="https://web.archive.org/web/20200102195729cs_/http://fonts.googleapis.com/css?family
   type="text/css" media="all"/>
72 <link rel="stylesheet" id="tribe-events-full-pro-calendar-style-css" href="https://web.archive.org/web/20200102195729cs_/http://www.deltas
   type="text/css" media="all"/>
```

Figure 9-3. *Output of the diffr Function*

`diffr` can work on any text file to create a difference report. It's not going to be your solution, however, for compiled files such as a PDF. As of this writing, there isn't a utility in R to compare PDF documents; however, it does exist for Python. And as hinted earlier, `diffr` is not going to be your solution if the document you download has specific data you need. For that, `rvest` is your best option.

However, as a caveat, `rvest` or any other package is going to be pretty worthless if the data you download doesn't include the data you need. Many web pages today use JavaScript to download data after the page is loaded, through an Asynchronous JavaScript and XML (AJAX). When you download a web page using the `download.file()` function, it downloads the raw HTML. That HTML might just include placeholders for the data that you want, because that data gets loaded later in your web browser. This means that `rvest` won't be able to find anything. Later in this chapter, we'll look at a solution for this in our ChangeAlert script, by emulating the page loading experience in a "headless" web browser. For now, let's turn back to the basics of detecting change. Because once we can get the data one time, we can get it in the future as often as we like to compare against that first copy.

Schedules, Interruptions, and Resuscitations

In a perfect world, we'd always do what we want to do at the time we want to do it. As I write this, in the midst of the COVID-19 pandemic, my morning routine looks a lot different than it usually does. I wake up around 6:50 AM, and I'm at the "office" (a.k.a. my wife's craft room that I'm given a corner of) after a 10-second commute. Around 7:10 AM I make a trip to the coffee shop (my kitchen), and I am back by 7:15 AM. If I need to do something every morning, I can easily think about it based off my schedule – "right after coffee".

But normally my days are a bit more chaotic – I get to my office at 8:00 AM, bounce between meetings, classes, conferences, lunches with friends, and more. I don't have anything to hook on to that's constant, so if I have to download a report and compare it against the previous day's version, I will forget on more days than I will remember. Thankfully, we have a few ways in R to schedule our task to run on a schedule that we set once, and only update as needed.

Scheduling with Cron or Later Function

When it comes to scheduling, we have two options: having our script run at a set time or having our script run on an interval. We may also do a combination of the two. In the first scenario, we use the task scheduler on our operating system (Cron for most Linux, Unix, or macOS users) and tell it to run the RScript command we discussed in Chapter 8. Additionally, packages exist that help schedule tasks from within R – with cronR for our non-Windows users and taskscheduleR for the Windows crowd.

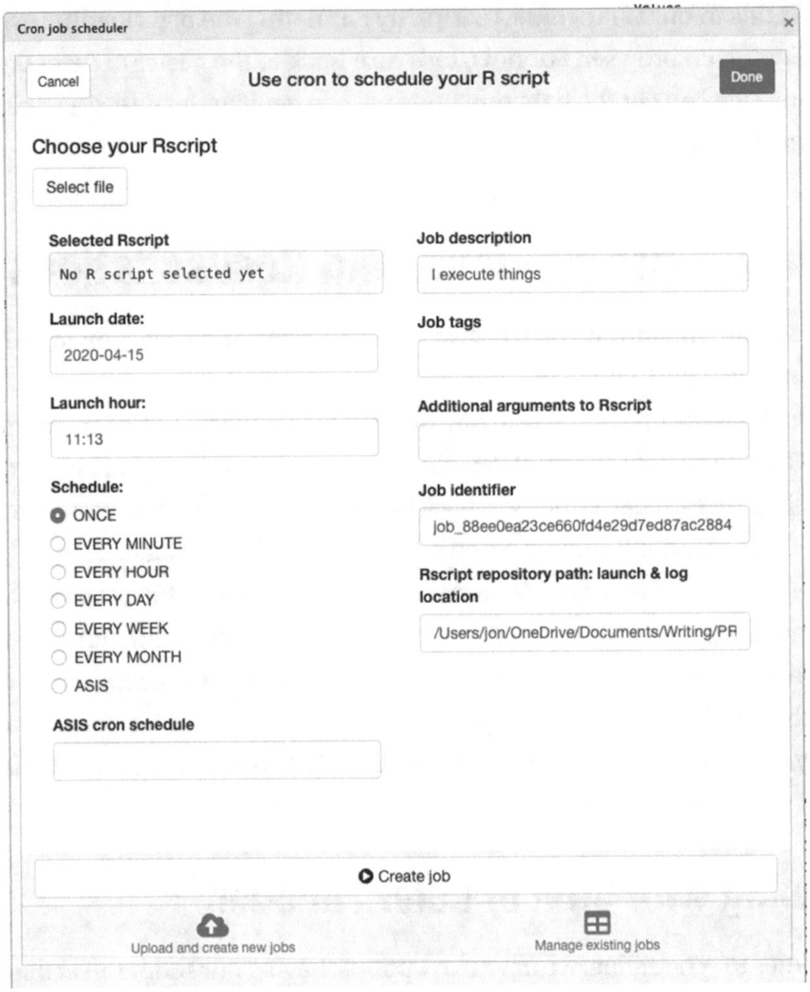

Figure 9-4. *cronR Running Inside RStudio*

This is great if I know I want to run something at 8:00 AM every workday, or every hour on the hour. It's not so great if I want to run something over a shorter period of time (e.g., every 10 seconds) or if I want to monitor the output in real time, able to start and stop the task as needed. For that, we need a package that will let us run something on a loop. Enter the aptly named later package and function.

later() allows you to specify a function and a delay. Take a look at the following code:

```
install.packages("later")
library("later")

loop <- TRUE
```

```
myfunc <- function() {
  print("This is the output of the scheduled later loop")
  while(loop) { later(myfunc, 10); break;}
}
```

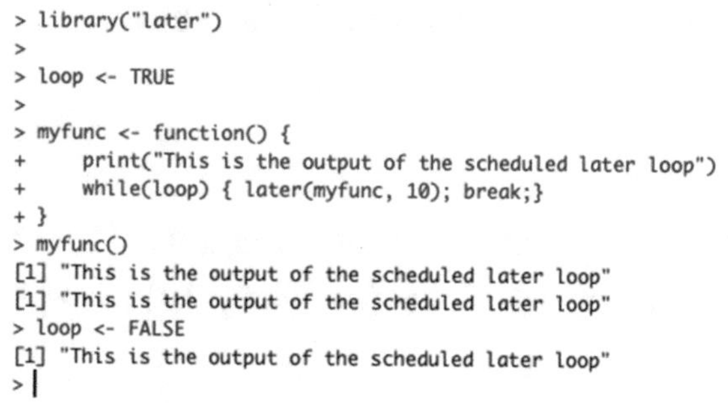

```
> library("later")
>
> loop <- TRUE
>
> myfunc <- function() {
+     print("This is the output of the scheduled later loop")
+     while(loop) { later(myfunc, 10); break;}
+ }
> myfunc()
[1] "This is the output of the scheduled later loop"
[1] "This is the output of the scheduled later loop"
> loop <- FALSE
[1] "This is the output of the scheduled later loop"
> |
```

Figure 9-5. *Output of the Later Loop*

Typing myfunc() into R after running that code will print "This is the output of the scheduled later loop" repeatedly while the loop variable remains true. Type loop <- FALSE and press Enter, and you'll get one more loop of the myfunc() command and then it will be done.

We can also interrupt the later() function by using code such as this:

```
myfunc2 <- function() {
  cat("this is the output of the scheduled later loop, run at ",
  format(Sys.time(),"%a %b %d %X %Y"))
  cancelfunc <<- later(myfunc2, 10)
}

cancelfunc <- later(myfunc2, 10)
```

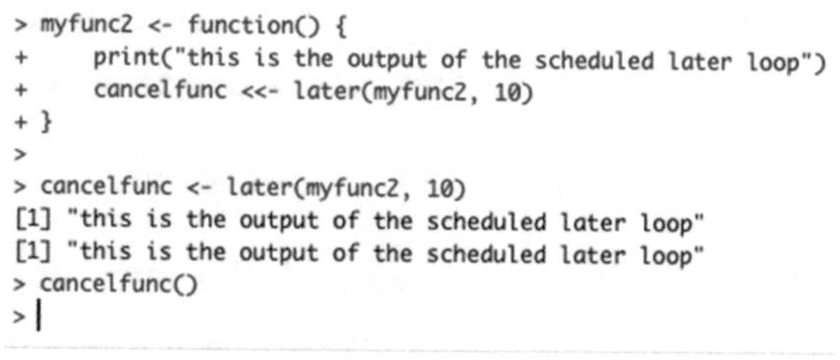

```
> myfunc2 <- function() {
+     print("this is the output of the scheduled later loop")
+     cancelfunc <<- later(myfunc2, 10)
+ }
>
> cancelfunc <- later(myfunc2, 10)
[1] "this is the output of the scheduled later loop"
[1] "this is the output of the scheduled later loop"
> cancelfunc()
> |
```

Figure 9-6. *Output of the Second Later Loop*

That code will start the function, and it will keep going every 10 seconds as it "reschedules" itself each time it runs. However, typing `cancelfunc()` into R and pressing Enter will cause the loop to be cancelled. Unlike the first method, you don't get an additional run out of the code – it stops as soon as you execute `cancelfunc()`. If you'd like the option to cancel after the next run (using the `loop` variable) or before the next run (using `cancelfunc()`), you can modify the code to this:

```
loop <- TRUE

myfunc3 <- function() {
  print("This is the output of the scheduled later loop")
  while(loop) { cancelfunc <<- later(myfunc3, 10); break;}
}
```

The best of both worlds, at least in terms of loop flexibility. And flexibility is important, because just like humans don't always wake up at the right time of the morning, our computers can have off days as well. Power outages, data connectivity issues, confused system administrators who reboot the system while people are using it, and more all mean that your script might not keep running in perpetuity as you intended. Let's talk about a little bit of redundancy.

Building a Redundant Script

In the R world, we have a few choices for how to store data for either short- or long-term retrieval. In some cases, I can simply declare a variable with the data I want and then compare my data to that variable later. Imagine that I write a function to get the top hot thread on Reddit, named `gettophot()` (if you can't wait, you can see this code later in our ChangeAlert script). Running `gettophot()` returns whatever the top hot article title is at that moment. In that scenario, the following code can be very helpful – it checks to see if I had a `tophothist` variable in my R environment, and if it does not (because this is the first run of my script), it creates it and saves the current top hot thread to `tophothist`:

```
ifelse(!exists("tophothist"),tophothist <- gettophot(),"")
```

As long as my R environment is saved when I exit R, I can always come back and compare against this. It's fast, and it's also easy to modify if I want to test my script – I don't have to wait for the top hot title to change, I simply need to change `tophothist` to something new and my script will detect it as a change.

However, as you may have guessed, this can be problematic if my R environment isn't saved by default or if I'm working on multiple machines that don't replicate my R environment. For this scenario, I might want to store my data in file format. Options for this vary depending on the type of data you're storing. In the following example, where I'm storing web pages, I might use `download.file()` to get the original copy of my file and `read_html()` from the `rvest` package to load it. I could also store R objects into a `.RDS`. Saving `tophothist` to an RData Object file would be done using `saveRDS(tophothist, file="tophothist.rds")` and restored using `readRDS(file="tophothist.rds")`.

Finally, you can also programmatically save and restore your entire R workspace image using the `save.image()` function, which stores your image in a file named ".RData" by default. However, you can specify a filename using the `file=` option. You restore the image by using the `load()` function.

You'll have to give some thought to how you want to store your "baseline" data – the data you want to compare new data against. In some cases, you may have files always on your hard drive that you're comparing. In other cases, you might need flexibility to have a new file downloaded in either by your script or through another means. For example, many cloud storage providers such as Dropbox and OneDrive allow you to keep files in sync across many devices with a local copy stored on each. In this way, you could run your R change script from multiple places, and it won't matter where you last ran it if it's always writing to the same file.

Once you've decided what you want to track and how you want to schedule it, you next need to decide how you want to alert yourself to a change! Once we talk about that, we can see all of this in action in the ChangeAlert script!

Notification and Acknowledgment

So how do you want to be disturbed? Or how disturbed do you want to be by technology? That's the question for this next section. We'll talk about various ways that we can learn about our change.

In the R console

Perhaps the simplest way to learn that something has changed is for R to let us know about it directly in the console. We've seen this in the `later()` example, with R using the `print()` command to output a notification. We'll also see it a bit in the following ChangeAlert script. It's simple and a great backup method if you aren't quite sure your other methods are 100% reliable.

If you want to get a little bit fancier than a simple print output, you can use one of the several packages that R has for logging information. `futile.logger` has a ton of features for multiple logs and different notification thresholds. Combining those together, you could choose to silently log certain levels of change, without disturbing you until you want to check on the results later. Another option would be to have a pop-up dialog box or alert. Something like the `svDialogs` package will do the trick:

```
install.packages("svDialogs")
library(svDialogs)
dlg_message("This is a test")
```

```
> install.packages("svDialogs")
trying URL 'https://cran.rstudio.com/bin/macosx/el-capitan/contrib/3.6/svDialogs_1.0.0.tgz'
Content type 'application/x-gzip' len    R Message
==========================================
downloaded 185 KB                           i    This is a test


The downloaded binary packages are in
        /var/folders/nt/z82_3xdd3m9fd                              OK
> library(svDialogs)
> dlg_message("This is a test")
```

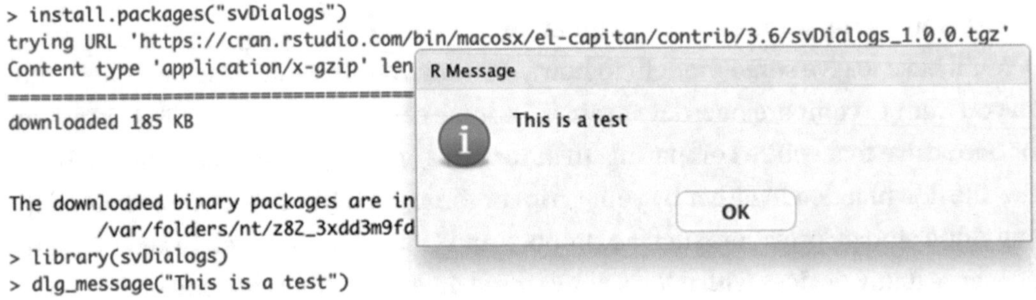

Figure 9-7. *Output of the svDialogs Test*

These methods are great if you are running your code in a machine you can easily access and view; however, they might not work if you're scheduling your script (or at least not work in the ways that you would find useful or intuitive). Thus, you may want to send a notification elsewhere, in a few different ways that we'll explore.

Email/Text

Perhaps the most intuitive way to be notified would be through email or text message. These methods are fairly well used and accepted. We've seen how to send emails in Chapter 6, and dedicated texting options do exist. While this might be your knee-jerk notification go-to, it's worth pointing out a few potential problems. First, email can be held up or dropped for looking untrustworthy. Sending a message that says "This is a notification that your job has finished" will look rather suspicious to most email filters. Your message may be dropped without you even realizing it. The same goes for text messaging. Unless you're using a commercial service designated for texting, you might run into the same "suspicious" problem. At the very least you'll have to figure out how to get your email to text, which can be confusing as this feature isn't as widely used as it once was.

At the end of this section, we'll talk about a method that I endorse over email and text for its reliability and customizability, named Pushover. However, there is one more way you might get your notification across – updating your web page.

Push a Status File to a Web Server

A final "basic" method to notifying yourself comes in a simple solution: push an update file to a server that you can access to check. This works best in situations where you want a status update when you want it, not when it wants to send. After a change is detected, your computer could write a text file with the status update and use a package such as `ssh` to move the file to a web server. Alternatively, you could place the file in a cloud storage folder and let the cloud client on your computer (e.g., Dropbox, Google Drive, OneDrive) push the file up to the cloud. You can then browse to that folder at your leisure and check the results. I'd suggest putting a timestamp into any message, so you know if it's new or old. The stamp that I like to use looks like this in R: `format(Sys.time(),"%a %b %d %X %Y")` – or in human speak, something like "Tue Apr 14 22:05:50 2020".

We've just discussed three ways to send notifications, with each one having a strength. Outputting to the console allows you to output a lot of information – some urgent, some just informative. Sending to email or text is intuitive and simple – one line of code (after you're set up) and the email can go out. But email can be unreliable. A status file to a web server or cloud storage is nice, but it means you need to keep track of a lot of different filenames to check. The service I'll discuss in the following, Pushover, can do all of those previous things. Sadly, unlike most everything else I've mentioned in this book, Pushover isn't free – it's $5 for a lifetime license on your choice of platform, iOS, Android, or Desktop. And it's worth the very small price, as we shall discover.

Pushover

To understand Pushover, you need to think back to a time when push notifications were first being widely used, almost 10 years ago. To get a push notification, you needed to be a developer with an infrastructure to send these notifications. You also needed to pay to access the notification APIs, either directly or by having an app in the Google Play Store or the Apple App Store that supported push. It wasn't really accessible for individuals. Pushover changed that.

At its core, Pushover is a push notification service that offers a variety of customizations. You purchase a Pushover license for a one-time cost of $4.99 per platform. I bought my Pushover license for iOS in 2012, and it's the same one I'm using today. No subscription costs, no ads, just a reliable service.

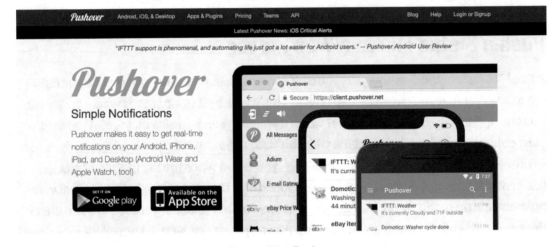

Powered by Pushover

Figure 9-8. *Pushover Homepage*

To send a notification, you can simply email a special email address Pushover assigns to you. But you won't want to do that if you're using R, because you can use the pushoverr package! Here's a small listing of use scenarios that Pushover supports, with R code:

- Simple setup: Create an app to get an API key (see Figure 9-9). Then put your API key and user key at the top of your script:

```
install.packages("pushoverr")
library("pushoverr")
set_pushover_app(token="ad7w7uqezsfd3v81sze7znjhaz1")
#Change this to your API key
set_pushover_user(user="GnoCrXCawlXUwcBDFDkhKBUgC1IMSO")
#Change this to your user key
```

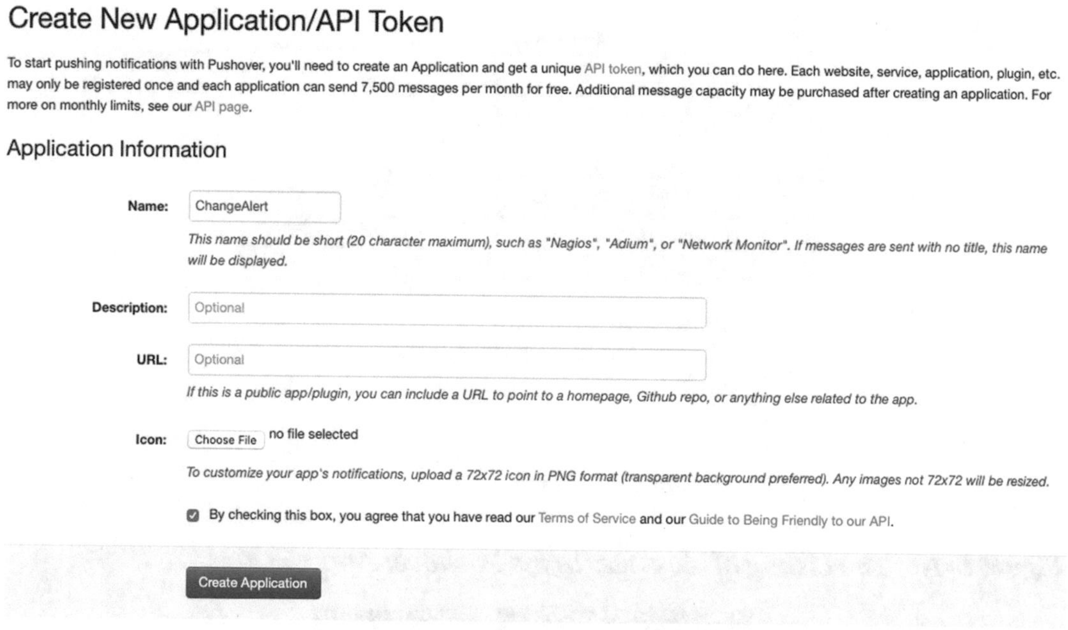

Create New Application/API Token

To start pushing notifications with Pushover, you'll need to create an Application and get a unique API token, which you can do here. Each website, service, application, plugin, etc. may only be registered once and each application can send 7,500 messages per month for free. Additional message capacity may be purchased after creating an application. For more on monthly limits, see our API page.

Application Information

Name: ChangeAlert

This name should be short (20 character maximum), such as "Nagios", "Adium", or "Network Monitor". If messages are sent with no title, this name will be displayed.

Description: Optional

URL: Optional

If this is a public app/plugin, you can include a URL to point to a homepage, Github repo, or anything else related to the app.

Icon: Choose File no file selected

To customize your app's notifications, upload a 72x72 icon in PNG format (transparent background preferred). Any images not 72x72 will be resized.

☑ By checking this box, you agree that you have read our Terms of Service and our Guide to Being Friendly to our API.

Create Application

Figure 9-9. *Creating an App in Pushover*

- A simple one line of code notification that will be delivered within 10 seconds (or so): pushover(message = "This is a test message") (Figure 9-10, at the bottom).

- The ability to send silent notifications: They will be delivered to the Pushover app on the person's device, but won't pop up: pushover_quiet(message = "This message doesn't vibrate or pop up on an Apple Watch") (Figure 9-11).

- The ability to send priority notifications: They will be delivered and cause the device to make a noise (even if on mute, as long as you've given the client permission): pushover(message="High priority message",priority = 1) (Figure 9-12, on an Apple Watch).

- The ability to require the user acknowledge the notification, or the client will keep notifying them on a regular interval. This is great if you're prone to forgetting that you got a notification. The pushoverr package can also track these acknowledgments, so that you can check to see if you have acknowledged yet (Figure 9-13, on an Apple Watch).

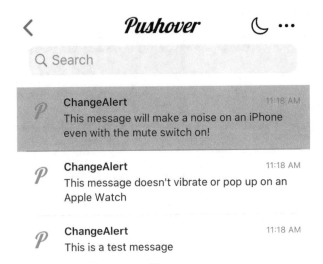

Figure 9-10. The Listing of Messages in the Pushover App

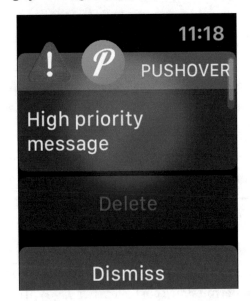

Figure 9-11. A Priority 1 Message

```
# send an emergency message
emer_msg <- pushover_emergency(message = "This message will make a noise on
an iPhone even with the mute switch on!");

# Check to see if the emergency message was acknowledged
is.acknowledged(emer_msg$receipt)
check_receipt(emer_msg$receipt)
```

- The ability to set "quiet hours" in your settings, so that Pushover won't wake you up with notifications that could wait until morning.

- Group support: If you have multiple people who you want to be notified, each of them can send you their Pushover user key, and you can create a "group" key that will contact everyone.

- Support for different sounds and the iOS Critical Alerts features.

I've been a user of Pushover for a number of years, which is why I recommend their service when you need a notification that's reliably delivered and trackable. Over the years, I've used Pushover for the following situations outside of R:

- Server monitoring, making sure that the load on a particular machine doesn't get too high

- Weather alerts

- Alerts through IFTTT.com's network of sources

- A custom button on my website that sent an alert when it was pressed

And I'll likely use it for others. But before that, let's put everything we've discussed together in this chapter and create our ChangeAlert script!

The ChangeAlert Script – Tracking What's Hot, and When Email Tops 130,000,000,000!

Now that we've talked about all of the things you might want to track and how you'd like to track them, let's look at putting it all together. There are two ChangeAlert scripts that are provided in the book's code download. We'll walk through both of them: in ChangeAlert-JSON.R, we see how to download JSON data and alert ourselves that something has changed. In ChangeAlert-Rendered.R, we look at a situation where a raw download won't work.

ChangeAlert-JSON.R

```
# Get Top hot Reddit Thread
install.packages("jsonlite")
install.packages("later")
```

```
library("jsonlite")
library("later")

# Track the change of the top hot
gettophot <- function() {
  hot <- "https://www.reddit.com/hot/.json"
  hot.df <- fromJSON(hot);
  return(hot.df$data$children$data$title[1])
}
tracktophot <- function() {
  ifelse(!exists("tophothist"),tophothist <<- gettophot(),"")
  #If it doesn't exist, start tracking it.
  same <- tophothist == gettophot()
  if (!same) {
    tophothist <<- gettophot()
    cat("\n at ",format(Sys.time(),"%a %b %d %X %Y"), " New Top Hot: ",
    gettophot())
  }
  cancelfunc <<- later(tracktophot,3600)
}

tracktophot()
```

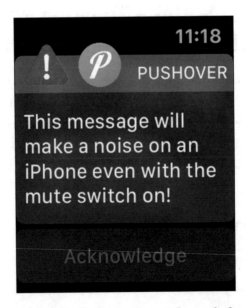

Figure 9-12. *An emergency alert that requires acknowledgment*

The preceding code takes an example I mentioned earlier in the book and fully develops it out with other concepts introduced. It first installs and loads the `jsonlite` and `later` libraries. Next, the code creates a function named `gettophot()`. This function first declares the URL for the JSON download of the top hot threads from Reddit and then returns the top hot thread. Theoretically, we could always just call these three lines of code, but by putting it in its own function, we make things a bit more elegant in the following section.

In that next section, we create another function, `tracktophot()`. This function first checks to see if we have a variable named `tophothist`. If we do not, it creates it and puts the current top hot thread title into it. If we didn't have this line, R would complain that we were referencing a variable that didn't exist when we compare the current top hot thread to our `tophothist` variable. Next, we ask R to compare the current top hot thread (by calling the `gettophot()` function) to the history that we've saved. The variable `same` now is either True (if the current top thread is the same as the history variable) or False (if it's different). If it's true, we don't need to do anything – there hasn't been a change. But if it's false (which we test by using the `!same` statement), we then need to alert someone to its change.

In this example, I'm simply writing to the console that, at a given time, the top hot thread changed. I then output what it changed to. Technically here I'm being a bit wasteful – I'm calling the JSON URL twice and downloading it twice. I could modify my code to store the variable temporarily in a variable in the function, but since this only runs infrequently, the difference is pretty minuscule in processing time, bandwidth, and API usage.

Finally, I use the `later()` function to schedule my loop to run every hour (3600 seconds). I then launch it by calling `tracktophot()`. If I want to cancel my running loop, I can by calling `cancelfunc()`. When I resume, because `tophothist` is a global environment variable, it will compare based off of my last unchanged thread title.

In thinking about what you would like this type of script to do, obviously you can swap out the console logging for any of the other notification options. For example, changing `cat(` to `pushover(` after loading in the `pushoverr` library and setting your user key and API key will cause the message to get pushed to your cell phone instead of written to the console.

ChangeAlert-Rendered.R

```
# Monitor the number of emails sent on the internet, alert me when it's
above 130 billion
library("pushoverr")
library(rvest)
library(later)
set_pushover_app(token="ad7w7uqezsfd3v81sze7znjhaz1")
#Change this to your API key
set_pushover_user(user="GnoCrXCawlXUwcBDFDkhKBUgC1IMSO")
#Change this to your user key

# This Function downloads the live stats, and checks them. It then
# notifies you if the number of emails sent is above 130,000,000,000
checkmail <- function() {
system("./phantomjs get_internetlivestats.js")
page <- read_html("livestats.html")
node <- html_nodes(page,"span")
# The number we want, Emails sent Today, is element 22
# html_text(node)[22]
num.emails <- as.numeric(gsub(",","",html_text(node)[22]))
# we can now alert if that number is above our critical cutoff (130 billion,
130,000,000,000)
if (num.emails > 130000000000)
{ pushover(message = "It's Above!") } else { pushover(message = "It's Still
Below!") }
cancelfunc <<- later(checkmail,300)
}

checkmail()

# This modified function downloads the live stats, and checks them. It then
# notifies you if the number of emails sent is above 130,000,000,000
# It also will require that you acknowledge it or it will keep sending
checkmail <- function() {
  system("./phantomjs get_internetlivestats.js")
  page <- read_html("livestats.html")
  node <- html_nodes(page,"span")
```

```
# The number we want, Emails sent Today, is element 22
# html_text(node)[22]
num.emails <- as.numeric(gsub(",","",html_text(node)[22]))
# we can now alert if that number is above our critical cutoff (130
  billion, 130,000,000,000)
if (num.emails > 130000000000)
{ if (exists("msg")) {
  if (!is.acknowledged((msg$receipt))) {
  pushover(message = "It's Still Above, and No One Acknowledged") } else
{ pushover(message = "It's Above, but someone has acknowledged. No Further
  } else { msg <<- pushover_emergency(message = "It's Above!") } }
    cancelfunc <<- later(checkmail,300)
}

checkmail()
```

Our goal in this script is to monitor the web page InternetLiveStats.com and let us know when the daily email sent total reaches 130 billion and notify you with Pushover (with a second version that's pushier than the first). There are a lot of other stats on that page we could also use, but given how much email I feel like I send and receive, the email number seemed darkly comedic. There is a lot going on in this script, including calling another application to do some heavy lifting, so let's walk through it!

First, we need to load our libraries and set our Pushover values. Next, we create a function that downloads the live stats and checks them. This is actually a lot harder than it sounds. Thus far we've downloaded static web pages, where the data we need lives in the raw HTML files. If you download the raw HTML of internetlivestats.com, you get a page with placeholder values. That's because the authors of internetlivestats use JavaScript to load the values in using AJAX calls in the background. This lets them keep the numbers rolling higher and higher as the person views the page, but it also means that the data lives somewhere other than the raw HTML.

Our way around this is to emulate the same thing we would do if we went to the web page in our browser and downloaded the fully rendered page. We can do this using a piece of open source software named PhantomJS (https://phantomjs.org). PhantomJS is a command-line "headless" browser, which will take a URL and render it, saving the output. To instruct PhantomJS what we need it to do, we use the system() function in

R to call a small JavaScript file that I've named `phantomjs_get_internetlivestats.js`. That file is included in the book code download as well as in the following data. You'll need to download the version of PhantomJS for your operating system in order to get it working and put that file inside the project directory so R can find it.

```
// get_internetlivestats.js

var webPage = require('webpage');
var page = webPage.create();

var fs = require('fs');
var path = 'livestats.html'

page.open('https://www.internetlivestats.com', function (status) {
  var content = page.content;
  fs.write(path,content,'w')
  phantom.exit();
});
```

Once you have that code saved and the PhantomJS browser downloaded, calling the `system()` function takes about 3–4 seconds to load up the page and save it as `livestats.html`. From there, we can use our old friend the `rvest` package to open the file, find the number of emails that were sent, and save it to a variable, `num.emails`.

From there, we simply compare `num.emails` to the value we've set (130 billion), and if it's higher, we push the message it's above. If it's lower, we push the message that it's below. We then schedule using the `later()` package to have the check run again in 5 minutes (300 seconds) and launch the whole thing using `checkmail()`.

Lower down in the code, you'll see that I've modified the `checkmail` function to be a bit more insistent in notifying the user that we're above 130 billion emails. Specifically, we've changed the following code:

```
if (num.emails > 130000000000)
{ if (exists("msg")) {
  if (!is.acknowledged((msg$receipt))) {
  pushover(message = "It's Still Above, and No One Acknowledged") } else {
  pushover(message = "It's Above, but someone has acknowledged. No Further
} else { msg <<- pushover_emergency(message = "It's Above!") } }
```

Now we use the `pushover_emergency()` function to send a high priority message. We then check, one each fun of the function, first if we've sent an emergency notification before (`exists("msg")`) and then to see if it's been acknowledged (`!is.acknowledged...`).

```
at  Sun Apr 12 00:01:52 2020  New Top Hot:  What do you genuinely not understand?
at  Sun Apr 12 02:01:56 2020  New Top Hot:  [Giveaway] $100 Xbox Gift Card
at  Sun Apr 12 03:01:59 2020  New Top Hot:  Varnish brings an oil painting back to life
at  Sun Apr 12 04:02:02 2020  New Top Hot:  My wife and I started watching movies listed on this Top 100 Movies scratc
h-off poster when we started staying at home because of the Coronavirus. We just hit the halfway mark with 50/100 watch
ed! 50 more to go!
at  Sun Apr 12 05:02:04 2020  New Top Hot:  [Giveaway] $100 Xbox Gift Card
at  Sun Apr 12 08:02:09 2020  New Top Hot:  When the UK government use the same font as cards against humanity!
> cancelfunc
```

Figure 9-13. *The Output of the tracktophot() function*

A few things to note in this code that you may have noticed but not understood. First, you'll see that when we send the emergency pushover, we use `<<-` instead of `<-`. This is so that the `msg` variable lives in the global environment, not the local environment inside the function. By default, R keeps local variables inside the scope of the function only, so that they don't mess with other functions that might use the same variable names. However, when we want something to live in the global environment, we need to use `<<-` to indicate that.

Similarly, you'll notice the remove function (`rm()`) has a `pos` option for `.GlobalEnv` – this tells that function to delete the global environment variable `msg` and not a local variable inside the function named `msg`. Same idea as using the `<<-` – we need to know if we're talking about a variable that only exists locally inside the function or if it's in the global environment.

Conclusion

We've come a long way in this chapter – we've broken down the types of things we might want to be notified about changing, we've talked about how we'd build in some redundancy, and we've talked about notifications. We've then seen examples of tracking several different items, including fully rendered web pages. From here, you should feel confident to mix and match based on your needs in tracking the things that someone never bothered to tell you changed!

## CHAPTER 10

Project 6: The R Personal Assistant

If you are like me, you probably have a morning routine that involves information. Perhaps before you even get out of bed, you grab your phone or tablet and hit your "cycle" of apps: email, news, social media, and perhaps company reports and analytics. Sometimes it seems like you spend more of your time cycling through things than actually reading them. Wouldn't it be nice to tie all of that together? In this chapter, we'll do exactly that by having R build a daily briefing for us, and we'll discuss ways to get it to us in the morning (or anytime we need it) as quickly and easily!

Planning Part 1: Choosing Your Sources

Each person reading this chapter will probably have a different idea of what is essential and vital to them every morning. When planning the chapter, the following thoughts came to my mind:

- I generally need to know what the **weather** is for the day.

- I always check my **calendar** to see how long I can stay in bed before my first meeting!

- I tend to be curious about how some of my **investments** are doing – the most recent stocks I've bought, or the market in general.

- Reviewing the **top news stories** is always important, especially when you don't watch or listen to news.

- It would be nice to start things off with a bit of **inspiration** as well.

© Jon Westfall 2020
J. Westfall, *Practical R 4*, https://doi.org/10.1007/978-1-4842-5946-7_10

To a lesser degree, it might be important to someone to

- Receive *reports* from their analytics software, perhaps most recently software or unit sales

- Have a summary of *social media* interactions

- Have their *to-do* list items present and accounted for

- Hear about specific *news items* such as content about their local town or favorite sports team

- Monitor the progress of *ongoing jobs* on their computers, such as backups or network activity

And the list could go on and on. For the following example , I've focused on the five items that were in my first list. But the second list is completely doable as well; it just might take some ingenuity. Let's take a moment to think about where we get the data that goes into these lists:

1. Through API calls, like we saw with the Reddit examples in Chapters 8 and 9.

2. Through web scraping, for when an API is not available.

3. Through internal reports – you may have a piece of software that runs nightly and creates a report, dropped onto your hard drive or RStudio Server.

4. Through command-line calls – you can use something like the R ssh package to run a command on a remote computer and capture the results, perhaps the uptime command on all of your machines to verify their load levels and status.

5. Through communication from others – you could draw in emails and tweets from your friends to put in your report as well.

Each of those items is going to require a bit of planning to pull off. For our example, we've limited ourselves to the API calls; however, you can imagine using the code examples from previous chapters in this book to scrape websites and create reports. If you wanted to be especially daring, you could script an email to be sent out every afternoon at 4:30 PM to your employees reminding them to fill out a form with the day's report. You could then have an R script download that form data (see Chapters 2, 3, and 7) every evening and compile a report. You could finally have your daily briefing script at 8:00 AM every morning pull portions of that report to put into your briefing. All of this could happen after you programmed it one time, without you having to chase down reports every day or week and compile them by hand.

Once you've decided what sources you want to use, your next step is to figure out the format you'd like your daily report to be in. Let's talk about that next.

Planning Part 2: Choosing Your Format

As we have seen, R can output information into many different formats. For your daily report, you might want to consider the following options. I've discussed each one in the following and noted the pros and cons of it: plain text, HTML/PDF, or data frame/graphs.

Plain Text

Perhaps the simplest and most effective way to communicate in the world is just through words. It's how I'm communicating in this book, and it's how you're taking in the information. While infographics, charts, spreadsheets, and PowerPoint slides are useful, sometimes they add more clutter than information. Plain old text can sometimes be king for its brevity, its ability to be specific using small changes of phrase, its reliability, and small size. Plain text is also extremely easy for a text-to-speech (TTS) synthesizer to use. Thus, your smartphone or personal assistant can easily read your daily report without having issues navigating around photos, images, and formatting blocks.

However, text can fall short in some key spaces. First, for very complex thoughts, a picture can really be worth a thousand words. Thinking about how I explain certain statistics topics, such as three-way interactions, the graphs I use are way more intuitive than simply explaining it in words. Plus, there are certain things I cannot communicate in text. If I'm a product designer and part of my job is to review the latest design sketches every morning, I really can't depend on text for my daily briefing. And finally, text does take longer to parse than many other formats. Indeed you may notice in the daily briefing script as follows that while the text version of the script is shorter in length, the visual appeal of the HTML/PDF version makes it more palatable to the eye.

HTML/PDF

Rendering text in a rich environment while also adding formatting, images, and color can produce a stylish and professional looking report that you will enjoy reading each morning. It also has the added benefit that it's a report you will probably not hesitate to share if needed – especially if it's information that could appeal to others in your circle of friends or co-workers. UI/UX designers use the term skeuomorphic to describe the emulation of a real-world object virtually, such as the older version of applications on iOS that looked like their paper counterparts (e.g., notes, contacts, and calendar).

While not many of us will go "all out" with our skeuomorphic designs, there is something to be said about beauty as well as information. One example of this is the Tufte Handout style that one can actually create in RStudio using RMarkdown. This style is beautiful and simple and harkens back to a clean textbook style of decades past. However, while it may be visually appealing, a TTS synthesizer may have issues with it, and it could also be overwhelming to the reader who just wants to get what they need and get done with the document. Pretty may equal professional, but it doesn't always equal fast.

Data Frame/Graphs

Our last manner of rendering data is probably the most well developed in R, given its roots as a statistical software package, but also the trickiest to pull off effectively: exporting data as a data frame or in graphical representation. I won't spend a lot of time on this here, because it's likely that if your daily briefing depends on statistics and numbers in columns, you probably already know exactly what graphs you want and what tables of text you expect to see. I will note that some of the formatting that we'll see in the HTML version of the daily briefing R script is very useful if you are going to be working with these areas. And don't forget the `officer` package we talked about in Chapter 7 – it can be used to write and read Excel workbooks. I shared an example of an office having to put together the same report daily for 2 weeks and how this could be easily done using `officer`. I could see a similar scenario for someone in an organization that reviews metrics each morning designing an R script to create an Excel workbook with several sheets that could be shared.

Once you have decided what format you want your daily report in, it's time to glue it all together. In the next section, I'll walk through the daily briefing R script, how it pulls in its data, and how it exports data out in either plain text or in HTML through RMarkdown. Once we're doing walking through it, I'll talk about how we might distribute it to ourselves for the easiest "digestion" of our briefing.

Bringing It Together: The Daily Briefing R Script

At its core, the daily briefing R script ties together a lot of what we've seen already in this book; however, it does bring together more elements at one time than we've seen before. Thankfully, they all work together fairly seamlessly. I'll discuss each of the sources first, and then we'll build the plain text output and the RMarkdown output.

Packages You'll Need

Make sure you've installed the following R packages and their dependents before running the following code:

- owmr
- tidyquant
- jsonlite
- devtools (to install the Google Calendar library, gcalendr)
- markdown
- knitr

Weather from OpenWeatherMap.Org

Weather is a necessary consideration for most of us when we're not sheltering in place or quarantined (as you can imagine, during the month I'm writing this, April 2020, I'm not as interested in the weather as I usually am). OpenWeatherMap.org offers several weather APIs that you can choose from, with their basic forecast API for free for up to 1000 calls per day. You will need to sign up and get an API key in order to access their data remotely. Once you have yours, you'll need to replace the example APPID that I have in the following code. You'll also want to change your ZIP code to your location. Their API also allows you to specify city and latitude/longitude.

```
library('owmr')
Sys.setenv(OWM_API_KEY = "a91bb498c90bcd09f445039a88474ec5")
weather <- get_current(zip="38733", units="imperial")
weather$main$temp
```

Name	Type	Value
◔ weather	list [13] (S3: list, owmr_weath	List of length 13
◔ coord	list [2]	List of length 2
◔ weather	list [1 x 4] (S3: data.frame)	A data.frame with 1 rows and 4 columns
id	integer [1]	800
main	character [1]	'Clear'
description	character [1]	'clear sky'
icon	character [1]	'01n'
base	character [1]	'stations'
◔ main	list [6]	List of length 6
temp	double [1]	70.72
feels_like	double [1]	67.6
temp_min	double [1]	69.01
temp_max	double [1]	71.6
pressure	integer [1]	1015
humidity	integer [1]	53
visibility	integer [1]	16093
◔ wind	list [2]	List of length 2
◔ clouds	list [1]	List of length 1
dt	integer [1]	1587520615
◔ sys	list [5]	List of length 5
timezone	integer [1]	-18000
id	integer [1]	0
name	character [1]	'Cleveland'
cod	integer [1]	200

Figure 10-1. *Downloaded Weather JSON Object*

As you can see from the last line of code, we now have a data frame named `weather` that contains our forecast data. Later we'll mine out the current weather conditions to put in our report. And while we'll only be using two of the variables that we're given, we could use much more. See Figure 10-1 to see all of the information that was downloaded through OpenWeatherMap.org's API.

Stock Quotes from `quantmod`/`tidyquant` Packages

Grabbing our financial data comes via the well-established `tidyquant` package that will install `quantmod` along with it. These pieces of financial data come from Yahoo! Finance. Here we are grabbing the current stock quote; however, we could expand out to get as many ticker symbols as we like, and as you'll find investigating the `quantmod` package, you can also get options, dividends, financials, splits, and more data as you find it useful.

```
library("tidyquant")
dji <- getQuote("^DJI") #Get Current Dow Jones Industrial Average
aapl <- getQuote("AAPL")
goog <- getQuote("GOOG")
```

Previously, we've loaded the library and downloaded three quotes – the current Dow Jones Industrial Average, Apple, and Alphabet Inc. (Google). We'll slot them into our report as we find it useful. Figure 10-2 shows an example of the data downloaded for one quote, in this case, for Apple.

```
> aapl
                Trade Time    Last    Change  % Change   Open     High     Low    Volume
AAPL 2020-04-21 16:00:02  268.37  -8.559998 -3.091033  276.28  277.244  265.44  45247893
 ~ I
```

Figure 10-2. *Apple Stock Quote*

News Headlines from NewsAPI.org

The world we live in is changing at light speed, so knowing what's going on can be crucial. NewsAPI.org provides a free developer account that allows you to get live headlines and articles with a 15-minute delay up to 500 requests per day. Definitely, a really nice deal when you realize you can also search their API for news that fits a certain keyword, publishing date, source (by name or domain name), and language. You'll need to sign up to get an API key from their website and replace my "APIKEY" example here with yours. Once you do that, the following code will download the top 20 headlines in the United States, saving it to a data frame (see Figure 10-3):

```
library("jsonlite")
url <- "http://newsapi.org/v2/top-headlines?country=us&apiKey=APIKEY"
news.df <- fromJSON(url);
```

news.df	list [3]	List of length 3
status	character [1]	'ok'
totalResults	integer [1]	38
articles	list [20 x 8] (S3: data.frame)	A data.frame with 20 rows and 8 columns
source	list [20 x 2] (S3: data.frame)	A data.frame with 20 rows and 2 columns
author	character [20]	NA 'Katie Conner' 'Stella Chan and Theresa Waldrop, CNN' 'The Associated Press' ...
title	character [20]	'Coronavirus Live Updates: Trump Pauses Issuing of Green Cards; Senate Passes Ai ...
description	character [20]	'A 60-day pause in immigration will not apply to guest workers. The House is exp ...
url	character [20]	'https://www.nytimes.com/2020/04/21/us/coronavirus-live-news-updates.html' 'http ...
urlToImage	character [20]	'https://www.nytimes.com/newsgraphics/2020/04/09/corona-virus-social-images-by-s ...
publishedAt	character [20]	'2020-04-22T00:46:08Z' '2020-04-22T00:22:43Z' '2020-04-21T23:43:00Z' '2020-04-21 ...
content	character [20]	'Heres what you need to know:\r\nVideo\r\nBack\r\nPresident Trump said he would ...

Figure 10-3. *Headlines from NewsAPI.org*

Daily Inspiration Quote from TheySaidSo.com

After reading the news, you may be feeling a little depressed. TheySaidSo.com has an API that allows you to pull ten calls per hour to get their Quote of the Day, which is all we really need. And it doesn't even require an API key. The following code will pull it and store it in a data frame for us (see Figure 10-4):

```
library("jsonlite")
url <- "http://quotes.rest/qod.json?category=inspire"
quote.df <- fromJSON(url);
```

quote.df	list [4]	List of length 4
success	list [1]	List of length 1
contents	list [1]	List of length 1
quotes	list [1 x 11] (S3: data.frame)	A data.frame with 1 rows and 11 columns
quote	character [1]	'Winning isn\'t everything...it\'s the only thing.'
length	character [1]	'47'
author	character [1]	'Vincent van Gogh'
tags	list [1 x 2] (S3: data.frame)	A data.frame with 1 rows and 2 columns
0	character [1]	'inspire'
2	character [1]	'winning'
category	character [1]	'inspire'
language	character [1]	'en'
date	character [1]	'2020-04-22'
permalink	character [1]	'https://theysaidso.com/quote/vincent-van-gogh-winning-isnt-everythingits-the-on ...
id	character [1]	'B7OFzrXc4MXRTfb4Ga0fxQeF'
background	character [1]	'https://theysaidso.com/img/qod/qod-inspire.jpg'
title	character [1]	'Inspiring Quote of the day'
baseurl	character [1]	'https://theysaidso.com'
copyright	list [2]	List of length 2

Figure 10-4. *The Daily Quote Downloaded*

Calendar Information from Google Calendar

The last piece of the puzzle can also be the most useful – our calendar data from Google Calendar. To get up and running with this code, you'll need to enable the Google Calendar API (see Figure 10-5) and download an OAuth 2.0 Client Key. Thankfully, the steps for that are almost identical to the steps we took in Chapter 6 to set up gmailr email sending – so just follow those and enable the Google Calendar API instead of the Gmail API. Once you have your client_secret.json file, you can put it into your working directory and run this code. The first time that you authenticate, you will have to allow the unverified application, same as you did in Chapter 6. From that point on, you're able to download your calendar events.

Figure 10-5. *The Google Calendar API*

If you have multiple calendars, use the `calendar_list()` function to get a list of them, and then replace the `my_cal_id` with the ID of the calendar you'd like to pull. Figure 10-6 shows the day I used for my example throughout this chapter (ironically filled with things I would do on an average Sunday, but didn't do on this particular Sunday!).

Finally, the last line of code here sorts the events in order from earliest to latest; otherwise, they'd be alphabetical, which might cause your After Dinner Conference Call to show up first on your list before your Zither Breakfast Meditation!

```
devtools::install_github("andrie/gcalendr")
timezoneoffset <- -4 #Set to your distance from UTC
library(gcalendr)
calendar_auth(email="examples@gmail.com",path="client_secret.json")
```

```
my_cal_id <- "examples@gmail.com"
events <- calendar_events(my_cal_id, days_in_past = 0, days_in_future = 1)
events <- events[order(events[,3]),]
```

Figure 10-6. *The Day I used, As Viewed in Google Calendar*

With all of the piece put together, we can now create our text report! And we'll do that in a very basic yet easily changeable way – by building a paragraph.

Plain Text Output

The following code may look rather intimidating, but at its core, it is simply building a paragraph, line by line. Each paste(txt line uses the output from the previous line (txt as its starting point. In some cases, we use sep="" to override paste()s default behavior of putting in an extra space between each element. In other cases, we want the space, so we leave the sep option out.

Reading through this, you'll notice a few features. First, you can re-arrange the order with ease by cutting and pasting the various blocks. If you don't want the Calendar Block first, you can put it after the stock or world news block. If you want the URLs for the news articles, you could create a new block at the end and paste them out. And you could always add and remove content as you need to.

Finally, you'll notice a few nice touches – first, the Calendar Block will format the text properly depending on if this is one of many items or the last item in the list (e.g., by adding the ", and" and by placing a period at the end instead of a comma). The Stock Block also checks to see if the percentage change was positive or negative, so it knows whether to say increased or decreased.

```
txt <- paste("This is your automated daily briefing for ",format(Sys.
time(),'%a %b %d %Y'),"! Today the high temperature will be",sep="")
txt <- paste(txt,as.character(round(weather$main$temp,digits=0)))
txt <- paste(txt," degrees and ",weather$weather$main,".",sep="")
# Calendar Block
txt <- paste(txt,sprintf("You have %s events today.",nrow(events)))
txt <- paste(txt,"The first event,", events$summary[1], ",starts
at",format(events$start_datetime[1]+timezoneoffset*60*60,'%H:%M'))
i <- nrow(events)-1
txt <- paste(txt,sprintf(".The remaining %s events are: ",sprintf
(as.character(i))))
j <- 2
while (j <= nrow(events)) {
  txt <<- (paste(txt,ifelse(j == nrow(events)," and ",""),events$summary[j],
  " at ",format(events$start_datetime[j]+timezoneoffset*60*60,'%H:%M'),
  ifelse(j == nrow(events),".",","),sep=""));
  j <<- j+1
}
```

```
# Stock Block
txt <- paste(txt," In stock news, the Dow Jones closed at ",as.
character(dji$Last)," a change of ",as.character(round(dji$`%
Change`,digits=2))," percent.",
if (aapl$Change > 0) { txt <<- paste(txt,"Apple Stock increased") } else {
txt <<- paste(txt,"Apple stock decreased") }
txt <- paste(txt,as.character(round(abs(aapl$`% Change`),digits=2)), "
percent. Google stock ")
if (goog$Change > 0) { txt <<- paste(txt,"increased") } else { txt <<-
paste(txt,"decreased") }
txt <- paste(txt,as.character(round(abs(goog$`% Change`),digits=2)), " percent.")
# World News Block
txt <- paste(txt,"In world news, the top 3 headlines and their
sources are:",news.df$articles$title[1],"followed by",news.
df$articles$title[2],"and finally",
# Optionally, include news.df$articles$url at the bottom of your text
briefing so you can easily get to the full story.
# Inspirational Quote Block
txt <- paste(txt,". Finally, to wrap up your briefing, today's
inspirational quote comes from ",quote.df$contents$quotes$author[1], "and
is '", quote.df$
```

When I ran this code today, my output looked like this:

This is your automated daily briefing for Sun Apr 19 2020! Today the high temperature will be 63 degrees and Clouds. You have 3 events today. The first event, Lunch with Karey ,starts at 12:00 .The remaining 2 events are: Podcasting (Mobileviews.com) with Todd at 14:00, and FaceTime with Nate & Kristen at 19:30. In stock news, the Dow Jones closed at 24242.49 a change of 2.99 percent. Apple stock decreased 1.36 percent. Google stock increased 1.57 percent. In world news, the top 3 headlines and their sources are: As coronavirus cases rise in U.S. hot spots, governors tell Trump it's too soon to reopen America - Reuters followed by The coronavirus pandemic will likely leave a lasting legacy on retail: Fewer department stores - CNBC and finally Pence defends Trump's 'LIBERATE' tweets - POLITICO . Finally, to wrap up your briefing, today's inspirational quote comes from Brene Brown and is ' What's the greater risk? Letting go of what people think or letting go of how I feel, what I believe, and who I am? '. That's today's briefing, have a great day, Jon

For good measure, I'll use the following code to save that output to a text file, which I can easily distribute later. I'll also save my workspace image to a file, so that I can save some time (and API calls) later.

```
fileDB <-file("db.txt")
writeLines(txt, fileDB)
close(fileDB)
save.image("daily-brief")
```

While text is perhaps not the prettiest, it is easy for a text-to-speech synthesizer to read to me. If I want it prettier, well, then I'll just create an HTML version!

The HTML Markdown Version

To create the more polished version, we'll use RMarkdown, which we briefly discussed at the end of Chapter 5. Markdown, with R integrated into it, can make for some extremely rapid report writing, as you can see in the following code:

```
---
title: "Daily Briefing"
output: html_document
---

```{r setup, include=FALSE}
knitr::opts_chunk$set(echo = TRUE)
load("daily-brief")
```

`r format(Sys.time(),'%a %b %d %Y')`

Welcome to your daily briefing. Today the high temperature will be `r round
(weather$main$temp,digits=0)` degrees and `r weather$weather$main`.

```{r echo=FALSE, results='asis'}
library(knitr)
kable(events[c(1,2,3,5)], caption="Your Schedule")
```
```

In world news, the top 5 headlines and their sources are:

```{r echo=FALSE, results='asis'}
cat(paste(
  '<ul><li><a href=',
 news.df$articles$url[1],'>',
 news.df$articles$title[1],'</a></li><li><a href=',
 news.df$articles$url[2],'>',
 news.df$articles$title[2],'</a></li><li><a href=',
   news.df$articles$url[3],'>',
 news.df$articles$title[3],'</a></li><li><a href=',
   news.df$articles$url[4],'>',
 news.df$articles$title[4],'</a></li><li><a href=',
 news.df$articles$url[5],'>',
 news.df$articles$title[5],'</a></li></ul>'))
```

Here are your stock quotes from the last trading day:

```{r echo=FALSE, results='asis'}
stocks <- rbind(dji,aapl,goog)
kable(stocks)
```

Finally, to wrap up your briefing, today's inspirational quote:

>`r quote.df$contents$quotes$quote` -*`r quote.df$contents$quotes$author`*

Walking through the code, we can see that it starts with a commented title and output type. RMarkdown then sets options by using the triple back-tick (`) to indicate code and then putting a brace ({}) and the letter r – this tells the R compiler that it shouldn't just show this code, it should actually execute it. We can see an example of r code execution in Line 11, where we put in the date of the report. We can also see it on Line 13 when we slip in the temperature and the weather conditions.

Moving into Lines 15–18, we can see a nicely formatted table (using the kable() function). In Lines 20–35, we iterate out the five top stories. We could do this with a loop as well; however, I wrote it out in longer form for easy modification. But it would be more efficient to do this with a for() loop as we did with the text output earlier.

Finally, we finish with our stock quotes and our inspirational quote in block quote format. With the file completely written, all that's left to do is write the Markdown and HTML versions of my report, using the following code:

```
## Write the Markdown Version
knitr::knit(input="daily-briefing.Rmd")

## Write the HTML version
library(markdown)
markdownToHTML("daily-briefing.md",output = "daily-briefing.html")
```

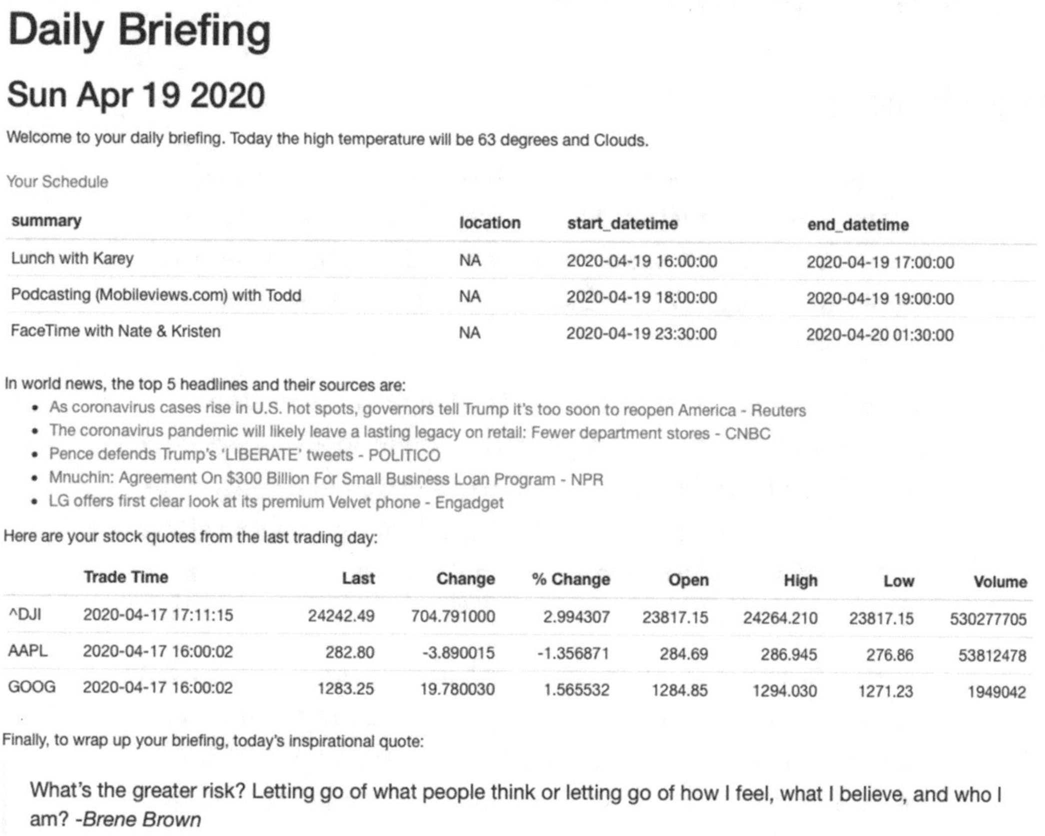

Daily Briefing

Sun Apr 19 2020

Welcome to your daily briefing. Today the high temperature will be 63 degrees and Clouds.

Your Schedule

summary	location	start_datetime	end_datetime
Lunch with Karey	NA	2020-04-19 16:00:00	2020-04-19 17:00:00
Podcasting (Mobileviews.com) with Todd	NA	2020-04-19 18:00:00	2020-04-19 19:00:00
FaceTime with Nate & Kristen	NA	2020-04-19 23:30:00	2020-04-20 01:30:00

In world news, the top 5 headlines and their sources are:
- As coronavirus cases rise in U.S. hot spots, governors tell Trump it's too soon to reopen America - Reuters
- The coronavirus pandemic will likely leave a lasting legacy on retail: Fewer department stores - CNBC
- Pence defends Trump's 'LIBERATE' tweets - POLITICO
- Mnuchin: Agreement On $300 Billion For Small Business Loan Program - NPR
- LG offers first clear look at its premium Velvet phone - Engadget

Here are your stock quotes from the last trading day:

	Trade Time	Last	Change	% Change	Open	High	Low	Volume
^DJI	2020-04-17 17:11:15	24242.49	704.791000	2.994307	23817.15	24264.210	23817.15	530277705
AAPL	2020-04-17 16:00:02	282.80	-3.890015	-1.356871	284.69	286.945	276.86	53812478
GOOG	2020-04-17 16:00:02	1283.25	19.780030	1.565532	1284.85	1294.030	1271.23	1949042

Finally, to wrap up your briefing, today's inspirational quote:

What's the greater risk? Letting go of what people think or letting go of how I feel, what I believe, and who I am? -Brene Brown

Figure 10-7. *The HTML Version*

Opening up the HTML version (Figure 10-7) in a web browser, we can see that it's nicer than the text (and more functional, since I can click the news headlines) – not as easy to read if you're a computerized voice in a smart speaker, but easier on human eyes. With that, we have two versions of our daily briefing. I could easily set up an R script to run db.R every morning at a set time and have the two files written on my RStudio Server or my desktop and ready to go whenever I wished. Now the final question is – where? Where do I put them so that I can access them when I need them?

Distribution Options

Once you have your daily briefing, it's up to you how you would like to either access it or have it delivered to yourself. Depending on your workflow, you may be more comfortable with a "pull" method (where you go out and initiate the action of reading the report) or a "push" method (where it's sent to you automatically). Here are a few options for both that you might want to consider.

Pull Methods

- Perhaps the most basic would be to have it write the file to a spot on your hard drive that you would access each morning. It may be easiest to have this in a cloud storage folder, such as OneDrive, Dropbox, or Google Drive. That way you could also easily access it from your phone or tablet.

- Saving it to a dedicated "notes" application such as OneNote or Evernote may also be an option. Some of these apps support "watch folders" – folders that they monitor in the background and look for changes within. If your software supports that, you could easily have the R script write it to that location, and let the note software do the rest.

- Saving it to a public location, such as your web server. This is likely easy but not very secure unless you secure with a username and password. However, if your daily briefing contains no sensitive information (e.g., perhaps you take out the schedule), then there would be no harm in putting it somewhere that someone could stumble upon it. It might even allow you to create a record of them for future posterity.

- Speaking of posterity, if you use any sort of journaling or diary application, you might find it useful to have R write directly to it. For example, the application that I use for my personal journal, Day One, has a dedicated command-line interface. I could use that plus the system() function in R to auto import my daily briefing to my journal – a great way to both access it and archive it for the future.

- To make pulling your report easier, you will likely want to create a shortcut in some way depending on the device you're using. On iOS, for example, you might use Siri Shortcuts to create a custom home icon that will take you to your report location. In Windows, you might create a shortcut to the file.

Push Methods

- You could attach your daily report to an email as seen in Chapter 6 and have it emailed to you daily. This also will be useful for archival purposes as well.

- You could use Pushover as discussed in Chapter 9 to alert you to your daily briefing. Pushover supports image attachments, HTML, and messages up to 1024 characters. My text version earlier was 1070 characters, which would be just a little too long. However, if you shorten your briefing, you may be able to put the whole thing in one Pushover message. At the least, you could include a URL to wherever you publish your briefing.

- Various text-to-speech options exist. For example, a quick Siri Shortcut on iOS can be created to download and read your report to you (Figure 10-8). Scheduling these can be tricky though. Initially, I wanted to include code in this chapter to have your Amazon Echo device automatically read your briefing to you each morning. This proved to be nearly impossible for an independent, small, home-brew project. The only API, at this time of writing, that would allow this would be the Echo Announce feature, which (because it interrupts you and reads an announcement) is restricted to verified and validated apps. As a completely automated workaround, you could have a text-to-speech engine convert the text to a Wav or MP3 file and use it as your alarm clock tone.

- Depending on your financial resources and position in society, you might also be able to get this information pushed to you via an administrative assistant or secretary. They could receive the report emailed to them every morning and have it printed or loaded up for you when you get into the office.

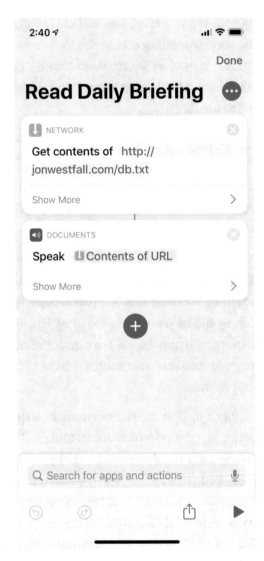

Figure 10-8. *The Siri Shortcut to Read Your Report to You*

Conclusion

As you can see, having your own daily briefing facilitated by R can be a fun project to build out and create as well as a useful timesaver for you during the day. As the final project in this book, I hope that it's inspired you beyond the limitations of what I've shown.

This book has had a central goal of introducing you to ways to use R in your life that you might not have considered. I would challenge you to dream up ways to use the building blocks that we've seen, whether they be statistical analysis and basic data manipulation, to offloading daily work to R automation solutions, to allow you to spend more time creating and enjoying the fruits of your creation, rather than simply being a slave to pointing, clicking, and typing the same things over and over again. If that's been accomplished, even if by just inspiring you, then I've done my job. I look forward to hearing from you through your feedback to my social media accounts (principally @ jonwestfall on Twitter, a full list available at `http://jonwestfall.com/contact`) and old-fashioned communication such as email. And if you're looking for new ideas, you can always check out my blog at `http://jonwestfall.com` and hear my thoughts nearly every week on the MobileViews podcast (`mobileviews.com`) with my good friend, Todd Ogasawara. Keep learning, keep creating, and keep growing!

Index

A

as.Date() function, 159
as.numeric() function, 115
Asynchronous JavaScript and
    XML (AJAX), 274

B

blockMessage() function, 23, 24
Built-in datasets
    base installation, 30
    ChickWeight Structure, 35
    data() command, 30
    histogram, 33
    linear model output, 37
    linear regression, 38
    output, 34
    releveling, ChickWeight, 38
    USArrests, 32

C

calendar_list() function, 301
cancelfunc() function, 278
casino package, 212
cbind() function, 157
ChangeAlert-JSON.R, 285, 287
ChangeAlert-Rendered.R, 288, 289, 291
ChangeAlert script, 275, 279

Change detection
    API data, 271, 272
    code running, 270, 271
    R data formats, 268
    web page, 272, 275
checkmail() function, 290
Command line, SSH, 249
comparedf() function, 268, 271
Content management system (CMS), 3
CRAN package, 175
cronR running, 276
Customer satisfaction survey, 62

D

Daily briefing R script
    Google Calendar, 301, 302
    HTML Markdown version, 305, 307
    NewsAPI.org, 299, 300
    OpenWeatherMap.org, 297
    plain text output, 303, 304
    R packages, 297
    stock quote, 299
    TheySaidSo.com, 300
Database servers
    can't connect error, RMySQL, 46
    code blocks, 48
    combined financial records, 44
    connection set up, 45
    core tunnel routing, 45

© Jon Westfall 2020
J. Westfall, *Practical R 4*, https://doi.org/10.1007/978-1-4842-5946-7

S